EXACTING CLAM No. 16 — SPRING 2025
CONTENTS

I0641239

Front cover: "Water Only When Coil Droops" by Mike Silverton

© 2025 Sagging Meniscus Press
All Rights Reserved

ISBN: 978-1-963846-40-9 (paperback)
      978-1-963846-41-6 (ebook)

exactingclam.com

Exacting Clam is a quarterly publication from Sagging Meniscus.
Contributing Editors: Jake Goldsmith, Tomoé Hill, Kurt Luchs, Melissa McCarthy, M.J. Nicholls, Mike Silverton, Thomas Walton
Contributing Metaclamician: Christopher Boucher
Senior Editors: Jeff Chon, Elizabeth Cooperman, Tyler C. Gore, Doug Nufer
Fiction Editor: Charles Holdefer *Poetry Editor*: Aaron Anstett
Reviews Editor: Jesi Bender
Assistant Editor: Gina DeMartino
Executive Editor: Guillermo Stitch
Publisher: Jacob Smullyan

Jake Goldsmith

On Knowing the Past

Most fail at history. The past cannot truthfully, without prejudice or an idealising influence, be understood by modern people applying contemporary epistemology and all the subsequent amendments of technology and custom. This failure occurs among cultural *conservatives* and with those who are not so regressive. Conservatives fail as they wish to return to a fake, glorified, and distorted past that never existed and never resembled their moral inclinations. Our currently prolific ex-conservative authoritarian ideologues make the same mistake and make it worse. Progressives fail as they too cannot conceive of the past, the ways people lived, how they perceived the world, not coloured by modern influences. Modern influences, of moral character, language, psychology, or epistemology, may derive from past philosophies and politics, yet whatever ways we have of perceiving the world today, the air we breathe, any latent assumptions on nature, life, or being, become disconnected and removed—having evolved into a new phenomenological species, with the past now extinct. For everyone here, and for too many in-between, the past is less something to be studied and learnt from than something to be selectively mined for acutely contemporary concerns, thus assuring current moral superiority.

Is the past, then, unrecognisable? No, hopefully not, but I see no-one, or no more than a scant few, who can imagine history and embody the minds of our ancestors without deference to the epistemological traps of today. We are always stuck in our time. Whatever morality I myself may agree with is modern, my conception of politics and philosophy is modern, and its past influences still result in a view of life that is, through time and change, distant and even unrecognisable to the dead. I cannot begin to ever thoroughly understand, say, medieval life as I cannot truly escape today. This may seem banal, but it is worth remembering. We cannot render the past with unimpeachable accuracy, overcoming all our significant linguistic, cultural, political, and technological developments.

I see representations of the past that align with my moral and philosophical sensibilities, but they do not reflect accurate history. I do not think this history is impossible, with true feelings and ideas now beyond us, but it is at any rate more difficult to address.

Read many current accounts of history and it is easy to tell, from language, attitude, ideological maps, and any view on how life functions, that it was written in the 21st century by people tempered, or trapped, by present-day thoughts—to the extent that they are alien to their historical subjects. This does not mean we are necessarily morally wrong, nor does it mean we should replicate the morality of the past, but our ability to understand the biography of historical people is tremendously limited. Our world is that of now. The past is not just a foreign land: if we stretch the analogy and repeat ourselves, it is a different planet inhabited by extraterrestrials. Resemblances in behaviour are superficial—I do not trust us to be able to reveal or accurately portray a different scope of knowledge, a different phenomenology, a different way of conceiving everything. We have evolved, though that does not mean we have progressed—only that we have changed. Language, and the limits of language determining thought, particularly shows just how different thought once was and now is. It is not impossible, while maintaining ourselves, to render this different life, yet it is harder to see when obscured by our own prejudices—and across the entire political spectrum. We all fail. The map of history we have, what dates are noted, who we are occupied with, none of this depicts life and events from a true view of the dead; rather, it shows life through several filters of modernity—basically a caricature. We do not have to go back far to corroborate this. What did Samuel Johnson think? How did he think? How was he able, given his influences, to think? What capacity did he have for thought? From any angle most are confined and unable to think beyond their current mores—stuck within our current paradigm. We can answer about ourselves, not Johnson.

Life is seen as a timeline, a chronological order, with events and a teleology bending towards justice, progress, or some other ideal. Moral regression or political upheaval are seen as temporary setbacks or necessary backwards steps in order to take two steps forwards; often for a nebulous historical goal. A sense of historical progress feels almost intuitive, to the extent that it is insulting and frightening for many to suggest otherwise. What we want, what is best for us, or what is morally good is not practically, politically, mechanically, spiritually, or metaphysically inevitable. It is unsatisfying to think that on the level of events there is *no automatic selection which conforms with our moral requirements*—though that is probably the case.

To gain a glimpse of what life was like for people in another era we need to understand our own time, how it developed and came to be, and know how removed—or not—any historical subjects are from it. This does not excuse or justify the past, and rather is an attempt, as much as possible, at experiential accuracy. It is fine to condemn the past as a contrast to our current moral grounds, but we should first be accurate. That the past was often horrific is obvious, yet this fact is treated as if it were a rare novelty, with those who relish in declaring it so for their own ego. Nasty history does not mean we are morally improved, or that we will progress. Many do not understand the present by understanding the past and our chronology. Instead, the past is understood in reverse, fixed with present customs, with a forgotten or obscure development, where comprehensible yet dull ideas are employed to make easy, comforting analogies. Almost all historical analogies are inaccurate in some way.

It is difficult to think like a medieval peasant. It is much easier to think of an observable, accessible modern image, deformed and twisted by time, as if left out in the weather and no longer recognisable, and think that was as it always was. I cannot suggest that someone from the past is really an alien, with a morality as well as a psychology that does not resemble contemporary humanity. Indeed, there are moral, ethical, and psychological resemblances that a 21st century person and a 13th century person share.

Instead, while we are alike, we underestimate how different we are—the past is transformed into a flat cartoon, holding our current thoughts while dressed in *cosplay*. We do not understand the past in forward gear, we learn it and comprehend it backwards, from the present, even if we do not wish to. Present ideas develop after a gestation, influenced by the past. But this development is hardly recognised. The current state of the world is as it is due to history, but few, myself included, understand this process. The historical narrative is constantly distorted by the end result; the long backwards shadow. A common phrase says that people are a product of their time. The overabundant equipment and overwhelming industry of modern life make this ever more so for us. The past as some pure form cannot exist. Cliché as it is, the past becomes an invention of the present rather than the present a product of the past.

B eyond real history, much historical fantasy and fiction face a similar impoverishment. Much *fantasy* is a Walt Disney act of historical fiction with old props on an old stage addressing contemporary sensibilities and conceived in a mind that can only recognise contemporary sensibilities (of whatever political, moral, or psychological persuasion). This is sometimes fine, yet it means modern fantasy moves beyond a purpose of older myth-making. It is familiar, agreeable, and far too obvious. Of course I may agree with and recognise an allegory for political autonomy and some other message I am happy with, yet dressed in Renaissance clothing. Nevertheless it is a modern story—a story that would be identical in a science-fiction future or in present-day Britain. It is the present day in fancy dress. I enjoy the clothing, the styling, the swords and the magic, but there is not much in the way of myth. We lose myth—which requires us, in part, to suspend understanding and tell a story regardless of our personal attachments. Sometimes I am eager for true escape, myths and allegories that may contain a moral lesson but are truly fantastical; psychologically, spiritually, existentially confusing; and not me. Not some easily accessible moral or message I agree with, but a creative story.

None of this is out of reach. For now, testimonies from the past still exist. History with more density, more depth, shared, and with more of an imagination about how our inner lives have changed is possible. The case for a more accurate picture of the past is banal but nonetheless true. Accurate history reveals social, maybe civilisational decay. Historians often play Cassandra, warning us of civil degeneration and the collapse, or at least the faltering and decline, of empires and kingdoms. We have a better description of our current malaise, institutional decline, a crisis of trust, and sociological devolution, if we can sense the echos of history. I'm not optimistic about what can be done, or prevented, but I'm not gloomy enough to give up. Much of the future will be like the past—similar tragedies, similar tyrannies, similar deaths. We cannot rely on our immediate environment alone. However uncomfortable it is, we deserve accuracy and something closer to the truth, as elusive as it may be.

Melissa McCarthy

Confidence and Consequence

Ahoy, here's the update from the far and near shores of marine/rhetorical life and death.

Orcas are still behaving badly, wiping out a whole population of great white sharks at Gansbaai in South Africa's Western Cape by hunting them down mercilessly to rip out their livers. Secondly, near Port Waikato, New Zealand, surfers were "stunned," reports the *NZ Herald*, to be "joined in the waves by a pod of playful orcas." "Everyone in the cafe above was screaming and going wild," said one of the surfers, approvingly, seemingly unaware that what they're probably screaming is, "No, don't do that."

And, because time ain't doing what it used to do, my concludingly tripartite item of "latest news" dates back to November 1970, when the state of Oregon's Highway Division was tasked with removing a dead, 14 meter-long sperm whale from the beach at Florence. Instead of burying, burning, or displacement, they decided that explosion was the way forwards, though the acting supervisor, engineer George Thornton, eschewed the advice of a passing military expert, and instead went profligate with his use of dynamite. Twenty cases were placed land-side of the corpse, and, to the grand entertainment of the news crew on the scene, and hordes of later internet viewers, the whale exploded all over the shop, spiralling huge chunks of blubber out into the surroundings, crushing cars and threatening onlookers. The best thing about the event, to my mind, is this Thornton, stylish in his '70s-camera-film-colour work jacket and little silver hard hat, saying, before the detonation, "Well I'm confident that it'll work." Would that we could all have the confidence of a highway engineer blowing up a dead sperm whale, half a century ago, forever.

That's in 1970. In 1973, Roger Moore debuts as secret agent James Bond, in the film *Live and Let Die*. Near the end, there's a sticky situation where Kananga, the villain, is just lowering Bond and the Bond girl into a shark pond. He has carved a wound (a Zorro-like slash) into Bond's right forearm, so that the blood will drip and enrage the shark. But Bond uses his fancy watch to magnetically snatch up a pellet of compressed gas, and to circular-saw through his ropes. Then he forces Kananga to swallow the gas, so that he inflates and explodes, and Bond is not eaten by the pretty shark (which also, I notice, has a slash mark on its right-hand side). See also, in 1975, *Jaws* the film, in which, again, exploding cannisters of compressed air are used to escape shark death.

But I was thinking of James Bond anyway, because of a particular rhetorical instrument that compelled me. It's the one used in the first, 1962, film *Dr. No*, in a conversation that takes place just before we, the camera/audience, actually see our hero's face (our introductory view of Bond is only of his surprisingly pink fingernails). In the casino, there's a beautiful woman at the some-sort-of-cards table, and she's playing against Bond, but her credit is getting over-extended. So before we ever see him, we hear Bond's voice saying, "I admire your courage, Miss . . ." And here the sentence tails off, because he cannot finish it correctly, because he doesn't know her surname, to wind up the comment. It's an incomplete sentence, considered under the lens of honorifical correctness. On the other hand, this sentence works perfectly for its second motive, which is to nudge her towards introducing herself. By providing her title, with an inquishitive intonation, then letting his speech fade out, Bond is actually asking, what's your name. (I suppose he's also checking whether or not she's married, but that's probably not important.) There's a sub-ulterior question involved in his phrase, too, which is, obviously, shall we have sex; Bond is good at multiple utterance. And the woman completes the sentence, she fills in the gap (or ellipsis) with, "Trench, Sylvia Trench. I admire your luck, Mr . . ." And it's only by absolutely copying her pattern of delivery that he then comes to give the now very famous reply that his own name is, "Bond, James Bond." (Theme tune—heavy eye contact—double entendres kick in.)

To labour the point, Bond coins his catch-phrase by: telling her his surname, then repeating it but preceded by his first name. In doing so, he specifies, expands upon the initial answer, intensifies, clarifies, elaborates. He reinforces, reduplicates, almost stutters, narrowing it down that though there might be a category containing many Bonds, he's this particular one. It's funny, the repetition of Bond's name, in this context, because it's a spoken, orthographic echo of the fact that he, bOndjamesbOnd, is a double O agent. Code named 007; the duplication meaning he's licensed to kill. Conversely, although he's specifying his particularity, Bond is also a sort of empty space, a hollow circle or gun-barrel-tunnel-vision, into whose ambit many different actors can besuitedly stride; he might be the only James Bond about, but we the viewers will learn that he's many and various.

And in this phrase, it looks as though Bond is using the rhetorical device of *diacope*, which is, I learn, a repetition with intervening parts. (It overlaps with *tmesis*, splitting in two [as though by an industrial laser]; it overlaps with *anaphora*, repeating at the start of successive clauses; it overlaps with *epanalepsis*, using the repetition to bookend. It runs alongside *epizeuxis*, pure repetition with nothing intervening, again and again and again.)

It's very effective. Once I'd discovered the technical term for the device, I started to think about where else it could be found. And I got waylaid by another phrase that implies diacope, without quite actually using it. It's not any grand quotation from literature or classic cinematic witticism; just an everyday comment. The phrase is, "Fuck around and find out," and it's used (sort of self-evidently) in a veiled-threat fashion, to suggest that the hearer really should not carry out a course of action they might be thinking about, because there will be bad consequences if they do. It's like "You'll be sorry," or "No, don't." I suppose it in theory comes after the question, "What would happen if I strayed off the straight and narrow?" (or perhaps, "Shall I go surfing with these orcas?"), though it doesn't in practice have to be such a direct answer to a direct question. This is nice; so much of language and communication is implied, is not res-

ident in the words that you actually say and reply straight back to.

But is "Fuck around and find out" an example of diacope? There's no repetition in this phrase, you might complain. I'd assert, though, that it has an implied repetition or perhaps recursiveness: fuck around and find out what will happen when you fuck around. In which case you don't need the first iteration; you could just say: I invite you to find out what will happen if/when you fuck around. But it's better in the original phrasing, with the direct activity at the start, then the consequence, the expansion on the repercussions, coming after. The phrase is telling the listener that if you do something, if you carry on (with the action OR the sentence) you will learn something more. That's why I read it as being in parallel to the first phrase: Bond,—then what?—James Bond; fuck around,—then what?—find out what happens when you fuck around. They're both invitations, in a way. As well as information, expansions on a theme. The listener learns more from the second half. And the listener, in the second phrase, will definitely learn more from the second half: they're going to be made to learn about come-back, repercussions, consequences.

It's vague what would actually constitute this fucking around. This is in keeping with the way that the swear word "fuck" expands to incorporate not just sexual but a near-infinite range of activity. (And to incorporate any part of speech, fulfilling any grammatical role in a sentence. Cf. the apocryphal Glaswegian factory worker's complaint about a non-functioning machine part: the fucking fucker's fucking fucked.) But more specifically, the term usually refers to anything transgressive, to do with misbehaving, messing around, fooling about.

My American editor wondered whether the phrase might be one of earnest instruction, or antisocial disruption, along the lines of the ubermensch mantra, "Move fast and break things." But in British English, what I speak, it doesn't have that humourless / eschatalogical overtone, and it's not really meant to be taken as helpful suggestion; it's not like, "Have you tried turning it off and on again?" There's a definite mischief involved; there's being stupid. There's trouble, but it's probably fun, nonspecifically.

And on reflection, there's another vagueness to the full phrase. Although I've described it as containing a threat, I suppose you could read it as being vague enough that there is no definite, detrimental repercussion. The statement is that you'll find out what happens when you fuck around. It's conceivable that the slightly bathetic answer is: nothing bad! You had fun, now it's over. Next! That's not how it's really used in practice, though.

I've described the phrase as recursive, but is that right? Meaning, I think, that it repeats itself at every scale, in smaller and smaller fragments, so that each tiny part gives you the information you would need to reconstruct the greater whole. Or, looking through the other end of the telescope, the situation stays the same as it diminishes towards a vanishing point of smallness. There's a vortex, a vertigo away to the very central kernel. Something at the heart that you're trying to get to. This, I want this.

And there's a third phrase or cliche on my mind, following those two, which is, "Play stupid games, win stupid prizes." This has definitely got repetition, variation, and it rolls off the tongue quite nicely. Is it diacope? I'd say so, as the adjective "stupid" is repeated in each mid-clause, linking the action-reaction of: play games—then

what?—win prizes. Those are the specific actions. The descriptive state, the stupidness, remains in place throughout. What does it mean? In general, that you can expect consequences that correspond to, follow inexorably on from, what you've done. That you'll get your comeuppance for behaving foolishly. One thing will come after another: after the action you'll gain the knowledge. But in particular, why games? Which, by most definitions, are things that aren't serious, they are playful, frivolous, outwith the official and the formally sanctioned; they are all stupid. Although not unimportant. And if the prizes, too, are stupid, well, that's ok, that's appropriate and fitting. Stupid prizes are still prizes; they're not necessarily bad.

There's something about this phrase, about all three of them actually, that appeals to me. Maybe to do with vagueness, the sense that the meaning might depend on your frame of mind. Is "Play stupid games" an invitation, like the activity over which Bond, James Bond meets Sylvia Trench (they go on to play mini-golf in his apartment, and to smooch)? Or is it a warning: you might think this is a suave invitation, up until it all explodes round you; in language, there's always the risk of its going wrong, of injuries, as from the blubber from an ill-judged sperm whale disposal unit. That is perhaps the epitome of stupid prizes. But there are worse things.

CHRISTOPHER CLAUSS

SUSPECTED SPAM CALLER

Hello, valued customer **The phone is**
congratulating you **vibrating**
with much excitement **from a front pocket**
because you have been **an unpleasant disruption**
selected to receive one **during what is no longer this**
exclusive offer to get in on a **pleasant afternoon**

Limited opportunity time share unit- **The number**
I am calling today **is not recognized**
and I want to let you know **Don't bother**
with your credit score **picking up**
you should really consider crypto **because I know**
Unfortunately **it will be about**
your car's extended warranty **something stupid**
is about to expire **and probably**
you should know **it's non-existent**

M Sarki

Two Poems

I Gave My Love a Cherry

Being a nymph
of no conscience,
it appears your

mother is sadly
no lady. And those
bitter cowards

that drink as well
from the same pail
as thirsty peasant

girls. But others
wish to climb inside
her robust garden

too. And unwittingly
be tried with
serrated fish knives

secretly planted in
her crowded farm
to table plot

duly designed
for just green beans
and asparagus.

The Mistitled Prostitute

Their hollow horns
of knowledge speak
waterfalls of pity.

And naked apostles
criticize each life
of one's own

making. Shadows
eclipsed with phony
slips disguised by

tongues so freely.
As ready numbers
of handmade blades

corrode as much,
completely.

David Winner

Nazi Lovers

John Carter and Putzi sitting in a Tree, K-I-S-S-I-N-G

Years after the death of my great aunt Dorle Soria in 2001, I discovered five sets of love letters written to her from different men hidden in her apartment, all from the '30s. Researching these men for *Master Lovers*, a book I've written about Dorle, has sent me on a long, twisty journey, making me question both my own connection to evil and the nature of evil itself. Coming from a Jewish family that arrived in the United States between the Slave Trade and the Holocaust, I thought I was ethically in the clear, but several people connected to Dorle, including her lover, John Franklin Carter, were linked to dark mid-century forces. And those dark forces could be absurd. Carter, a suspected Nazi, and his sidekick, Ernst Sedgewick "Putzi" Hanfstaengl, an actual Nazi, had farcical adventures reminiscent of a movie I loved as a kid, *The In-Laws* (1979), in which dentist Alan Arkin's life gets overtaken by his CIA agent brother-in-law, Peter Falk. Carter and Putzi deserve a prequel though the backdrops to their lives—Nazism, the Holocaust, the Japanese internment camps—are even more sinister than the Cold War Latin America of *The In-laws*.

Carter was a journalist/civil servant/spy connected to Franklin D. Roosevelt. Putzi, a half-American advisor to Hitler, introduced the ecstatic pep rally chants of his alma mater Harvard to the Führer's early speeches. The two materialize like jokers, Zeligs, at key moments in the 1930s and the 1940s. The mild-looking Carter, the tall, tussled Putzi were like Steve Bannon, Roger Stone, and Tucker Carlson today, apologists for fascism accepted into the firmament of American society.

Dear Aunt Dorle, a liberal Jew who donated to the defense funds of Sacco and Vanzetti and the Scottsboro Boys, is implicated by association. A force in classical music in her day, instrumental to Maria Callas and Leonard Bernstein's careers, she had drifted perilously close to an evil that would likely have annihilated her if her family hadn't made their way from Poland to New York in the 1880s.

Carter: A Bolshevik in Rome

In 1932, *The New York Times* will claim that Carter had been deputized by Herman Goering to bring Nazism to the United States. But several years before, after an affluent childhood as the eldest son of a cleric in Williamstown, Massachusetts, he went to Yale and worked on a controversial issue of *The Record*, the university's humor magazine, called "The Bolshevik Number." Its cover, bearing the caption "Down with the Dean's Office," depicts a Soviet peasant manhandling an elderly academic in a white suit. "The purpose of the Bolshevik number," proclaims Carter in an early example of his petulant prose, "is to register one, final, uncompromising and perfectly open protest at certain conditions as they now exist in college life and certain personalities and customs which to us appear ridiculous."

Carter re-emerges in Rome a few years later as a stringer for U.S. and British newspapers. My grandfather, Percy Winner, is there, too, covering Mussolini sympathetically for the *New York Herald*. Two larger-than-life American journalists in summer suits drink white wine at a café off the Piazza Navona, gazing at the Bernini fountains, comparing notes about fascism.

Back in America at the end of the decade, John loses his post as an economic advisor to the Coolidge Administration because, in the words of his FBI file, "Articles revealing secrets of the State Department began to appear in newspapers and magazines under [his] name, resulting in an investigation." 1932 finds him and his wife Sheila back in Europe, Germany, trying to interview Hitler at the behest of Fredrick Birchall of *The New York Times*. This is where Putzi enters the story, tasked to take the Carters around the country.

Putzi and the Carters in Germany

Putzi graduates Harvard in 1914, but the First World War prevents him from returning to Germany. When he finally gets back to Munich, his fluent English and aristocratic connections make him the perfect conduit between American diplomats and German politicians. By the time he's met John and Sheila Carter, he's become Hitler's close friend and foreign press secretary. At private gatherings at Hitler's house, he bangs away at the Liszt piano transcriptions of Wagner, beloved by the Führer, who also liked a piece by Irving Berlin, unaware that he was a Jew.

The Carters' time in Germany with Putzi is relayed in brisk detail in Sheila's 1932 diary. They attend a Hitler rally. "He was accompanied," she reports, "by guards, flags, music, quite a good show."

Then "Putzi persuaded us to go to Berlin for the dissolution of the Reichstag."

"All of Berlin," writes Sheila once they've arrived, "feels electric over showdown in Reichstag—where all the traffic has been stopped, heavy police guards posted."

She feels cross when John and Putzi leave her to meet not with Hitler, who rarely dealt with Americans, but with Herman Goering.

Carter wires what he claims to have been an interview with Goering to Birchall at the *Times*, but the *Times* publishes a news story instead, claiming that "John Franklin Carter, a young American now traveling in Europe, has been appointed chairman of an organizing committee for a New National Party that is to introduce Hitlerism in the United States."

The article goes on to say that Carter was heading to "Geneva and Lausanne to investigate what developments for Hitlerism are possible in those directions."

Sheila reports getting bitten by mosquitoes on Lake Geneva but does not suggest that John is off laying the foundation for a Nazi Switzerland.

It took me several years of amateur sleuthing to get at least some idea of the slippery truth.

John *did* try to establish a political party upon his return from Europe. He rented an office space in Manhattan. He sought donors. But nothing suggests the party was "Hitlerest" and by the time of Roosevelt's victory in November, an event which left Sheila and John "tired but happy," he seems to be losing interest.

But what happened between Goering and Carter? How do we get from the wild tale, hiding in plain sight from historians, of an American dispatched by Goering to bring Hitlerism to the United States to a bureaucrat and Roosevelt-apparatchik happy about the 1932 elections? Carter's own answer to these questions can be found in his archive, a motley collection of documents at the University of Wyoming in Cheyenne, where I found Sheila's 1931–1932 diary, mislabeled as John's.

Carter wrote to a man named Weinstein in 1937, claiming that Fredrick Birchall, the editor who sent him to Germany, had "substituted his [Birchall's] garbled dispatch [the story about Goering and Carter actually published in the *Times*] for the signed interview which he had commissioned," a dispatch with "two entirely untrue statements": that "Hitler had appointed me to head a Nazi movement in the United States," and that "I left Berlin to look into the possibility of a Nazi movement in Switzerland."

That explanation takes an even weirder turn. Carter insists that both Birchall and Arthur Sulzberger, the publisher of the *Times*, had sent him letters admitting to their error but that he had "lent" the letters to a man from the "Jewish Telegraph Agency," which sounds like an antisemitic concoction but did and does exist. When the man failed to return the letters, Carter contacted the organization, but they had no knowledge of him, a fraud or phantom.

Sulzberger, whose letter to Carter is among his papers at the New York Public Library, complains that "the tone of [Carter's] letter makes it difficult for me to answer," particularly the accusation of the intentional "falsification of the news from Berlin," but grants that "as far as the facts of the particular matter of discussion are concerned, the indications are that you are right and we are wrong."

The heart of the "misunderstanding" appears to lie in the following phrase, "The Interview was accorded me in my capacity as chairman of the organizing committee of the New National Party of the United States," which apparently indicated to Birchall that Carter's party was concocted by Goering to bring Nazism to America.

Dorle and John

After interviewing Goering in Berlin, Jon takes the Île de France back to New York by himself, conveniently stranding Sheila in Le Havre and meeting Aunt Dorle aboard ship. Their turbulent affair will last, on and off, for the next five years.

Carter's Organization

The cloak-and-dagger tale of the phantom JTA member brings us to the next phase in Carter's career, which will ultimately reunite him with Putzi. While John spent most of the 30s working on New Deal farm programs, by the early 40s he was trying his hand at espionage. Carter also wrote novels that echoed his political life. In *Murder in the Embassy* (1932), he had created a fictional secret service working for "the liveliest cripple in American politics [who is] as easy to pin down as a live eel on a sheet of oilcloth."

Unaware or unoffended, in the lead-up to America's entrance into World War II, Roosevelt granted Carter the authority to create his own spy agency, which the FBI referred to as "Carter's organization." John was tasked with rooting out potential German subversion, ironic given his own subversive German connections. Which went beyond Goering and Putzi. In a letter to Dorle towards the end of their affair, John announces that he has met with a man named George Viereck. John, Viereck tells him, has been included in a list of Nazi Agents gathered by the McCormack-Dickstein Report. McCormack-Dickstein, a Committee in the House of Representatives that investigated German propaganda, does *not* actually mention Carter, but Carter's buddy Viereck was referred to by Rachel Maddow in her Ultra podcast in the fall of 2022 as the "top banana" of German infiltrators in the lead up to World War II.

As part of his espionage for FDR, Carter dispatched Henry Fields, an heir to the Fields department store fortune, to Trinidad to investigate the longstanding French community because Carter deemed it somehow "vulnerable to [German] espionage." Another agent, investigating Café Society, an early integrated nightclub in New York, racked up a $750 (1941 dollars!) bill that Carter asked the FBI to pay.

"Absolutely not," scrawled J. Edgar Hoover on the memo requesting funds.

"We know Carter well and most unfavorably," Hoover later concluded. "He is a crackpot, but a persistent busybody bitten with the Sherlock Holmes bug and plagued with a super exaggerated ego."

Putzi's Fall from Grace

Back in Germany, Putzi's relationship with Hitler is deteriorating. Putzi keeps insulting Goebbels, as Goebbels grows closer to the Führer. Putzi stumbles upon Goebbels without shoes to hide his clubfoot and thereafter refers to him as a "satanically gifted dwarf." Putzi takes his son Egon and Unity Mitford, Nancy's sister and a Nazi acolyte, out on Lake Starnberg in Bavaria. On the boat, Putzi complains vociferously about Goebbels and other members of Hitler's inner circle that he didn't like.

But Mitford, who could not brook the slightest hint of disloyalty and was famously indiscreet, repeats Putzi's words to Hitler and Goebbels over lunch soon afterward and falsely claims that Putzi had disparaged the bravery of German soldiers fighting for Franco in Spain.

Like lethal seventh graders, Hitler and Goebbels hatch a punishment for Putzi, which may or may not have been a species of practical joke.

Every year, Putzi held a large party for Washington's birthday, which fell in February like his own. This one promises to be even more elaborate, as Putzi is turning fifty himself.

A week beforehand, Putzi receives word that he is to be dispatched on a secret mission. He protests but is told that the Führer is insistent. The plan (an assassination attempt or practical joke; the verdict is still out over eighty years later) involves Putzi parachuting into Spain, Franco-controlled Salamanca, to assist German journalists covering the war.

Rather than the comfortable Lufthansa crafts on which Putzi had flown with Hitler during his political campaigns, he boards a military plane and is expected to withstand the long journey strapped into a metal seat.

He complains to the pilot and learns during their conversation that he is not to be parachuted down into Salamanca but behind loyalist lines, a likely death sentence.

As Putzi clings miserably to his parachute in his cramped seat, he hears the engine failing. The plane is forced to make an emergency landing at a small airstrip between Leipzig and Dresden.

At the airstrip bar, Putzi plies his fellow travelers with vermouth, and, once they are lubricated, slips away. He finds a country road (he later writes) on which a friendly peasant woman directs him to a small train station where a train is just then leaving for Leipzig. From there, he catches another train to Munich, and, finally, a night train to Zurich.

In Zurich, he stays at a luxurious hotel and summons his sister Erna from Germany. She only reluctantly complies as she doesn't believe that Hitler really wants to eradicate him. She sees Putzi as paranoid, delusional. They had only been flying him towards Spain to scare him and would have returned him safely to Germany.

Once Erna arrives in Switzerland, she and Putzi create a ruse of their own. Communicating with people back in Germany, they suggest that Putzi has gone to Switzerland for treatment, a cure, rather than to escape the regime.

Putzi does seek treatment, therapy with Carl Jung still practicing in Zurich at the time. Erna wants Putzi to speak to Jung about what she believes to be his paranoia, but Putzi, feeling himself entirely right in the head, only consents to *pretend* to be crazy. A suspicious Jung quickly cuts off therapy.

Erna returns to Germany, but Putzi goes into exile in England.

In London, his money runs out, and he supports himself (barely) by writing about Hitler and the Nazis for various newspapers. Once war breaks out, the British imprison him along with other Germans. And pack him off to be interned in Canada.

BUSH HILL

Carter, still working on espionage, convinces FDR that Putzi is an asset with useful information about the Nazi war machine. Overcoming British resistance, FDR clears the way for Carter to bring Putzi down to the United States for questioning.

Apparently, something goes awry when John and Sheila Carter cross over the Canadian border on their way to Ottawa to reach Putzi. Carter asks the FBI and the State Department for assistance in returning to America. No one wants to help, a State Department official declaring that "in all probability, Carter, being the type that he is, insulted some immigration inspector on the way up and anticipates an argument on the way down."

The Putzi that John and Sheila encounter in Canada is hardly the same. Once impeccably, often extravagantly dressed and coiffed, he is haggard, dirty, losing his teeth. He's been through a lot since his 50th birthday got canceled and he fled the country. Once high-spirited, ebullient, he's sour, erratic.

While the war was going on in Europe, German prisoners (minor Nazis at best) were detained in miserable conditions. But once he reaches America, Putzi is put up in a dilapidated but grand eighteenth-century estate called Bush Hill in northern Virginia.

Where he begins to behave strangely.

Infuriated by the disorderly landscaping—trees, bushes, undergrowth run wild—he sets a bonfire to contain it that creeps dangerously close to the house. When a revolver is discovered poking out from his pillow, he announces that he presumed that "you stupid Americans would never notice it."

He's allowed to attend a dinner party at a neighboring house if he doesn't reveal his identity or say anything political. Late in the evening, presumably intoxicated, he plays the piano for the other guests, moving from innocuous Debussy to the Liszt Wagner transcriptions so beloved by Hitler.

"*Mein Führer, mein Führer,*" he apparently declaims, his eyes full of tears, begging Hitler to make peace even at the cost of surrender so that Putzi's beloved fatherland won't get destroyed.

Very little useful intelligence emerges from the interrogation. Never privy to military secrets and years out of the loop, Putzi can only come up with sensational personal claims. Geli Raubal,

Hitler's niece and presumed mistress, had not taken her own life, as was suspected, but was murdered by the Führer, himself, after she'd had the temerity to fall in love with her Viennese Jewish singing teacher. Hitler's own megalomania, opines Putzi, was the result of getting venereal disease from another Jew from Vienna, a prostitute, that rendered him unable to maintain an erection or ejaculate or both.

As the interrogation of Putzi, titled the "S-project" for Sedgwick, Putzi's American name, was expensive and unsuccessful, FDR gave in to British pressure and sent Putzi back to the U.K.

Putzi and Carter may never see each other again. The bromance was over, but what was it about? They shared large personalities and grandiose ambitions. They were simpatico politically, both having odd relationships with fascism, and they were useful to each other. Putzi brought Carter into the orbit of prominent Nazis to interview Goering. Carter provided a respite from a period of internment for Putzi. Putzi would have been living in Munich when he heard of the passing of Carter in 1967. Did he shed a tear? If he wrote a condolence letter to his old pal Sheila, it was not among the Carter papers that landed in Wyoming.

In Britain after the shuttering of the S-project, Putzi is remanded to the Isle of Man. He's pleased to find himself on a Gestapo death list, but the British still don't release him until 1946, whereupon, weak, dispirited, and broke, he returns to Munich.

Carter: An Important Task

In the months before Pearl Harbor, as conflict with Japan grows likely, FDR asks Carter to determine the loyalty of the Japanese community in California: an investigation that will impact hundreds of thousands of American lives.

Carter dispatches a former military officer named Curtis B. Munson to California. Despite a plethora of racist assumptions and terminology ("the Japs"), Munson susses out the basic trustworthiness of the *nisei*, Japanese born in America, though he is more skeptical about *isei*, Japanese born in Japan. The Munson Report, which was sent to Carter to present to FDR, suggests that the *nisei*, rather than white outsiders, should be called upon to govern the community. What that would have looked like exactly we don't know, but it would certainly be less intrusive than what ultimately occurred, the uprooting and interning of the entire Japanese community.

I'll hit pause. Carter's politics are creepy, his prose bombastic, but having seen so many of his letters and books, having read his wife's diary, having spent so much time in his virtual company, I feel connected to him. I want to think the best of him for his own sake and for Dorle's, whose great love seems to have been on the just side of history at least once. The Munson Report was a breath of fresh air. Carter had commissioned a document that contained suggestions that could have prevented or at least minimized a great American tragedy.

I'd learned about Carter and the Munson Report by rudimentary Internet digging, and after Greg Robinson's book *By Order of the President: FDR and the Internment of Japanese Americans* arrived in the mail, my brief faith in Carter came crashing down. A summary penned by Carter that may be all that FDR read of the Munson Report, "minimized and distorted Munson's endorsement of community loyalty."

"There are still Japanese in the United States," wrote Carter, losing Munson's crucial distinction between loyal *nisei* and foreign-born agents, "who will tie dynamite around their waist and make a human bomb.'"

From the Bolshevik Report to the Goering interview, the run-ins with Hoover, the fruitless interrogation of Putzi, Carter has bounced from one inanity to the next, but this time he may have caused irreparable harm, though (under pressure from xenophobic California politicians) FDR may have ordered the internments regardless.

Carter does, however, join with Munson and Kenneth Ringle, a naval intelligence officer, in proposing a plan to safeguard the Japanese in California after the violent backlash post-Pearl Harbor, but the Ringle Report, like the Munson one, is ultimately ignored.

The real Carter may not have helped the Japanese, but a fictional Carter bravely argues for them in another of his novels, *The Catoctin Affair* (1949). Placing himself, Roosevelt, Churchill, and others in a fictional Camp David, he demands of the president: "In 1941, a government survey [indicated that] the Japanese Americans were fully as loyal as the Southerners or Mid-Westerners. . . Why sir did you let the army [imprison] them?"

John and Dorle Again

In the late '50s, over twenty years after their breakup, John gets back in touch with Dorle. He visits her and my Uncle Dario, her husband since the late '30s, in the same 55th Street apartment where I will stay myself just a few years later, not far from the metal filing cabinet where John's letters to Dorle are hidden.

John elegiacally describes saying goodbye to Dorle after cocktails. "When the elevator arrived, I was about to deliver myself of a profound remark—at least if not really profound, one which represents a good many years' reflection. So for what it is worth it is that people never fall out of love. Sometimes love falls out of people, but only if the love or the people are not real."

Memento Mori

Carter died seven years later in 1967, a heart attack while at work in the National Press Building in Washington. But Putzi was alive and well enough by the early '70s to publish a memoir in which he claims, yet again, that Hitler's plan for him in Spain was a death sentence rather than a joke. For someone tough enough to get close to Hitler and wily enough to escape, it's no wonder that he doesn't slip easily away from this Earth.

Back in Bavaria in 1974, he is diagnosed with prostate cancer and given only weeks to live. He falls into a coma, and the end seems near, but he emerges from it and lives for several more months before his world goes dark.

Traces

As of the fall of 2024, as I write, I have spent over a decade with Dorle's lover and his old German friend, and I've begun to wonder about their de-scendants, not that their descendants would wish to hear from the likes of me. Before this piece of writing, members of Carter's family could safely Google him to hear about an august figure, a journalist, an FDR ally, but now they may run across extramarital affairs and Nazi ties.

Ancestry.com reveals that John and Sheila's daughter died in Santa Barbara in 2004. Obituaries and lists of survivors have proved illusory, but I found a woman on Facebook with her name living in Santa Barbara who could have been related except her conventionally ideal body and unconvincing facial features suggested that she was an AI creation.

Putzi's son, Egon, was Hitler's godson. He was born in New York in 1920, died somewhere in the United States in 2007, but was buried in Bavaria. While his father was at Bush Hill, he tried to rescue the family's American reputation. When his offer to go to Germany to kill Hitler was ignored by FDR, he went off to fight in the war, urging fellow German Americans to do the same "to find out for certain which side they were on."

Several years after the war, he taught at Brooklyn College and attended faculty meetings, leaving me to wonder if his many Jewish colleagues knew who his godfather had been. Egon's son, Eynon, born in 1950, was Hitler's god-grandson, if such a category exists. A minor actor, he played in German movies before taking his own life in 1988 at the age of 37.

Cocktails on 55th Street

Putzi came back to America for a Harvard reunion in 1974.

He probably flew through New York; perhaps he lingered before going up to Cambridge.

The name Putzi recalls the exotic-sounding names of Dorle and Dario's friends: Ismail, Henri- Louis, Kazuo, Boris, Giorgio. My favorite was a German one like Putzi, Gustl. Memory provides Gustl, an Austrian music producer, with a short pudgy body and wild mane of white hair, though he's thinner and better coiffed in a photo that I found. Unlike Dorle and Dario, he strayed beyond the confines of classical music. Led Zeppelin were awful to work with, but David Bowie, with whom I was enamored, was charming, immediately grasping that Gustl Breuer was the son of Josef Breuer, an associate of Freud's.

Not only Jews like Gustl came over for cocktails. Dorle was also close with Germans and Austrians who had enjoyed early success during the Third Reich. Often enough Jewish musicians and German/Austrian ones active during the Reich performed together.

Karl Böhm (G/A) conducted Yehudi Menuhin (J).

Lorin Maazel (J) conducted Elizabeth Schwartzkopf (G/A).

Wilhelm Furtwängler (G/A) conducted Jascha Heifetz (J).

Furtwängler, not a believer in Nazism, had nevertheless been Hitler's favorite Wagner interpreter, and Goebbels championed Elizabeth Schwarzkopf. Very close with Schwarzkopf and well acquainted with the others, Dorle surely had both G/A's and J's over for cocktails.

The doorbell rings, and Dorle rushes to answer it, pecking Putzi on both cheeks and showing him into the living room. Dorle and Dario serve him a martini but do not encourage him to play the baby grand that the pianist Rudolf Serkin had inaugurated at a party years before because the amateurish Wagner banging that enthralled Hitler would not pass muster with Dario.

Few people these days (including me) think that we can ignore an artist's behavior or beliefs (particularly if they're a Nazi), but Dorle, who wrote romances in her teens glorifying pedophiles like Gauguin and wife-beheaders like Henry VIII, surely felt otherwise.

She could easily have invited Putzi, but present-day fascists might not have cut impressive enough figures to gain admission for cocktails. Frumpy Steve Bannon, bizarro Roger Stone, preppy Tucker Carlson also lacked other talents to distract us from their evil ideologies, but, along with their leader, our once and future president who enjoys sharing classified Iranian attack plans in country club bathrooms, they'd fit very well in an *In-Laws* redo set in Trump-era United States.

Where does this leave us, what kind of executive summary like Carter's ill-conceived one for the Munson Report would fit here? Something about the inextricability of good and evil, comedy and tragedy, fascism and democracy.

At one point in the sixties, Dorle haughtily dismissed my father's concerns about her old friends' Nazi involvement with the declaration that great art lay outside the realm of politics as if Nazism were merely some disagreeable political view. Many years later after a book came out revealing Elizabeth Schwarzkopf's deeper ties with Nazism, I asked Dorle my father's question and received a very difference response. Learning this about Schwarzkopf had pained her. When my father had asked Dorle, she had been at the height of her powers, a baldly driven ambitious person, but by the time I asked her, she had softened and lost much of her short-term memory. I wonder how she would have responded had I asked her about John Franklin Carter. Or confronted her more explicitly about the Nazis she knew in America and those that she did not in Poland, where members of our family must have died in the Holocaust.

W. J. Davies

On Not Reading Thomas Hardy

What makes us decide not to read an author or text? Sometimes, an author's writing can put you off. The sounds of their words can ring wrong in your ears. Politics, reputation, even popularity, be it of author or book, can all derail a reading. A book can meet you at the wrong moment in life. Sometimes, you're too tired or distracted to give what is left of your attention span. I am guilty of avoiding books recommended to me, which has never stopped me recommending books to others. A powerful force for not reading is when we are told a particular work or writer is good for us.

I was in Dorset earlier this year, flitting about in Hardy country. I've not done the Hardy Trail, but my wife did get a potted biography as we drove past the bronze statue in Dorchester on the way to Mapperton House for a food festival. Mapperton was used in the 2015 film adaptation of *Far from the Madding Crowd*, though it trades more on the Earl of Sandwich thing (disappointing egg mayonnaise on white). Apart from the usual habit of being a literary bore, I was keen to tell my wife about Hardy because her dad and I have spoken about him frequently. In a postscript to the 1912 Wessex Edition of *Jude the Obscure*, Hardy said it was the book that cured him of novel writing. My father-in-law has told me on at least two occasions that *Jude the Obscure* cured him of reading Thomas Hardy. It's an enviable turn of phrase and a quick Google search says it's his.

The first time I remember my father-in-law mentioning *Jude* was at a family dinner. We were talking about how he had been discouraged from reading widely as a teenager by a mixture of bad teaching and an English curriculum that thought reading Hardy and learning Shakespeare by heart was morally improving. The idea that *literature* is good and if you fail to read it you are yourself a failure scarred countless schoolchildren and still does, particularly those like my father-in-law who grew up working class in a world where telling a child they were thick or worthless for not getting on with a novel from the previous century was commonplace. Fortunately, the sciences took him under their wing and he became a successful geologist (a vocation Hardy would certainly have approved of). His journey back to being a reader required a degree of self-enrolment, an auto-didactic spirit reflected above all, I think, in his love of Clive James.[1]

James is an excellent writer to turn to when faced with cultural elitism: a writer who believed writing should 'get itself heard in the wider world', who took literature seriously and found it funny just how seriously people could take it, particularly when they got it seriously wrong.[2] He could be savage. When James read the phrase 'my gesture towards *Finnegans Wake* is deliberate' in Ronald Bush's book *T. S. Eliot: A Study in Character and Style*, he pounced. The drubbing came in the poem 'A Gesture to James Joyce' in the *London Review of Books* in July 1984. Here is the second-to-last stanza:

> The gesture towards *Finnegans Wake* was deliberate
> And so was my gesture with two fingers.
> In America it would have been one finger only
> But in Italy I might have employed both arms,
> The left hand crossing to the tense right bicep
> As my clenched fist jerked swiftly upwards—
> The most deliberate of all gestures because most futile,
> Defiantly conceding the lost battle.[3]

An aside. In the seventies, James weighed in on several literary spats during the decade, one concerning Hardy's legacy. Actually, it was about Philip Larkin and his edi-

---

[1] Reflected also, since retirement, in his acquired expertise in astronomy and beer-making, as well as exceptional taste in son-in-law.

[2] The quotation is from James' remarks on poetry in the introduction to his *Poetry Notebook* (2014), but it holds true for his views broadly, I think.

[3] I read this for the first time in David Collard's *Multiple Joyce* (SM, 2022). More on that later.

tion of *The Oxford Book of Twentieth-Century English Verse*, but Hardy mattered because Larkin included a generous helping of his poems in the volume and, to some readers, rather neglected one or two big players. But Larkin's choice of Hardy over, say, Ezra Pound, should have come as a surprise to no one; 'it helps us neither to enjoy nor endure' was his view of modernism.[4] In an enraged review of the *Oxford Book*, Donald Davie barked that Larkin was neglecting his duties as the unofficial post-war laureate:

To be, as Philip Larkin is, the author of many poems generally esteemed and loved brings with it certain responsibilities. And in this anthology Larkin shirks those responsibilities quite shamefully. The poems that we have loved, that we love and cherish still, turn out to have been written by a man who thinks that poetry is a private indulgence or a professional entertainer's patter or, at most, a symptom for social historians to brood over. It is a grievous misfortune that in him an exquisite talent for poetry seems to go along with a mocking scepticism about the possibility of critical discrimination among poems. Perhaps the right word is not scepticism but cynicism.

According to Davie, Larkin's allegiance to Hardy blinded him to the contribution modernism made to Anglophone culture, which Davie had tried to show in his book *Thomas Hardy and British Poetry*. This is where Clive James comes in, who reviewed *Hardy + BP* for the *Times Literary Supplement* after the mudslinging over Larkin's *Oxford Book*. As James points out, Davie does some bizarre critical contortions to claim that Hardy was the most crucial influence on Larkin's poetry, something which seemed fairly obvious given Larkin was pretty open about his debts to Hardy. He even kept a volume of Hardy's poems at his bedside. Davie was having none of this, or was, but only on his terms. Either way, he felt that he needed to show that not only was Hardy the most important figure in Larkin's poetry but that this also generated

the conditions, read *limitations*, of Larkin's choices in the *Oxford Book*. Davie's skin in the game was two-fold as both a famous critic who habitually backed the wrong horses (Yvor Winters, Ezra Pound after it was cool) and a (then) famous poet who, unlike Larkin, rarely stuck the landing (Davie's *The Shires*, published in '72, had not been well-received). He has since been all but forgotten as a poet. James wasn't much of a Hardy fan—'I didn't catch on', he wrote in the essay 'Interior Music'—but he knew his Hardy and Larkin well enough to declare Davie's evaluations of both poets as 'thunderous misreadings.' The problem with reading, of course, is that you can misread; not reading solves this instantly. Ultimately, Davie was trying to articulate how values can be defined and transmitted through traditions, poetic style and diction and therefore was trying to emphasise the political stakes of Larkin's editorial choices. Fair enough, but it's a long-winded way to complain about not being picked to edit a book of poems.

Meeting the writing of Clive James was fortuitous for my father-in-law. They share many qualities: shockingly well-read, wary of pretentiousness, a good nose for bullshit and deeply thoughtful about art in ways that are worth returning to again and again. This brings me to another time when my father-in-law made his Hardy quip. My wife and I were staying by Corfe Castle, near Swanage, which Hardy rendered as Coorvsgate Castle in his 1876 novel, *The Hand of Ethelberta*. Both early risers, the FIL and I were texting over our morning coffees. We were talking about the weird world of cultural cachet and literary snobbery. I had started this particular conversation by passing on a remark by David Collard about *Ulysses* in his excellent *Multiple Joyce*, which puts into words what I've always felt about reading *literature*: 'it's not for everybody, but it is, and should be, for *anybody*.'[5] I quote, with permission, my

---

[4] *All What Jazz: A Record Diary, 1964-68* (London: Faber and Faber, 1970), pp. 16-17.

[5] For my money, it is one of the best critical books on Joyce and a kind of accessible writing about literature more writers should emulate.

father-in-law's response (formatting preserved):

> Like it . Captures it really nicely . I'm starting to think criticism would be more helpful if it was less about "is this good or bad ", rather "would anyone like it and why would that be"
>
> I really like Bach, and I really like the JCB song .
>
> I'd be very happy to have a musician tell me why , or an English scholar why I don't like Thomas Hardy and I do like Clive James .
>
> Now , if the question were "why do you like Tottenham , and don't like Arsenal " , that's easy , one lot are shitbags and that's the end of it .

Much less succinctly, I replied that I like the idea that criticism can help us understand a work and why someone might like or dislike it. From there, conversation and debate can flow, and from there, mutual understanding. I also mentioned that a friend of mine who is a Hardy scholar would like the challenge of unpicking why someone isn't a fan of 'the little old gentleman', as Larkin called him, and would love to have a go at convincing them to take a different view. If that gets anywhere, I'll report in. On the football remark, I offered nothing. FIL again:

> Yeah this is good bud . It's Broad Brow in spades .[6]
>
> I never liked French white wine because of a litre bottle from a Norwich branch of Spar . Then my Maths teacher bought me a bottle of Pouilly Fuisse and the rest is ...
>
> So , to your mate who writes about Hardy ....
>
> Apparently he said something like "Jude cured me of novel writing" , whereas I said "Jude cured me of Thomas Hardy" . Discuss.
>
> Also ...If you've got any mates who can help me with why I like Miles Davis and not John Coltrane, that would be a good one , but now I'm just being pretentious .

'I never liked French white wine because of a litre bottle from a Norwich branch of Spar . Then my Maths teacher bought me a bottle of Pouilly Fuisse.' I mean come on, just give him a publishing deal already. (In a recent 'A Writer's Diary' Substack entry, Toby Litt, responding to comedy writer David Schneider, said 'don't try to be funnier, try to be more and more specific.' That's why it's funny that the white wine was French and came in a litre, the shop was Spar, and it all happened in Norwich.)

While I've always enjoyed Hardy's books (if enjoy is the word I want), and despite becoming increasingly acquainted with 'Hardy country', I've never found a way to convert a non-believer. I find his novels and poems quite beautiful, often there when I need them. Still, you must accept they're a touch bleak (aside from *Ethelberta*, which, sticking with the theme, I've never finished), which doesn't appeal to as many people as you think. The argument that they're even better when you read them in 'Wessex' falls flat if your respondent isn't on board already or willing to come with you to Dorchester. Should I keep working on the FIL, or am I making the mistake of his wretched teachers? Sharing a bottle of Pouilly Fuissé sounds like a better idea.

I've one more notable experience of failing to encourage someone to read Hardy. This time, it was because I completely forgot what it is like to be a teenage girl. I should explain. About three years ago, my job as an academic dissolved with my employing institution's finances when the pandemic lockdown bit. To keep the wolf from the door, I took up private tutoring, mostly the GCSE English curriculum for overseas students. I also took on a student in London who, her parents told me, was feeling let down by her English classes and had lost her passion for reading. She was thirteen and had, in recent years, devoured books like *The Turn of the Screw* and *The Strange Case of Dr Jekyll and Mr Hyde*. That should tell you about her tastes. So, I was happily employed as a sort of reading buddy, meeting her once a week to close-read a book of her choice. In our first session, I offered half a dozen opening pages from various novels and poetry volumes. She picked *The Return of the Native*, which I think is still occasionally an A-Level English text. On we went. We did a few chapters at a

---

[6] This is a reference to J. B. Priestley's notion of the broadbrow from a thirties radio talk entitled 'To A Highbrow' I had shared with my FIL. Those interested in hearing a lightly dramatised reading of the broadcast can find one in the BBC Radio 4 documentary 'The Battle of the Brows', which I consulted on. It is on BBC iPlayer.

time. She was a careful, funny, inquisitive reader who concluded that the novel was the equivalent of today's soap operas, only better. She treated the book like a mixture of *The Archers*, *Coronation Street* and *Inside No. 9*. Those were *her* comparisons.

As we went on, she developed powerful likes and dislikes of various characters, casually praying that Mrs Yeobright would succumb to a terrible death (I know!). The problems started, however, when we went from term-time to the summer holidays. Suddenly, sessions were cancelled at the last minute, chapters went unread and, at one point, the family went away for three weeks, after which she revealed that she had left the book at home. It was then that the inevitable altering of the deal, *à la* Darth Vader in *Empire Strikes Back*, started to come from the parents. Could we touch on essay writing? It would be great if she could start to get a bit of homework. What about past papers? I became depressed about the whole thing and invariably failed to notice that she had lost interest because her parents started to demand results from her reading. I could not convince them that simply having a reading companion was doing her wonders; that what they had asked me to do was reignite a love of reading in their daughter, who was clearly gifted at it. Our last session was just before Mrs Yeobright is bitten by the adder. She would have loved it.

Why read Hardy, then? Why read anything? And why am I worrying about that question? Reading is a way of communing, with authors, with other readers, but I think there is something fascinating in what we choose not to read or finish, and what this says about us. Why did I performatively reveal that I haven't read Hardy's comic novel? Am I making some point in an essay supposedly about Hardy? Is that like when literary folks make a big deal about not reading *Ulysses* or *Infinite Jest*, as though it makes them *more* culturally profound? I'm genuinely unsure. Donald Davie was right that our reading shapes us, that Larkin was moulded by his love of Hardy's poems, just as my father-in-law was by his frustration with *Jude* and how he was forced to read it. Hardy helped make him the reader he is today. The books we give up on, wander away from, throw across the room, those are as revealing as the well-thumbed volumes we keep by our bedsides. I'm considering setting up a "What I'm Not Reading Book Club". Any takers?

Allan Peterson

Two Poems

Revelations

How snow devils
make vortices in corners
otherwise wind is invisible
though it knocks you down

How pointing is a language
like me in France like dark to harken
Stablehand is not a condition
affecting balance dizzy is

How with a hand inside it
a sock talks

Exoticism

The treasure of reason resides in a box
not everyone can open or wants to

The heat of unreason is insufficient
to create light yet produces hotheads

A phone used to rest in its cradle
ears down to hear the infantile

Easy to see compass in compassion
as exploration provides oration

That Noon to me sounds Persian
is an exoticism

like a toad using its eyes to swallow

JACK FOLEY

SIN, NOT TIME

SATAN'S FIRST SPEECH IN *PARADISE LOST*

" **I** f once they hear that voice," Beelzebub assures Satan in Book I, "...they will soon resume / New courage and revive, though now they lie / Groveling and prostrate" (274–279).[1]

In *Surprised by Sin* (1967) Stanley Fish argues that the true movement of *Paradise Lost* is the movement of the reader's consciousness and that this movement is in fact *away* from the splendors of Satanic rhetoric, despite the tendency, not only of the fallen angels but of many readers as well, to regard Satan's voice as the dominant one in *Paradise Lost*.

I should like to appropriate a good many of Mr. Fish's insights and techniques and apply them to what seems to me to be a particularly difficult and complicated moment in the poem: the entry of Satan and his first speech. In doing so we can, I believe, discover something further about the nature of Satanic rhetoric, both as a theme of the poem and as its instrument: discover, that is to say, something further about the "voice" which at one point Milton compares to the rod of Moses.[2] In doing so, however, we will also discover some difficulty in holding fast to a distinction which appears to be much simpler than it is: the distinction between Sin and Time and—even further—the distinction between Time (or Mutability) and God: "There was a place," Milton writes in Book IX, "Now not, though Sin, not Time, first wrought the change" (69–70). If we leave out the Epic Voice's introduc-

tion, Satan has the first word in *Paradise Lost*, and that word is "If":

> If thou beest hee; But O how fall'n! How chang'd
> From him, who in the happy Realms of Light
> Cloth'd with transcedent brightness didst outshine
> Myriads though bright: If he whom mutual league,
> United thoughts and counsels, equal hope,
> And hazard in the Glorious Enterprise,
> Join'd with me once, now misery hath join'd
> In equal ruin: into what Pit thou seest
> From what highth fall'n, so much the stronger prov'd
> He with his Thunder: and till then who knew
> The force of those dire Arms? Yet not for those,
> Nor what the Potent Victor in his rage
> Can else inflict, do I repent or change,
> Though chang'd in outward luster; that fixt mind
> And high disdain, from sense of injur'd merit,
> That with the mightiest rais'd me to contend,
> And to the fierce contention brought along
> Innumerable force of Spirits arm'd
> That durst dislike his reign, and mee preferring,
> His utmost power with adverse power oppos'd
> In dubious Battle on the Plains of Heav'n,
> And shook his throne. What though the field be lost?
> All is not lost; the unconquerable Will,
> And study of revenge, immortal hate,
> And courage never to submit or yield:
> And what is else not to be overcome?
> That Glory never shall his wrath or might
> Extort from me. To bow and sue for grace
> With suppliant knee, and deify his power
> Who from the terror of this Arm so late
> Doubted his Empire, that were low indeed,
> That were an ignominy and shame beneath
> This downfall; since by Fate the strength of Gods
> And this Empyreal substance cannot fail,
> Since through experience of this great event
> In Arms not worse, in foresight much advanc't,
> We may with more successful hope resolve
> To wage by force or guile eternal War
> Irreconcilable to our grand Foe,
> Who now triumphs, and in th' excess of joy
> Sole reigning holds the Tyranny of Heav'n. (84–124)

Filled with the rolling and insistent rhythms hat so frequently carry us through the complications and intricacies of Milton's syntax, and giving voice to sentiments which we can immediately and easily share, the speech is no doubt a brilliant one, and critics as different as C.S. Lewis and William Empson have singled it out for praise. [3]

Yet even on a first reading—and despite the fact that it contains nothing so obviously ironical as Satan's "Awake, arise, or be for ever *fall'n*" (330, my italics)—one might find in it certain elements

[1] The text I am using is John Milton, *Complete Poems and Major Prose*, ed. Merritt Y. Hughes (New York: The Odyssey Press, 1957). All line citations, unless otherwise indicated, are from Book I.

[2] Book I, 337–343. The lines in question are these:

Yet to thir General's Voice they soon obey'd
Innumerable. As when the potent Rod
Of Amram's son in Egypt's evil day
Wav'd round the Coast, up call'd a pitchy cloud
Of Locusts, warping on the Eastern Wind,
That o'er the Realm of impious Pharaoh hung
Like Night, and darken'd all the Land of Nile....

[3] See C. S. Lewis, *A Preface to Paradise Lost* (New York: Oxford University Press, 1961) and William Empson, *Milton's God* (London: Chatto & Windus, 1961).

which ought to be somewhat disturbing. In his very opening lines, the devil announces that he will not "repent or change," and as the poem progresses we come to see that that statement is true, though, like many of Satan's statements, in a way he does not intend. Satan's character does not undergo change so much as our awareness of it does. The disturbing elements in Satan's early speeches, present but easily disregarded, grow in importance as the poem moves forward, and we should not be surprised to discover—even in those speeches that remain most exhilarating—aspects of Satan that become explicit only much later in the poem.

One such disturbing element in the speech quoted above is the circumstances in which it is delivered. The Epic Voice tells us that "Nine times the Space that measures Day and Night / To mortal men, hee with his horrid crew / Lay vanquisht, rolling in the fiery Gulf / Confounded though immortal" (50–53), and the phrase "mortal men," recalling "that Forbidden Tree, whose mortal taste / Brought Death into the World" (2), hints at what it is that Satan will accomplish: there *is* an immense difference between "mortal" and "immortal," and it is Satan—first referred to as "Th' infernal Serpent" (34)—who will cause us to understand that difference all too well. Moreover, at the moment we first see him, Satan is himself in what he will later describe as an "abject posture":

> have ye chos'n this place
> After the toil of Battle to repose
> Your wearied virtue, for the ease you find
> To slumber here, as in the Vales of Heav'n?
> Or in this abject posture have ye sworn
> To adore the Conqueror?   (I.318–323)

At the very beginning of *Paradise Lost* the devil is totally defeated. He is not commanding his "Chaos" but floating within it, "Chain'd on the burning Lake" (210), and we will see more and more clearly that this chaos is not only external but internal: as Satan himself will say, "which way I fly is Hell; myself am Hell" (IV.76). In Book II, immediately after Sin opens the gates of Hell, both the devil and the reader are given a kind of revelation. Though Milton emphasizes the massive heaviness of the gates—"every Bolt and Bar /

Of massy Iron or solid Rock" (877–878)—they nevertheless open with shocking suddenness and

> Before thir eyes in sudden view appear
> The secrets of the hoary deep, a dark
> Illimitable Ocean without bound,
> Without dimension, where length, breadth, and
>   highth,
> And time and place are lost....   (890–896)

"Into this wild Abyss," the Epic Voice comments, "the wary fiend / Stood on the brink of Hell and look'd a while, / Pondering his Voyage" (917–919), and we must realize that Satan has a great deal to ponder here, that *any* "Voyage" begun by him is in fact begun in chaos. The primary trait of the Satanic character is not tragic heroism but simple confusion. When Satan actually plunges into the abyss he is again totally defeated: "all unawares / Flutt'ring his pennons vain plumb down he drops / Ten thousand fadom deep" (932–934). The devils are indeed—as Moloch puts it—"On this side nothing" (II.101), and our very first view of Satan "rolling in the fiery Gulf" is an indication of just that. But like so much in the early portions of the poem, it is an indication that we can hardly be expected to perceive on a first reading. In a sense, all of *Paradise Lost* may be considered a definition of the terms "awake," "arise," and "fallen," and it is only when we have experienced the poem in its entirety that we know the true meaning of Satan's cry. But it is the particular aim of the first two books to define what it means to "be for ever fall'n": "all unawares / Flutt'ring his pennons vain plumb down he drops." If it is the nature of the unfallen Adam to spring up towards Heaven "As thitherward endeavoring" (VIII.206), it is the nature of the fallen Satan to be forever—falling.

In the opening invocation Milton's epic question, "what cause / Mov'd our Grand Parents in that happy State...to fall off / From thir Creator," is answered emphatically with "Th' infernal Serpent: hee it was" (28–34). The answer is given with absolute authority—"for Heav'n hides nothing from thy view / Nor the deep Tract of Hell" (27–28)—and the emphatic quality of the verse has all the force of a direct accusation:

> Him the Almighty Power
> Hurl'd headlong flaming from th' Ethereal Sky
> With hideous ruin and combustion down

To bottomless perdition, there to dwell
In Adamantine Chains and penal Fire,
Who durst defy th' Omnipotent to Arms.(44–49)

There is, we feel, no doubt about *that*, and the heavy rhythmical emphasis on the alliterative "Him...Hurl'd headlong" tells us a great deal about the poem: Milton is already establishing, in no uncertain terms, the facts of *Paradise Lost*, and one of those facts is the complete authority of the Epic Voice. We are not in the world of Henry James' untrustworthy narrator. In a sense, we may say that it is "John Milton," a particular man, who asks the question but that it is Wisdom itself that answers. The phrase, "Instruct me, for Thou know'st" (19) is a kind of prayer. (That the poem will be dealing with the Tree of *Knowledge* is of course relevant here as well.) At the conclusion of *Paradise Lost* Satan will have *become* a serpent, but here, in the first reference to him, he is *already* a serpent. In a sense, the entire poem exists to prove to us that the Holy Spirit was right, and—again in a sense—we might think of *Paradise Lost* as an immensely involved commentary on what the Holy Spirit *means*. The rhetoric with which the poem begins—whatever else it may be—is magnificently self-assured: the poet, with what seems to be tremendous arrogance, asserts that he knows the cause of *all* our woe:

Of Man's First Disobedience, and the Fruit
Of that Forbidden Tree, whose mortal taste
Brought Death into the World, and all our woe....
    (1–3)

In this arrogance and self-assurance, the Epic Voice is astonishingly similar to Satan.

Indeed, the same voice that warns us against so many Satanic ruses also makes it easy for us to respond to Satan's first speech: we move from "Th' infernal Serpent" to "th' Arch-Enemy" (81) and finally to "Satan" (81), and though the name literally means "adversary," the effect is to suggest the idea of a beast, the idea of an enemy, and, finally, the idea of a particular man with a particular name: again, Milton makes it easy for us to ignore, "to lose / In sweet forgetfulness" (II.608–609), the basic fact that Satan *is* "Th' infernal Serpent." Moreover, Satan seems actually to be *created* for us at the very moment we first see him: the Epic Voice tells us that he is "thence in Heav'n call'd Satan" (82), and whatever words

the devil has previously spoken as Lucifer, these are to be his first words *as Satan*. (At this point, of course, we do not know that we will later be given the war in Heaven.) Furthermore, we are told that they will be "bold words" and that they will break "the horrid silence" (82–83).

The stage, then, is entirely Satan's: there is absolutely no other sound and, in effect, we are to hear the *first* words of the *first* fallen angel in the *first* poem inspired by a spirit that from the *first* was present; we are now to hear—for the first time—what it is like to *be* Satan. The stage is set for an entrance like Othello's, for a voice that will command our immediate respect if not our love. But Satan bungles the job entirely. His first words are an expression of utter uncertainty: "If thou beest hee." Coming as they do after so much certainty of tone and prepared for with so many careful dramatic effects, the words are almost comic. Indeed, in Satan's very first speech, we are not so far from the mock-heroics that will soon appear. (Later, for example, he will cry out to his followers, "Go therefore mighty Powers, / Terror of Heav'n, though fall'n; intend at home "—II.456–457; by that point the distance between rhetoric and fact has become explicit.) We do not notice that the words are an expression of uncertainty because we naturally assume that they are conditional; that is, we expect a sentence like the following: "If thou beest he who once dwelt in Heaven, *then* we still have a good deal of strength." But there is no *then*. Satan's first phrase is interrupted by the exclamation, "But O how fall'n! How chang'd," and his use of the word "fall'n" suggests that he understands his state. He is obviously not referring to the physical "fall," and though the sense of "fallen in battle" is clearly present, the echo of Isaiah 14:12, "How art thou fallen from heaven, O Lucifer," indicates that more than this is meant.

The sentence then begins again: "If he...." But again there is no *then*, though the word "fall'n" now appears completely divorced of its moral connotations and referring to the physical "fall" alone: "into what Pit thou seest / From what highth fall'n." The fact is that this is Satan's form of direct address! In contrast, Adam's first speech begins, "Sole partner and sole part of all these joys" (IV.411) and God's first speech begins,

"Only begotten Son" (III.80). Satan is the only one of them who doesn't know who he talking to—though later in the poem Adam, faced with a similar difficulty, will have recourse to a rather problematical past tense:

> O fairest of Creation, last and best
> Of all God's Works, Creature in whom *excell'd*
> Whatever can to sight or thought be form'd....
> (IX.896–898, my italics)[4]

Despite its almost comic elements, the problem raised here is a crucial one. In Book II, for example, Beelzebub will begin his speech with

> Thrones and Imperial Powers, off-spring of Heav'n,
> Ethereal Virtues; or these Titles now
> Must we renounce, and changing style be call'd
> Princes of Hell? (310–313)

The answer to the question—though it is not the one Beelzebub's rhetoric demands—is yes; like Adam, who will speak with "alter'd style" after the fall (IX.1132), the devils are indeed something quite different from what they were, and we must realize that they are *not* "Thrones and Imperial Powers"—they are even less "Ethereal *Virtues*"—that those titles refer to a place in God's order which they no longer occupy. The question of the identity of the fallen angels is a very important one in the poem. All I want to suggest here is that one possible answer is that they are very nearly nothing at all. Like Hell itself they are "on the brink" of the abyss, "on this side nothing." Satan's name has changed because *he* has changed, and it is very understandable that he should question whatever it is before him. But Satan—though just as "fall'n" as Beelzebub—will not admit to any difference: he is merely "chang'd in outward luster." When, in Book IV, he is himself not recognized, he is genuinely hurt:

> Know ye not then said Satan, fill'd with scorn,
> Know ye not mee? ye knew me once no mate
> For you, there sitting where ye durst not soar;
> Not to know mee argues yourselves unknown,
> The lowest of your throng; or if ye know,
> Why ask ye, and superfluous begin
> Your message, like to end as much in vain?
> (827–833)

The answer is: "Think not, revolted Spirit, thy shape the same, / Or undiminisht brightness, to be known / As when thou stoodst in Heav'n upright and pure" (835–837). "Lucifer" and "Satan" are not at all identical—no more identical than the angelic and diabolic Beelzebub. Yet the entire seduction of Satan's first phrase is that it contains an implied assertion of identity. I have said above that the phrase strikes us as a conditional, but it strikes us as a conditional of a particular kind. We assume that Satan is asking, "Are you the same person?" and that the question—like Beelzebub's "these Titles now / Must we renounce...?"—is a rhetorical one. The construction is both simple and familiar. A question such as "Are you the men you were?" is not really a question at all but a means of eliciting a response; the answer you desire, an emphatic "yes," is contained within the question and you are merely prodding your audience to assert itself. It is a very common rhetorical trick, and it is as familiar to us as it must have been to Milton's audience. Any good preacher would have made use of it on innumerable occasions.

But this is not at all what Satan means. Milton has gone to some trouble to tell us how hard it is to *see* in Hell—"No light, but rather darkness visible" (63)—and Satan is merely groping in the dark towards what he *thinks may* be Beelzebub: "If thou beest hee." His words are those of a man who has just regained consciousness after being struck very hard on the head, except that Satan has been struck harder than any man could be: "Nine times the Space that measures Day and Night / To mortal men, he with his horrid crew / Lay vanquisht...." He is slowly beginning to recover his perceptions, but as yet he is not sure of anything. The phrase "But O how fall'n!" indicates Satan's sudden—and genuine—surprise at what he sees: the Beelzebub before him is not only a different person but is different from anything Satan has ever seen before.[5] And, in his as-

---

[4] Adam's use of the past tense indicates his awareness that this mode of address does not apply to the fallen Eve, but his language has already begun to vacillate between his nostalgia for a woman who no longer exists and his awareness of the present fact. For a discussion of the entire passage see *Surprised by Sin*, pp. 262–265.

[5] It is true, of course, that Satan has seen Sin before, but Milton's reader can hardly be expected to know that when he comes upon this passage. In any case, Satan's inability to recognize Sin in Book II suggests that he has actually forgotten her during the course of his military maneuvers: to use Mr. Fish's phrase, the devil is "surprised by Sin," and it is only after she has grown "familiar" that he is able to feel comfortable with her.

tonishment, Satan quite rightly calls the thing he sees "fall'n," though he immediately recoils from the word and replaces it with the far less loaded term "chang'd." The initial impulse, however, is not essentially different from the impulse that prompts the newly created Adam to name what he sees in Paradise: "My tongue obey'd and readily could name / Whate'er I saw" (VIII.272–273). The difference between Adam's experience and Satan's is that everything Adam sees is good and he is overjoyed by it whereas everything Satan sees is bad and he is horrified by it. The recoiling from the word "fall'n" is a recoiling from the fact of evil itself and the shift to "chang'd" is Milton's version of the first euphemism.

Satan's first words, then, are an indication of how very little he knows, but those same words change meaning so quickly that we hardly notice it. The phrase, "If thou beest hee"—which in itself may express either a kind of certainty or total uncertainty—soon emerges from this ambiguity and defines itself as something entirely different from its original meaning: "If he whom mutual league, / United thoughts and counsels, equal hope," and so on. But—and the point would be abundantly clear if Milton had written a play rather than an epic—it should be obvious to Satan that Beelzebub is not the same person: Beelzebub is standing—or floating—directly in front of him. Yet Satan *forgets*. The sentence he speaks—if it can be called a sentence—ends with an overwhelming certainty of tone: "him, who in the happy Realms of Light / Cloth'd with transcendent brightness didst outshine / Myriads though bright." But the certainty of tone has nothing to do with the Beelzebub who now exists. Satan begins in uncertainty—"If thou beest hee"—reaches certainty—"But O how fall'n"— recoils from it—"chang'd"—and moves on to describe a Beelzebub who exists no longer. Yet in the very description of the dazzling, heavenly Beelzebub, the fallen Beelzebub tends to become transfigured; Satan's rhetoric literally illuminates the "dark" aspects of "fall'n" with phrases suggesting an immense amount of light: "happy Realms of Light," "transcendent brightness," "didst outshine / Myriads though bright"—and the fallen Beelzebub who is not described begins to take on the characteristics of the unfallen angel who is.

Beginning with a juxtaposition of the two Beelzebubs, the sentence goes on to remake the fallen angel into his former self. The facts of the fall are so unbearable to Satan that he takes refuge in language, and his words move further and further away from the truth: from accuracy to euphemism and finally—by suggestion—to an astonishing lie: for Beelzebub the angel is the absolute *antithesis* of Beelzebub the devil. Yet—and this is even more astonishing—the attempt to find refuge in language is completely successful, both for Satan and for the readers of the poem: though we are *told* about a fallen angel, what we *see* is an angel of light.

As Satan goes on, we progress from darkness to a specious sort of brilliance, and the speech that begins in uncertainties and is interrupted by a sudden exclamation now achieves a new assertiveness: "didst outshine / Myriads though bright." Indeed, though the past tense, "didst," might conceivably alert us to what is happening, it seems instead to prevent us from noticing that anything is very wrong. The present tense here would be utterly disastrous because Satan's ruse would then be immediately apparent, and the fact that the word is "didst" rather than "did" serves to bring us even closer to identifying the fallen angel with the unfallen. The dichotomy Satan originally sets up is between "thou"—who is fallen—and "hee"—who is unfallen. But though the word "didst" would have to have "thou"—not "hee"—as its subject, the phrase with which we are presented is "him, who...didst." Thus, though "who" seems to refer back to "him," the verb which follows it seems to refer back to "thou"! Even on a grammatical level, then—and we hardly notice it because "who" is separated from "didst" by two very seductive phrases—it would seem that "thou" and "hee" are tending to become interchangeable.

In any case, Satan's verbal pyrotechnics now enable him to pass on to a new tone:

If he whom mutual league,
United thoughts and counsels, equal hope,
And hazard in the Glorious Enterprise,
Join'd with me once, now misery hath join'd
In equal ruin: into what Pit thou seest
From what highth fall'n, so much the stronger prov'd
He with his Thunder....

At this point we are given something much closer to the sort of rhetorical question with which we thought Satan began: here there is no disturbing juxtaposition of what Beelzebub was and what he is, and if Satan began his earlier speech with "how *chang'd* / From him," he now begins with "If he whom mutual league...." The difference between the two Beelzebubs is no longer being emphasized—though to be sure we are still in the past tense—and the image of the unfallen angel has become dominant. Satan is moving further and further away from the horrible reality in front of him. It seems that once the image of the unfallen Beelzebub has cemented itself in Satan's mind, he is able to relive, in chronological order, the events that have led to his downfall. The effect is almost dreamlike. Beelzebub was originally an angel who outshone "Myriads though bright"; he then joined with Satan in "mutual league, / United thoughts and counsels"; the two of them had "equal hope"; and finally—as Satan seems to be re-experiencing that "hope"—they joined with equal "hazard in the Glorious Enterprise."

At this point the word "Glorious" brings us once again to the light imagery with which we began, and the extraordinary ring of the line indicates that it is the climax of Satan's rhetorical upsurge: we have experienced the early conniving, the "hope," the "hazard," and finally, the dazzling ideal for which the devils were willing to risk all. (Though the brilliant Beelzebub outshone "Myriads," his "Enterprise" seems to have been the even more brilliant ideal towards which he strove.)

Indeed—momentarily at least—we seem almost to have achieved the ideal: the passage does not end with darkness but with an intensification of the light with which it began.

But, as always in the first two Books, our sense of achievement—or near achievement—is immediately dissipated and it is necessary to descend from the heights we have almost reached: "into what Pit thou seest / From what highth fall'n." But the descent here is not nearly as horrifying as we might have expected it to be. If, for example, we compare Satan's line with the Epic Voice's "hideous ruin and combustion down / To bottomless perdition" we can immediately perceive

the difference: Hell is not "bottomless perdition," merely a "Pit"; Satan is not totally defeated—"vanquisht"—but able to relive with delight the events of his life; his enterprise was not totally hopeless—as the lines "Him the Almighty Power / Hurl'd headlong flaming" might have suggested—it nearly achieved success; and the word "fall'n"—from which Satan earlier recoiled with horror—can now be spoken with ease and it is perfectly clear that it now refers merely to a physical fall. While it is true that there has been some rhetorical drop from the line, "And hazard in the Glorious Enterprise," it is nothing at all compared to the sense of sudden downward movement conveyed by the phrase "Him.. .Hurl'd headlong"; the mock-heroics—which will be so noticeable later in the poem—are hardly present here at all. Satan has not been "Hurl'd" in any case; he has merely "fallen," and Milton seems to go out of his way to lessen the rhetorical distance between "hazard in the Glorious Enterprise" and "into what Pit thou seest / From what highth fall'n": the phrases "Join'd with me once" and "now misery hath join'd / In equal ruin" interpose themselves between the two lines and, while somewhat anti-climactic, they can hardly be said to deflate the line preceding them; instead, the word "join'd" suggests that the devils have *not* lost everything, that the bond between them—like the bond between Adam and Eve at the end of the poem—still remains. At this point "Hell" is merely a particularly unpleasant place, but its unpleasantness is entirely a matter of physical discomfort and, like all places, it seems to be morally neuter. Satan is quite able to look around himself and merely—grumble: "into what *Pit*"—and the word is spoken with disgust, as if it were an epithet, but not with horror. Moreover, what has earlier been called "the Almighty Power" is now merely "the stronger," and the reference to "Thunder" inevitably suggests the Pagan Zeus, not the Christian God. We are no longer dealing with a poem in which there is *literally* an "Almighty Power": the word "mightiest," which will appear later in the speech, seems to be a rhetorical exaggeration, a kind of title; [6] Hell is not both a place and a con-

---

[6] In connection with this point, the peculiar ambivalence of the word "omnipotence" has often been noted. As A. J. A.

dition, and "fall'n" has no moral implications at all. We are dealing with a poem about two men, one of them "stronger," to be sure—indeed, "god-like" in his strength—but the other cleverer, more intellectual, opposed to brute force. It is Ulysses and the Cyclops all over again, and our sympathy naturally goes to Ulysses. As we now see, Satan is in fact very far from being a mere grumbler: the very words "stronger" and "with his Thunder" seem to give birth to a new idea. He is suddenly struck by the thought that his "fall" has been in some ways *fortunate*: "and till then who knew / The force of those dire Arms?" And the implications of "stronger" are not yet exhausted: if God is merely extraordinarily powerful, "stronger," power can be defied—"by force or guile." Satan's speech now takes on a new air of determination and defiance:

> yet not for those,
> Nor what the Potent Victor in his rage
> Can else inflict, do I repent or change,
> Though chang'd in outward luster; that fixt mind....

But the phrase "chang'd in outward luster" should remind us of something we have nearly forgotten: what has become of the two Beelzebubs with which the speech began? The answer can be found, I think, in the second appearance of the word "thou": "into what Pit thou seest / From what highth fall'n." The tone here is conversational, familiar—the line is almost an aside—and Satan clearly has no uncertainty about who he is addressing: it is the person in front of him, a person who can see for himself

what Hell is like. The dichotomy at the beginning of the speech was absolute: the fallen Beelzebub was the antithesis of the unfallen Beelzebub. Here, however, we have no such dichotomy. It seems as if Satan had begun to deliver a highly formal speech—"If he whom mutual league..."— and has now broken off to make an informal comment to the person addressed. But the person has not "chang'd": *"he" and "thou" are merely formal and informal ways of referring to the same person*. At this point, then, both Milton and Satan— the one consciously, the other unconsciously— have managed to execute an extraordinary verbal maneuver: the difference between fallen and unfallen, between Heaven and Hell is reduced to the difference between formal and informal, between physical comfort and physical unpleasantness. But Satan's horror at the word "fall'n" is itself disproof of this! Hell is *not* merely a place—"myself am Hell"—and the distance between the fallen and the unfallen is immense: these are the facts, the "given" of the poem.

To see where we went wrong it is necessary to return to the beginning of the speech. Satan has described Beelzebub as "him, who in the happy Realms of Light / Cloth'd with transcendent brightness didst outshine / Myriads though bright," and I have called the effect Milton creates here "dreamlike." But the effect is more than "dreamlike"; it is infinitely nostalgic: this is the Beelzebub who *was*. The seduction of the words is that we do not take them as a description of literal reality at all: they seem to create an idealized portrait of some splendid vanished companion; we feel that the light in which he exists has been shed upon him by our memories. Satan appeals to an easily comprehensible emotion: the nostalgia for lost youth. Beelzebub is Arthur Hallam, John Keats, Arthur Hugh Clough and Edward King all rolled into one, and the thing Satan sees before him is very nearly a decaying corpse: "But O how fall'n!" Once this frame of reference is established, it seems natural to us that the young should join in "mutual league," should "hope," should be ready to "hazard" everything for the sake of some "Glorious Enterprise." We ourselves have experienced something of the same thing, and—like Satan and Beelzebub—we too have realized that the ideals of youth have faded, that

Waldock put it, "there is a certain equivocation in the use of the word 'omnipotent.' When it is convenient to do so Milton uses it with the full literal force; but on occasion it can seem not much more than a grandiloquent synonym for 'supreme.' There is a certain latitude or 'play' in the use of the word; and this for the benefit of narrative" [*Paradise Lost and Its Critics* (Cambridge: Cambridge University Press, 1966), pp. 67–68]. It seems to me that "omnipotence" is always used "with full literal force" but that it is the temptation of the poem—both for ourselves and for the devils—to believe that it is "a grandiloquent synonym." One might compare Virgil's use of "omnipotens" as an epithet for Juno—who is definitely not "omnipotent"—in the fourth Book of *The Aeneid*:

> tum Iuno omnipotens, longum miserata dolorem
> difficilesque obitus, Irim demisit Olympo,
> quae luctantem animam nexosque resolveret artus.
>   (693–695)

The Aeneid of Virgil, ed. T. E. Page (New York: St. Martin's Press, 1967), p. 86. For "fallen" and the problem of language in general see chapter three of *Surprised by Sin*.

though we have certainly retained something, we have also lost a great deal. In this context, the lines "into what Pit thou seest / From what highth fall'n" strike us as metaphorical: we too might describe our present state as a "Pit" and we too might think of the progression from youth to maturity as a "falling." The emotion is universal because all men are caught up in time, and Satan's defiant words are thrilling precisely because they seem—as Yeats put it—to "spit into the face of Time / That has transfigured me": [7]

> yet not for those
> Nor what the Potent Victor in his rage
> Can else inflict, do I repent or change,
> Though chang'd in outward luster....

But it is the whole point of the poem that Satan is the *cause* of time's ravages: "Th' infernal Serpent; hee it was...." The entire passage is a fake elegy: it begins with the fact of "death"—the unconscious Beelzebub floundering on the flames—moves on to nostalgia—"him, who in the happy Realms of Light"—then to the realization that something remains—"What though the field be lost?"—and finally to a determination to go on—"We may with more successful hope resolve. ..." *Paradise Lost* is indeed a poem that will deal with death, "the Fruit...whose mortal taste / Brought Death into the World," as well as with immense loss and with the determination to go on, and here, at the very beginning of his poem, Milton presents us with an elegiac movement.

But the elegy is all wrong. Satan is not creating an idealized portrait of his friend; he is describing literal fact: Beelzebub *was* in "the happy Realms of Light," he *was* "Cloth'd with transcendent brightness," and so on. The fact that he is no longer so, that he is now extraordinarily ugly is due to his joining in the "Glorious Enterprise" itself: because he has rebelled, Beelzebub's moral nature is now indicated by his physical appearance. (We should, incidentally, compare this passage with Sin's description of her birth. The rebellious angels react to her in exactly the same way that Satan reacts to Beelzebub: "back they recoil'd afraid / At first, and call'd me *Sin*...but familiar grown, I pleas'd"—II.759-762.) The nostalgia *we* feel in reading the passage is the nostalgia

[7] William Butler Yeats, "The Lamentation of the Old Pensioner," *The Collected Poems of W. B. Yeats* (New York: Macmillan, 1960), p. 46.

for a dead friend or for lost youth, but the nostalgia *Satan* feels is for the condition of goodness itself. Beelzebub has not died—though he has suffered an astonishing military defeat: he has become *bad*. Satan's horror is not caused by the sight of Beelzebub's wounds, many though they may be: it is caused by the fact that Beelzebub now looks evil: "But O how fall'n!" (Again, we should compare Satan's meeting with Sin: "I know thee not, nor ever saw till now / Sight more detestable than thee"—II.744-745.)

Yet it is precisely because Beelzebub has *also* suffered physical wounds that this crucial distinction is easy to lose sight of, just as it is easy to lose sight of the moral implications of "fall'n" because a military defeat and a physical fall have taken place. The whole push of Satan's rhetoric is towards blurring this distinction, and, finally, destroying it altogether: quite understandably, he cannot bear to think of it and consequently takes refuge in words. But this should not dupe the readers of the poem into forgetting that the distinction exists. The entire progression from uncertainty to determination is not real at all: it is simply verbal. The huge edifice of Satan's speech rests on an extraordinary evasion: "But O how fall'n! How chang'd." (On this "rock" Satan builds his church!) When the devil utters the word "fall'n" he *knows* that Beelzebub is evil, but the word "chang'd" enables him to forget. Then, by means of a rhetorical trick, he is able to identify—or at least blur the distinction between—the fallen and the unfallen Beelzebub. This success brings him even further into illusion: as he surveys his defeated troops he refers to God's strength—"so much the stronger"—though God's "strength" is in fact "omnipotence." Yet Satan does not say "omnipotence": his newly acquired power of euphemism has already begun to become automatic, and in the very act of saying "stronger" he forgets that what he really means is "omnipotent": the word comes into its own and begins to suggest ideas that carry us even further away from the truth: "and till then who knew / The force of those dire Arms?" And so on throughout the entire speech. The euphemism, like the "Word" of God, creates—but it creates only other words that carry us further and further from reality. Though Satan begins with the loss of Beelzebub, moves on to address him as present and concludes with a statement of their reunion—"*We* may with more successful hope"—he is in fact the antithesis of an elegiac poet. It is true that Beelzebub, like Lycidas, is just as "fall'n" at the conclusion of the speech as he was at the beginning and it is also true that all that really happens at the end of both poems is that the speaker has discovered a way of dealing with an originally unbearable reality. But the progression of "Lycidas" is towards accepting that reality; the progression of Satan's speech is towards evading it entirely: in effect Satan's speech is an attempt to annihilate reality, to *make the mind its own place*. But of course the attempt is absurd. The logical lapses, the absurdities, the lies, the mock-heroics that appear in Satan's later speeches are all indications of the distance between rhetoric and fact, of the sheer obstinacy of the real, and they are all engendered in the devil's first words: *we are witnessing the birth of the Satanic mentality*.

B efore concluding I want to return to those words again: "If thou beest hee." To exhaust their implications would, I think, require an explication of the entire poem. All I intend to do here is to suggest a few of the many implications I have not yet discussed. The opening words of the Book of Genesis are:

> In the beginning God created the heaven and the earth.
> And the earth was without form, and void; and darkness was upon the face of the deep.
> And the Spirit of God moved upon the face of the waters.
> And God said, Let there be light: and there was light. (I: 1–3)

And these are the opening words of the Gospel according to Saint John:

> In the beginning was the Word, and the Word was with God, and the Word was God.
> The same was in the beginning with God.
> All things were made by him; and without him was not any thing made that was made.
> In him was life; and the life was the light of men.
> And the light shineth in darkness; and the darkness comprehended it not. (I: 1–5)

The parody is now complete: we are not only seeing Satan for the first time in the first poem of its kind, and so on; we are seeing him *in the beginning*. Like the Spirit of God, Satan too moves "upon the face of the waters," but he is floating unconscious after a terrible defeat and they are not "waters" but "flames." For him too, "darkness [is] upon the face of the deep," but here there will be "No light, but...darkness visible." And if Saint John may say of Christ, "In him was life; and the life was the light of men," we might say of Satan, "In him was death; and the death was the darkness of men." The entire description of creation is inverted, as is the fundamental creative act, the act of naming: "Let there be light: and there was light." For God, the name and the thing named are identical, and the newly created Adam is able to share in this: "My tongue obey'd and readily could name / Whate'er I saw"—though, of course, Adam merely names things which are already created. The closest Satan comes to this act is in his exclamation, "O how fall'n!"—but "fall'n" is an adjective, not a noun, and Satan immediately recoils from it. The exclamation is enough, however, to increase the parody even further: *"fall'n" is the "Word" that is in Satan's "beginning"*: it is from this one term that the immensely confused flood of his speeches flows forth.

If God says, "Let there be...," Satan says, "If thou beest," and the meaning of "thou" is already beginning to drift away from the fact in front of him. For the truth is that Satan has forgotten what it means to be, and his very first speech ends with attractive—but deceptive—images of defiance and destruction. (His desire "To wage by force or guile eternal War," for example, finds its true fulfillment in the landscape of Chaos, "where eldest *Night* / And *Chaos*, Ancestors of Nature, hold / Eternal Anarchy, amidst the noise / Of endless wars, and by confusion stand"—I-I.894–897.)

But Satan's defiance is not even real defiance. In "arising" from the lake he is fulfilling God's will: "nor ever thence/ Had ris'n or heav'd his head, but that the will / And high permission of all-ruling Heaven / Left him at large" (I.210–213). God *wants* Satan to be "created," wants him to take his place in the immense scheme of things.

The only possible defiance, then, would be to refuse to arise, to refuse to be at all. But that would be total defeat! Satan's position is absolutely impossible: in the universe Milton describes, one simply cannot do anything contrary to the divine will. It is therefore necessary for Satan to "create" another universe in which God is not "omnipotent" but "stronger": in order to do anything at all, Satan must believe that he can defy God, but his very speeches of defiance become in the end merely another euphemism for "fulfilling the divine will." Defiance of a sort is possible, but not on Satan's terms: it is possible to defy *Satan*, and that is just what the Epic Voice does: "Him...Hurl'd headlong." But the Epic Voice prays to God to "Instruct me, for Thou know'st," and it is through that prayer that he is able to undergo a metamorphosis from "John Milton" to "Wisdom." Satan, on the other hand, refuses to know anything—"the darkness comprehended it not"—and his attempt to "change"

Beelzebub is successful only in terms of empty words. Indeed, the "hee" to whom Satan reaches out in his beginning is, in the full scheme of the poem, ultimately Christ: "If thou beest *he*"—the savior. In his benightedness Satan chooses Beelzebub instead of Jesus.

Finally, I think, Satan's rhetoric refers only to himself: it becomes in effect a gigantic metaphor for Satan. The two are at last exact reflections of one another, and it is entirely proper that Milton's description of the serpent should serve also as an excellent metaphor for even the most moving of Satan's speeches: "Hee leading swiftly roll'd / In tangles, and made intricate seem straight, / To mischief swift" (IX.631–633). At the beginning of the poem he is also "rolling," but we hardly notice it then.

[written in the late 1960s, published 1970, *ELH*]

Kurt Luchs

Found in Translation: Homer Through the Eyes of Emily Wilson

We can never have too many translations of a great work of literature. There is always the chance, or the hope, that a new version will bring out some crucial aspect of the work that previous versions have missed. We want a new translation to be at the same time more faithful to the original and also more exciting in our own language, as if combining our wife and our mistress into the same being. Once in a lifetime a new translation achieves these goals on such a scale that it flattens the competition and rises to a whole different level, the

level of the original work. This is what Emily Wilson has accomplished with her translations of *The Odyssey* and *The Iliad* by Homer. It is impossible to imagine them being equaled, let alone surpassed, any time soon.

"Who is Kurt Luchs," you may ask, "that he dares torment us with his pontifications upon works written in a dead language that he doesn't presume to know?" Well, fair enough. I'll go so far as to forgive that your imaginary question is so laborious and stilted that it sounds as if it was brought over from an even deader language. It's still a fair question. And the answer is, you're right. My knowledge of Ancient Greek is limited to a scene from the Marx Brothers film *Animal Crackers*, where Captain Jeffrey T. Spaulding (Groucho) is dictating a letter to his secretary Horatio Jamison (Zeppo). Groucho criticizes Zeppo's diction, and adds, "You want to brush up on your Greek, Jamison. Well, get a Greek and brush up on him!" It is not known what connection there might be between this classic exchange and the later Cole Porter song "Brush Up Your Shakespeare" from *Kiss Me Kate*.

What I can say is that it is precisely because I have brushed up my Shakespeare, and my Milton, and all the other worthy poets in the English language who have created a centuries-old tradition of blank verse in iambic pentameter, that I do have some ability to judge Wilson's work as poetry in our tongue. Not only do her translations of Homer make these epics sing in a way they never have previously for modern readers, and thus reaffirm Homer's greatness. They also prove that she is among the finest poets of our time. That is not something she would claim for herself. On the contrary, in the last paragraph of her Translator's Note for *The Iliad*, she refers to herself as a "mere translator." Her humility is admirable and exactly the right spirit with which to approach the monumental task she undertook. But it must be said that it takes a great poet to translate a great poem, to recreate it line by line in another language in a way that does it justice, faithful like a wife, exciting like a mistress.

Even if these translations were less than magnificent, these books would be worth having for the introductions, probably the most entertaining and insightful musings on Homer ever penned. Further, she uses the introductions and translator's notes to explain her choices. And here we can see how she avoided the pitfalls of most previous versions.

The originals were written in dactylic hexameter, a line and rhythm that might make perfect sense in Ancient Greek but which sounds like horses galloping or the oom-pah-pah of a tuba in English. For better or worse, the only sensible English equivalent to the prosody of Homer is iambic pentameter. It sounds more like soldiers marching. By adding or subtracting a syllable here and there and occasionally switching up the beat, it can be capable of tremendous variety. Homer's poems were not rhymed, so there is no rationale for a translation to be (sorry, Alexander Pope, your version of *The Odyssey* is a nonstarter for this reason alone).

Blank verse it is then! Not, however, the blank verse of Shakespeare or Milton, wonderful though they are. Wilson takes pains to avoid any trace of archaic diction, unlike, say, the Technicolor biblical epics of the 1950s. The diction in

many of those films at least had some point, because it descended in a straight line from the translations in the King James Bible. Such a cliched device would do nothing to bring us any closer to the world of these poems.

And what a strange, incomprehensible world it is for those of us looking back from the 21st century. The founders of this nation took many ideas about democracy, the governance of republics and human rights from Ancient Greece and Rome. These poems, however, predate the Greece where the first stirrings of democracy and freedom were felt. In fact, though written in Greek, they predate Greece. Nowhere in them can be found any notion of essential human rights, the equality of women, the errors of racism and nationalism, and the evils of wars of conquest. By the end of *The Iliad* the characters have become deeply aware of the horrible suffering and destruction of war, but they cannot look outside the framework of their time to question the whole enterprise.

War was the means by which talented and ambitious men won honor. It was also the means by which they obtained wealth, through plundering and pillaging those they had defeated, and claiming every kind of trophy, up to and including human beings. That's what Helen was if you'll recall, a trophy. Every kind of theft was legal and even meritorious in warfare. *The Odyssey* contains multiple passages admiring the clever piracy of its protagonist.

The worst evil, from our modern viewpoint, was slavery. In the world of these poems it was ubiquitous. The most striking thing about it is that nobody questions it, least of all the slaves themselves. The slave rebellions of Rome were centuries in the future. When a woman is captured by the enemy in wartime, she knows she'll be enslaved, raped, and kept as a powerless concubine for the rest of her life.

Of course, slavery is far from extinguished even in our time. It is still practiced in Chinese gulags and in parts of the Middle East and Africa, and in a sub rosa form anywhere there is human trafficking. But it is quite peculiar to be immersed in the world of these epics where it is universal and taken for granted.

As readers from a different time with different values and social structures, we should feel alienated from these foreign tales. Yet we do not. Despite the gulf between us and Homer, we share many human feelings, and feelings are the basis of art. We too grow up in families, study, work, worship, fall in love and start families of our own. And when necessary, either to obtain honor or riches, or to defend them, we fight for what we love and believe in, to the death if we must, though most of our battles occur in boardrooms and the marketplace and are not immediately fatal.

Part of Wilson's achievement lies in how she has artfully tuned the English diction of these translations to bring out the same feelings in us as the original poems presumably did in their listeners. It's worth noting, also, that she is the first woman to translate these works in their entirety. For the first time, perhaps, we can be reasonably sure that the misogyny, racism and imperialism that we find in them are the creation of Homer alone and have not been unintentionally enhanced by a biased male translator.

I could go on about her canny and erudite choices and how well they serve Homer, but you can see that for yourself in her introductions and translator's notes. It's time for a look at some of the results. Wilson's personal favorite of the two epics is *The Iliad*, for reasons she explains well. Mine is *The Odyssey*, because it seems to me the more universal, though perhaps it is just a matter of which parts of the human experience Homer focuses on in each poem. For me, anyway, the premise of a long, fraught journey homeward to an uncertain reception resonates more.

I can't hope to cover the entire poem in an essay of this scope. Instead I will look at one of the 24 chapters (actually, they're called books). Let's examine some of the highlights of Book 22, "Bloodshed," which is the climax of the narrative. This is where Odysseus, after 20 years of wandering, is back in his own home in Ithaca disguised as a ragged beggar. He finally reveals himself to the suitors that have been hounding his wife Penelope for her hand (thinking her a widow), and slaughters them all with the help of his son Telemachus and some loyal longtime servants (okay, slaves).

The first thing one notices about this book is how aptly it has been titled. "Bloodshed" it's called and bloodshed there is, by the bucketful. Nor is Homer shy about depicting it graphically. His crimson-soaked telling makes *Macbeth* seem like a Sunday school pageant. I'm surprised that Sam Peckinpah and Quentin Tarantino have never filmed a version of this story. Here, for example, is what Odysseus has his men do to Melanthius, the goatherd who helped the suitors plunder the flocks of the household for their nightly feasts as they courted Penelope:

> Then the men took Melanthius outside
> and with curved bronze cut off of his nose and ears
> and ripped away his genitals, to feed
> raw to the dogs. Still full of rage, they chopped
> his hands and feet off. Then they washed their own
> and they went back inside.

Note the alliteration of "curved" and "cut," and also of "ripped," "raw" and "rage." Just enough to make a song of the narrative. The whole translation is like this: simple, subtle and supple. The directness of the brutal episode and its matter-of-fact delivery would make Hemingway proud. Right before this passage, Telemachus dispatches the twelve slave girls who betrayed their mistress and bedded down with the suitors:

> As doves or thrushes spread their wings to fly
> home to their nests, but someone sets a trap—
> they crash into a net, a bitter bedtime:
> just so the girls, their heads all in a row,
> were strung up with the noose around their necks
> to make their death an agony. They gasped,
> feet twitching for a while, but not for long.

Odysseus, Telemachus and a few loyal herdsmen prove enough of a force to annihilate every suitor. But the gods have been involved as well from the beginning of this tale. They have contributed to the hero's suffering and one of them will play a vital role in his victory. Athena, daughter of Zeus, and like Odysseus a master strategist, twice causes the suitors' spears and arrows to miss their marks.

We should pause here to consider how different the religion of the Ancient Greeks shown in these poems is from Christianity as preached, yet how similar to Christianity as practiced. The gods of Mount Olympus are simply humans writ large in both their virtues and vices, with Marvel superpowers added. They are temperamental, fickle, whimsical, and often vicious and cruel and vengeful. We of modern times, who fancy ourselves sophisticated and advanced, feel we would have trouble worshipping and obeying such beings whose moral sense is manifestly inferior to our own. The Judeo-Christian god, by contrast, is all-powerful and all-knowing but also all-loving and all-forgiving. Supplicants to Jehovah are urged to pray to be or become, not to get. The spiritual goal is to be more like him, not to get him to do things for us.

Well, saints like Augustine and Aquinas may live up to these ideals. The rest of us do not. Exactly like the characters of Homer's poems, we beg our god, we try to bribe him with offerings and promises of good behavior, and we implore him to give us what we want, no matter how impure or selfish our motives. Even worse, we subconsciously expect our god to understand this because the Old Testament shows him to be about as high-minded and emotionally stable as Zeus. All this to say, the emotional life and even the spiritual life of Homer's characters is not so far removed from us as it might first appear.

Back to the poem! The only other thing I want to touch on is the running theme of how the travels and travails of Odysseus have aged him and changed him in his 20-year journey. He expresses much anxiety over the twin dilemmas of how he can conceal his identity when he returns to Ithaca, and then how he can reveal himself convincingly before he exacts his revenge and takes back what is his.

Athena helps him with the first dilemma by using her powers to make Odysseus look even older and more ragged than his journeys have. This allows him to return to Ithaca unrecognized and to infiltrate his own household in the guise of an aged beggar. Athena helps with the second dilemma also, by removing the enchantments of age from Odysseus at critical moments, such as when he wants to be known by Telemachus.

More often, however, Odysseus reveals himself by letting the doubters see and touch the deep scar left in his thigh during his first wild boar hunt as a young man. There is nothing more intimate than a wound. While this wound is physical, it doubles as a symbol of the inner wounding of Odysseus during his unimaginable ordeals, his psychic suffering, his doubts, his fears.

And it has a curious echo in the New Testament account of the resurrection of Christ, when doubting Thomas must touch the wound in Jesus' side to be convinced that he's back. In fact, there is a remarkable parallel between these passages of *The Odyssey* and the inexplicable reactions of Jesus' followers when he reappears among them on several occasions after his crucifixion. It has always struck me as very odd that his disciples who have been with him constantly for three years don't seem to know him at all when they see him again. The women do, naturally, because women may see some things more readily than men.

Yet the men remain clueless. Aside from the general dull wittedness of the disciples, the most obvious explanation is that these unrecognized appearances of the risen Lord are not the risen Lord at all, merely misinterpreted and misremembered after the fact to fit the legend. Still, it is tantalizing to compare them with similar passages in *The Odyssey*, because they both employ one of the oldest religious tropes in existence, that of the trickster god. This too may help us relate to the emotional and spiritual world of Homer, as far removed as we like to think we are from everything else about him.

KURT LUCHS

THE SIGN OF ODYSSEUS

No one seems to recognize him
this ragged old man begging for scraps
in his own house like a feral dog

After twenty years away across the sea
fighting the Trojans to their doom
plundering foreign villages as any pirate would
watching his men be slaughtered
and servicing the pleasure of a goddess
he has returned to a home no longer his
his son not quite a man
his wife not quite a widow
the suitors wasting his substance
coming ever closer to a sanctified rape

Nobody knows him
nobody gives him a second glance
to see what's beneath the grime of decades
how can he announce himself
to a world that has stopped awaiting him

The gods can open the eyes of those he loves
the gods can do anything
and that's lazy writing Homer
much better to share secrets
things that only he would know
yet even that is not enough
an imposter could have heard these things
from his own dying lips
and returned in his place to claim his treasure

In the end there is but one sure sign
the wound given in his flesh
by the first wild boar he hunted and killed
the wound healed long ago but the scar remains
as personal as a signature
if you want them to know who you really are
show them your wound

Mike Marks

Calhoun

My pot smoking buddy Calhoun was a biology graduate student at Kansas State University, with his own lab and assistants in the penthouse of the old botany building. His coursework was completed. All that was left was a thesis that had most of the actual research completed.

Calhoun was a little guy, the product of a first-class prep school where all the other grads became doctors, lawyers, engineers, or captains of industry. At twenty-three years old, he was divorced and remarried, with two children from his first wife and one from his second, plus two stepdaughters came with his second wife. Five offspring was a bundle for a student in his early twenties. Besides, he was making payments on his loaded Camaro.

He lived in an apartment complex for married students with his new family. His wife worked at the university in a microbiology lab. Supporting five kids was expensive.

One day, a man appeared in Calhoun's private upstairs lab and asked him to supply him with chemicals for a small profit. The man wanted lithium aluminum hydroxide which is a powerful reducing agent. It has an ignition temperature of about forty degrees; that means you can hold fire in your hand without getting burned. The Sheik, a professional wrestler, used the stuff to open his act. It is sold in one-gallon cans, a necessary compound for the manufacture of amphetamines like speed. Some chemicals, like lysergic acid—the main ingredient of LSD—required a special permit to purchase, but not this stuff.

Calhoun pulled out his chemical catalogs, wrote a university purchase order, and bought a gallon dissolved in ether. The buyer insisted that the transfer of it for cash was made out in the farmland, where no one was following. Calhoun received a hundred dollars on the first transaction, then repeated the process once again. Then he bought five gallons at a time, saving one for his own use.

Calhoun tried making speed in his lab with the reducing agent. We tried the powder he made a few Friday nights. We put it on our tongues, but it never worked. He kept trying.

He mail-ordered a kit to assemble a fancy stereo system including amplifier and preamp from Allied Radio. He and I tried to slap it together one Friday night in his apartment. We worked on it all night. Early the next morning the last resistor was soldered in place. We plugged it in. The amp groaned for a second like a dog wanting to go out and do his business. Then it smoked and died. One transistor had failed and the rest fried like cascading dominos behind it. I went home to crash. In the meantime, Calhoun went to the local electronics store, bought the diodes and transistors he thought he needed and got the darn thing running before noon.

We were paranoid in 1969. I was busted for a small amount of pot the year before. Cops were keyed in on bringing down druggies. Calhoun told me how he ditched followers one night by cranking his Camaro over a hundred miles per hour with the lights off down narrow country roads. He detected cars slowing down suspiciously in front of his apartment complex. He claimed that the milkman took three hours to deliver at his building one morning. He suspected they were all narcs. We were all paranoid back then.

That summer was the only time I took acid. It wasn't a full dose and I never fully tripped. I understood where my hallucinations were coming from. I saw five stoplights, but knew that only the one in the middle was real. At 4:00 a.m., I filched someone's morning paper and walked onto campus to read it on a bench near Calhoun's lab. I thought it was normal for people to be constantly walking by. I guess I was high, but not totally zonked. I was tried to read the newspaper in the dim light.

I found out the next day that the Bureau of Narcotics and Dangerous Drugs (now DEA) was busting him that night. They admitted that they were watching him for a month. They were on to him because he bought so much of the reducing agent. They took movies of his lab. One fed even showed him what he was doing wrong in his amphetamine manufacturing process. Calhoun was charged with four federal felonies. They arraigned him in Junction City, a county to the west. It wasn't in the news. Without making any specific promises, the feds told Calhoun that the fed helps those who help the feds. They put him on a mission to bust a bigger fish. His buyer was part of a drug syndicate headquartered in Milwaukee that was trafficking a new designer version of speed called MDA.

He was banned from his lab just short of a master's degree. He spent his time putting over a hundred thousand miles on his Camaro getting tight with the Milwaukee contingent. In the end thirteen people were arrested in a sweep from Wisconsin to Kansas. The university had allowed him to stay on at the intervention of the Feds to protect his cover. Now that the job was done, the university told him he had to move on. In January, he talked me and my wife into moving two hours east to Kansas City with his family to get jobs. My wife was bored with college, ready for a change. I was starting graduate school in creative writing, but I wasn't learning about writing. I was paying tuition to write. I thought I would write no matter where I was. Surely, I could find a job that would pay me to write in the big city. Calhoun's wife grew up on a farm. We borrowed her dad's stake truck and relocated all our worldly goods to the city.

After testifying on behalf of the government, the drug phase of Calhoun's life ended with six months of probation on charges reduced to two misdemeanors. The same blind brazen attitude that got him into trouble got him out with little or no aftershock, not even from the men who were arrested.

He created a very lucrative profession selling blood to pharmaceutical companies that he collected from unborn calves at the Kansas City stockyard. But his success was short-lived as others cloned his business and squeezed him out. He went to see his sister in a small town in Alaska and never returned to the midwest.

Several years and wives later, Calhoun ended his three-term run as mayor of that small town in Alaska. Drug free for decades, he stays close with most of his previous spouses, twelve children and stepchildren, and all their children.

Kirsten Mosher

Dredging

You will feel a dull ache in your thigh, take the paring knife and peel a sliver of skin off a lemon. Lemon rind/espresso—blocks the bitter. Bent rind will microjet essential oils in your face. You'll take the spritz of fresh.

Your octogenarian father will be in the kitchen arranging the coffee cups. His turn to host. He won't be able to find the creamer. His friends will bring the pastries, flakey twirls topped with pink sprinkles. They will whisper loudly, say he seems lost, crumbly buttery tunnels filled with dark chocolate, say he should live closer to his family, donut holes.

"Oh, you're limping?" they'll say to you.

You'll pat your fresh nicotine patch in response. Your daughter will flit about the edges of the sunken living room offering packets of raw sugar. The box in the back of the cabinet, still here from your last visit, you insist on it, loving the way the brown crystals take longer to dissolve, adding crunch to the first few sips of coffee.

Cupboards slam shut, your father is still looking for the powdered creamer after setting it on the kitchen island five minutes ago, a reminder that this visit isn't just about sugar.

His friends will want to know what the plan is.

You won't recognize the one who is searching your face. She'll look at you unblinking, waiting for an answer. What's the plan? Her wrist will tremble causing ripples on the surface of her hot coffee. A sliver of lemon peel will rise to the top breaking through a layer of thick cream. Your stomach will sour at the site. You'll wonder, was that your mistake?

You take the red-eye, arriving with your daughter only hours before your father hosts his monthly brunch. He swivels away from the Her on his computer, relieved that at last you are here. His sigh fills the room. He's been looking for Her all his life, but he is glad to see you and his grand-daughter. He'd been pouring over trophy-wife-dot, fish-in-the-sea-dot, she's-young-enough-to-be-your-daughter-dot, a-man-needs a-maid-dot or just-take-care-of-me-especially-when-I'm-old-and-dotty-dot-com.

Eventually he says, "I have nothing to live for," and opens the bottom drawer, just enough for you to see inside.

He looks back at the computer screen, it's dark, but his den overflows with his collection of printouts, profiles with smiling portraits.

He opens another drawer: box of paperclips, box of ballpoints, box of bullets. "See, it's not loaded."

He's not sure why you're yelling at him, not sure what you're saying. All you can remember is the loud and the hurricane of your voice, how it comes out of your pores, the ends of your hair, how it wants to rake him over, wants to strangle him, help him end it right there, and then how it chokes, at the sight of your daughter, standing in the doorway, wet eyes whispering into your stomach, "why are you yelling at Grandpa?"

"Everything is fine," you say to her. "Everything is fine," you say it to him.

Everything is fine, because you are an expert hot chocolate maker. The trick is to melt the chocolate down first, slowly whisk in the milk, then only fill the cup half full, because the other half has to be whipped cream, so when you tilt the cup to your mouth your face is covered with cool thick cream before you finally get to sipping the steaming hot cocoa. The final sips are a matter of dredging a layer of dense sludge from the bottom of the cup.

Grandfather/granddaughter. One cup for him/one cup for her. Tuck in/tuck in. We'll talk in the morning/don't let the bedbugs bite.

The nicotine patch on your left arm is itchy, it's been time zones since you put it on. You stand at the front door and spit chocolate flavored phlegm into the garden, roll a plan between your fingers. Tomorrow he's hosting his friends here.

You go back to his den, open the drawer and grab the gun. It's lighter than you thought, feels like a toy. Your legs know where to go. Your feet walk into tall reeds. The house is a quarter mile behind. You throw the gun out into the wetland shit like you're some kind of Greek hero discus thrower, face blown off with centuries.

You look up at the stars. You have maybe a dozen back home, he has billions. Your eyes attach to the vast. Everything is fine.

Everything is not fine.

The wetland pond is too shallow. Guys fish there. Someone will find it. You should hand it over to the police. Don't hand it over to the police. It doesn't belong to you. It belongs to him. Fish it out of the shallow water, so you can throw it somewhere deeper.

You retrace your steps. The first layer of muck is warm, thick with reeds. You are getting suction cupped, with each move. The next layer is ice cold. Your memory plays back the splash. It was somewhere near here, where you're reaching, where you're elbow deep. You fish with your fingers, feel with your feet, kick something aside.

The blast is muffled, but it knocks you over, boils the shallow water. The muck, eight hundred times thicker, eight hundred times harder to travel through than air, slows the bullet.

You can hear yelling over the sound of ringing ears. Your voice, your hurricane. Your open mouth heaves wetland. A section of skin flaps off your thigh. The blood makes it seem worse than it is.

Yes, the mud, the stars, the cold will wash off, but you will be sweating yellow stomach slicing nerve juice until you come up with a real plan. A plan for the pain, your thigh is pulsing more than it should. A plan for the loaded gun, you are still clutching. A plan for your father.

Kat Meads

Spinoffs

People are such a commitment.
—Melissa Broder

Her traveling companion's college flight left earlier than Penelope's. Someone not Penelope would have continued to explore castles, towns and curiosities never again to be seen, but Penelope opted to return to the coastal bed and breakfast where she and her only friend in life had stayed at the beginning of their wander and there to wait out the remaining week before flying home. Because this was the end of Penelope's travels, funds were extremely tight. After the come-with breakfast, Penelope bided her time until two p.m. when she walked to a small shop and bought a packaged pastry, the last of her caloric intake for the day. To eat up time she walked, walked, walked the misty shore, drizzle or no drizzle, and repaired early to bed with a fat novel. On the second night of her stay, her reading was interrupted by a knock on the door and an invitation to head out for some "nightlife." Penelope declined; the inviter withdrew; Penelope finished the chapter and, stomach yowling, went to sleep. The woman who had poked her head inside Penelope's room the previous evening must have spotted Penelope from afar on the drizzly beach—obviously American, Penelope was supremely spottable—and soon fell in step, offering a native's view of the queen, the prime minister, the parliament and the historical and ongoing mistreatment of the working class. She was very tall with very red hair. She was Penelope's age. She was ebullient, gregarious, a dyed-in-the-wool mingler who did not mind drizzle. Penelope walked faster, then slower, on the crunchy sand. She stopped and stared broodingly at the churning sea. She failed to answer questions or answered evasively. None of these tactics dampened the other's enthusiasm for her company. To avoid sharing the breakfast room, Penelope began waiting until the last seating, her stomach outraged by the delay. To avoid predictable patterns, she began to vary the hour of her afternoon snack, yet again outraging her stomach. She gave up sea walks. Because she now remained in her room for much of the day, she finished the fat novel early, her carefully cal-

ibrated routine thrown completely out of whack by friendly overture. "I'm afraid, love, you didn't quite enjoy this visit," the proprietor said when Penelope checked out, ruefully leaving behind the finished novel. She would have nothing to read on the train or plane. People not reading looked available to chat.

—&&&—

There is nothing spiritually easier than being in opposition.
—Rebecca West

Adele's mother was a "have to" mother. According to Adele's mother, on an almost hourly basis, Adele *had to* do this and *had to* do that. Take out the trash. Clip her fingernails. Pay attention. Speak in full sentences. Stop picking at the mole on her leg. Avoid bacon—because Adele's mother had become convinced (utter nonsense) that her daughter had developed, sometime between the ages of ten and twelve, an allergy to pork. Adele's mother's endless, self-replicating "Have To" list had caused Adele to wonder what sort of mother her grandmother had been—specifically, if Adele's mother's mother had also been a "Have To" mother. Wondered, but did not follow-up. What did a dead grandmother have to do with her lot? Possibly quite a bit, but Adele was too young to go in for extended generational comparison. As it was, Adele spent far too much of a finite lifespan crafting deflections she would have uttered had she not been, by and large, a cooperative daughter. Spitting mouthwash into the sink, she parried: "No, Mother. I don't *have to* do anything except . . . breathe." Applying acne creme, she challenged: "Mother mine, I believe you are confusing necessity with choice." On a perfectly unextraordinary Monday, neither mother nor daughter besieged by migraine, menstrual cramp or indeterminate funk, Adele's mother pointed to her daughter's head and declared that Adele *had to* wash her (not all that oily) hair instantly and, while at it, *had to* apply extra conditioner to those proliferating split ends. Ask yourselves: who can predict at which point rebellion will kick in and claim its due? Neither shampoo nor conditioner touched Adele's strands for three weeks running, despite ferocious mother/daughter rows. In the mirror, Adele saw the visage of a savage cave girl emerge, one who would have been too busy hunting, fishing and starting smoky fires to bother with hair maintenance. Her scalp itched like a flea farm; still the cave girl look grew on her. She had begun to appear, to her notion, quite fierce.

—&&&—

What is the malaise? you ask.
—Walker Percy

It was this morning's job, family assigned, to take his aged aunt to the hairdresser's and afterwards, should his aunt be inclined to show off her smartened-up self to an unrelated public, to the coffee shop that served coffee at the scalding temperature she preferred. Sky analysis was slowing the operation. Once out the door of her garden apartment, his aunt planted her feet and stared balefully upward. "Ominous," she said, referencing the sky and not (he hoped) his attempt to, hand beneath her elbow, hurry her along. Ahead were fourteen increasingly elevated steps to the street and thereafter the further challenge of comfortably situating his aunt in the passenger seat of his Prius, run through the car wash just yesterday to avoid the importance-of-taking-care-of-one's-things conversation. "Ominous," his aunt repeated. Until he affirmed the sky summary, all motion would remain suspended. Dark clouds expanded above them. The sun was not to be seen. The dreariness also filtered down, both boxwood shrubs and Bermuda grass sporting a gray cast. "Whatever's blowing in from the Gulf won't be pleasant," his aunt said. "No," he said, meaning yes, the coming weather would not be pleasant. "But it should hold off till afternoon," he added, as if speaking as a trained meteorologist. His aunt redirected her scrutiny. "You miss my point," she said. He did not think he did. The longer they stood still, the greater the threat that grayness would further saturate his aunt's already gray hair and deepen the grayness of his crewneck sweater. Soon gray and grayer thoughts would begin to steep; helplessness would drag on his limbs, destroying his posture. The urge to crouch would become overwhelming. Suffocatingly trapped in a gray, gray bubble in which all speech in rotation echoed, he would cease to view struggle as noble, fulfilling or compulsory. Gradually breathing would become a chore and he would forget to blink. From the top step, his aunt scolded: "You'll make us late, nephew!" It seemed an insuperable distance: the gray top step, his gray aunt. Tremendous effort would be required to reach either. Also: desire.

—&&&—

The rest is almost history.
– Mary Ruefle

Whenever Octavia left home she felt convinced she would expire before returning. The house she feared never to return to wasn't much of a house, really. Approaching it after a day away anyone, even Octavia, perceived its limitations and discarnate air of melancholy. There was the busted front stoop. The splinter-wracked porch. Windows that did not live up to the reputation of windows. Around the foundation the limp and straggly weeds seemed infected by the house's ennui, "robust" not part of their character. And they were weeds. If not a fighting spirit, what is a weed? The spare interior failed to offer up anything to catch and hold the gaze in either pleasant or horrifying fashion. But because, after her demise, Octavia did not like to imagine anyone discovering the house in wild disorder and on that basis generalizing about its occupant, she never left the house without making the beds, sponging the counters, sweeping the floors and aligning the curtains, just as if she were a character in a fairytale fulfilling girl-tasks before venturing out into a deep, primeval forest. Octavia's actual house stood on a vast, open plain with unimpeded views of nothingness in every direction. It was a landscape with which a poet might equate forever, but Octavia had no poet friends and was not, herself, inclined toward metaphor. Because death workers were death workers, professionally immune to surprise, Octavia supposed they would make little of the terrain or its emptiness, driving the long, gritty path to the house, smoking a last cigarette before arriving and getting down to business—for Octavia had gradually come to accept that she might instead be found where last she lay, listening to creaking floorboards and whistling windows, her tired heart tiring of the pretense that life was good when for Octavia it had not been.

David Rose

Reaching Jackson

The Journey Perilous, right? When you start out, you never know where you'll end up. This blank canvas, it's *terra incognita*. You make your tracks, then begin to follow them. It's risky. You're creating from nothing.

What you're aiming for, always, is the Ultimate Picture—the one that releases you from life, that'll live in place of you. Destination Nirvana, right?

Help me tack it down, okay?

Aristotle said a work of art purges the spectator. Fact, it's the artist who's purged, if it's successful. The painting takes over, starts to come of itself. It's like the perfect shit.

I'll lay in some white first. Let it pool in there. Reminds me of whitewash on sacking. As a kid, every spring, whitewash the barn. Used to cut head and armholes in sacks for smocks, then just slosh it on. Know the Catskills in spring? Wouldn't want to go back, though. Your camera loaded?

How about a little antinomy here? Splash in some black before the white dries. Funny, you think, black is the darkest colour, fact it's the lightest, in weight. And white—it's pure, pure light, but most whites are lead, pure poison. It's these little quirks that make life, don't you think?

Click away but no flash, okay? The black's bleeding into the white, like marbling. We used to go to Utica once a month, for Pa to do his business, while Mom took us for our treat, for working hard. In summer/9A/'d go to this Italian ice-cream parlour. They had real marble-top tables, real Italian ice-cream, real Italian flies. Ice-cream came in tall glasses with long spoons. We smuggled one of the glasses out once, presented it to Pa on his birthday, for highballs. He didn't like us going there really, said he could get a bushel of feed for the cost of the ice-cream.

So let's have some ice-cream colours in this, just for Pa. Have to mix them off the canvas, get the exact shades. Pistachio. Scoop of strawberry.

A sleepy life and a painless death. Not such a bad thing, I sometimes think. Mom must have missed him, I guess, but she didn't show it. We kids just thought in terms of whinge-free treats, but of course, there were fewer of them, what with the hired hand, then the Depression.

We got to the ocean though. Mom took us to Portsmouth. I was around age nine, I guess. That first glimpse of it—the colour, sparkle. Ultramarine. Straight from the can.

Let's make a few waves. Feather in some white, monastral green.

Beginning to look like the sea in Botticelli's Birth of Venus.

I fell for Janine because of that. She had that long, corn-brown hair. She modelled for us, at the Art Students League. Probably why they took her on. I didn't think I stood a chance.

I said to her, If I blow in your ear, would you come out with me? That was a Botticelli Birth of Venus joke. She didn't get it either, but it broke the ice.

Yellow ochre. Dribble in some raw sienna.

Don't look right, somehow. You got a comb? What the hell, I'll leave the teeth in.

Darker now, almost umber, but she's still a good-looking woman.

Pass the brush, the six-inch, would you?

Band of cobalt. Another, mirror it. Splatter in some lemon. Cadmium red.

Our first date, League party. They'd hired a night boat up the Hudson. Jazz. Lights pepping up the river.

Lights went out, one by one, the shit-head had unscrewed the bulbs, completely dark, lamp black, he's top of the railing, yelling, I'm gonna jump, I'm gonna jump. I shoulda shouted, Jump, then. Asshole.

She asked me who it was, casual like, but I could tell she was intr/5/igued. Worked out okay, though, with the dark, the commotion, I kissed her, got my fingers into her hair at last, she didn't pull away, I knew it was going to be okay.

Dated steady after that.

Chrome oxide, mix in a little Prussian blue.

She had a dress that colour. Used to slip it over her head after modelling, run out to me, shoes in her hand. Felt proud. There were better painters there than me, better lookers too. I was plenty ambitious, but at that stage, you're un-focussed, know what I mean?

Texture's not right. Pass me a sponge, would you?

Trail in a little cerulean blue. Let's see how it's doing.

Bit too pretty, needs beefing up. How 'bout a few big swirls of ver/4/milion?

Blood red. *Sonofabitch.*

We were at this party, Artists Union. Janine's sitting on the sofa, he comes up from behind, leans over, says to her, You're in a period, right? I can te/2/ll these things, I like a woman when she bleeds. Motherfuckn shit-head. Janine's just rigid, sorta mesmerised. I /12 4 16 -/ taking a swing, but coupla guys pulled him away, out the door. Next thing, he's sickin up on the sidewalk.

We left early. I apologized, /00/ felt kinda re-sponsible, fellow-artist sorta thing. She just said, He is rather primitive, isn't he? I got to feeling she'd/ + / enjoyed it. I said, Okay, let's see you bleed both ends, sma/ 10 /cked her in the mouth. Only time in my life I ever hit a woman.

This is still too fuckn tame. Look, take these wire-cutters, get me a length of barbed w/49 =/ire from the fence, would you do that?

I'll coil it round the red, fence it in.

Used to go on picnics when we were first mar-ried. Only eating out we could afford, apart from gallery openings. She would lie there in the grass, I'd fan out her hair, plait it into the grass. She'd get up like Gulliver,/0/ pulling the grass with her, go home with it still tangled. /0/

Why don't I try that? Hooker's g/0 -/reen, lighten it a little, trickle it into the ochre.

Through the comb. Let it thicken out into roots, fronds.

Potted fuckn palms.

Two months later, gallery opening. W/89 /ent by myself, just in case. He looked straight through me, didn't seem to recognise me. He was with a crowd, they were laughing, he was quiet. He walks to the corner o/♂&♀ 1942/ gal-lery, unbuttons, pisses into the potted palms. Then he turns, looks straight at me as he buttons his fly, sorta smirk on his face. I wanted to strangle him.

Pass me the spray-gun. Can of black Duco.

Obliterate the green and ochre.

That look like a torso to you?

God, I'm going figurati/32/ve again. Thought I was through with that.

He used to curse Picasso. Everything he turned to, Picasso had been there first. Then he sorta broke through, found his own field.

Now we feel the same about him. Where do you go after Abstraction? Have to keep pushing against the fence, moving that much further out, get out from the shadow. Journey Perilous.

Sometimes I feel I'm almost there.

Life is how it is. Ever feel like crying because of that? The endless shimmering potentia/13A/lit-ies have settled into this particular pattern? And it's this absurdly particular shimmer you're after.

What the hell, let's give it a head.

Go the whole hog, stick on some buttons. Would you mind? Mine's a zip.

This is beginning to have possibilities. This could just be it. If I balance the red and black with a mass of white, impasto—

Into the void.

Ever read the coroner's report? Oldsmobile was doing seventy. He was catapulted out. Flew fifty feet, ten feet from the ground, straight into the tree, CKLOOLP. Christ. Straight through the sound-barrier, right?

Must've looked like one of Chagall's flying fig-ures.

Know the Falling Angel? /64 1943 / up in the top left, sailing through the air. I keep thinking of that.

This is beginning to come together, you know? I think I'm nearly there, I think I'm reaching it. Just needs—

Cut me another piece of barbed wire, okay?

I'll just—/5 7 10 14 27/a halo to you?

Andrew McKeown

She Lived in a Tree

He wasn't sure what she'd said.

'Sorry?'

She continued looking at him, as if *he* had engaged the conversation. Her clothes were dirty, he noticed. Not exactly like someone living on the streets, but unclean. There was a smell about her, too.

He had been thinking about yesterday. She had been walking around the other tables, her movements entering his thoughts at random: approaching a table, reaching into her bag—it had gone rather well, they might well offer him the job—leaning across a table, showing something—how would that affect his holiday plans with Angela?

The spring sky above the water and the sounds of distant traffic converged.

'Great day for it,' she repeated. Listening to her now with greater care he was surprised to notice her voice was light and inviting. He shifted his weight on the chair. 'You're not from round here?'

'I came for a job.' His answer sounded like an apology. He narrowed his thoughts against her— she must be begging—and made to select change from his pocket, aiming for a small coin, maybe two, before realising he had no cash on him.

'Is it ok if I sit?' Her body seated on the chair seemed to alter. A curve now ran through her hips, he observed. 'I live not far. Near the station. But sure you wouldn't know the place, would you?' He heard himself say he didn't. A moment passed. He was still holding a bunched hand in his pocket.

'I came for a job at the university.' He'd hoped to remove his hand unseen as he spoke; but she was too quick for him:

'Scholar, eh?' She was smiling. 'What's your subject?'

'English.' Again he felt that he'd spoken against his better judgment. He wanted to arrange the conversation into pleasantries, direct them toward a comfortable exit. Ideally, one with a joke.

'Books, eh? *Jane Eyre* and all that. Very romantic.' He saw an opening and felt his confidence return:

'No, linguistics, actually.' The woman mouthed his 'actually', lifting her eyebrows. He went red. The young man taking orders at the tables appeared.

'Now you know I can't serve you here, Bernadette.' He waited then turned away, looking back over his shoulder as he went to another table.

There was a further pause.

'Here.' The woman had taken a worn photograph out of her bag and placed it on the table between them. 'I was young then.' The black and white picture showed her sitting on a bollard on a quayside, not unlike the harbour where they now were, dressed in a former fashion, an air of which she still had about her. She was attractive, he found—somehow against his wishes—his gaze switching from the picture to her eyes, then quickly away.

'Not bad, eh?' She reached back into her bag. 'How about these?'

This time she brought out a sheaf of colour polaroids and wedged them into his right hand. 'Barry took those. He used to do all sorts.' He had passed one—then another—through his fingers before he realised that it was her again. In a bare interior somewhere overexposed skin stood out against a pink bedspread. Her face was painted, emotionless; the poses were inculcated, cold. She leaned forward on her chair, inclining her head to his line of vision. He put the pictures down, away from him.

'A real gentleman, Barry was. And all those friends he had.'

He gathered himself. He wanted to take his leave but had no idea what to say. The woman went on:

'Never laid a hand on me, though. Not like the other one, the one from Wales. He liked a bit of rough-house to get him going, *he* did.' She paused, checking his expression. 'Some of them do.' He looked away.

Behind the woman, people were looking at their phones, fingers swiping up and down the screens.

'Here, look at this one.' Reaching again into her bag, the woman withdrew a battered notebook. From between its pages she produced a single photo-booth picture. It showed a woman with a young child on her knees. The upper half of the woman's head had been cropped by the frame, leaving just a broad smile and a nose. 'I haven't seen her since she was nine.' He looked back at her, then down at his shoes. The woman began again:

'They wanted to put her into care.' Her face went still. 'They sent a letter saying they'd received information. Something about *duty of care* and *negligence*.' She giggled, like a perverse child. '*Negligence* or *negligees*, something like that, anyway. They were going to look after her. They'd find her somewhere nice.' A breeze momentarily lifted the other pictures lying on the table. 'That was when Barry offered to take her away. Said he'd look after her. Said he'd keep in touch.' There was another gap filled by the sound of a couple laughing gently at another table. 'Haven't heard from him since.' The woman placed the monochrome picture of herself on top of the others, leaving her hand there:

'I wonder I don't miss her some times.' The other realised he hadn't moved for some time. 'So then they said they'd take care of *me*.' She spoke as if this were an irony. 'All those noisy women along the corridors. And the stories they tell. But at least they fed you every day. And there was always something to do.'

The waiter was heading back in their direction. The woman stood up and held her bag open to her interlocutor:

'Go on.' He looked in. There were clothes and a certain smell. 'It won't bite.' Beneath the clothing there was a plastic shopping bag. Inside a hard, egg-like shape joined to a tangle of strings and sticks filled his fingers. It felt like some sort of marionette. For a split second it was like holding the remains of a child. 'It's for you.' The woman was laughing as he snatched back his hand.

*

She collected her pictures, making a neat deck of them then spoke again, as if returning to a point she had been making all along. Her voice had a practised measure to it:

'If you could help. Maybe some money.' He raised his open palms. At this the woman brandished the stack of samples in her left hand, taking out first one, then another with her right: 'Like this? Or this?' He was immobile. 'Nancy boy, eh?'

She put her things back in her bag and turned to go. The young waiter was standing behind her, watching her leave.

'She usually goes away for 50p,' he said.

Hank Kirton

Preposterous Spleen

Tom constantly talked about this weird guy who hung around subway platforms with a banged-up banjo. He wore a filthy cable-knit sweater that he claimed was gifted to him by Marianne Faithfull in 1968, which would have meant that she gave a large men's sweater to a two-year-old child. Maybe she did. It's never been thoroughly investigated or debunked. Faithfull hasn't been contacted for comment.

The sweater may have started its knitted country life nice and clean and white but it later became charcoal gray from years of particulate matter and diesel soot. His lungs were probably the same color.

Tom said the guy changed his name with every person he met: Bob, Floyd, Kelsey, Graham and so on. Wilbur, Horatio, Bill, etc. Tom said that he'd been doing that for so long that he'd forgotten the actual name on his birth certificate.

"If he ever even had one!" Tom once exclaimed.

Evan, Antonio, Willie, Clarence and so forth, ad nauseam. Tom said that the first time he met him he introduced himself as Phineas Q. Butterscotch.

And then the next time he met him it was merely *Brian*.

Tom liked him at once, back when he was Phineas Q. Butterscotch and later when he was Brian. He would eventually become Larry Pym the 3rd.

And Tom liked him too. Tom was obsessed with the man.

Tom said the guy never actually played the banjo. He just held it over an open case at his feet and people would drop in money anyway. He said the banjo didn't even have strings. He'd salvaged it from a dumpster behind the Irish cafe, O'Toolies, on Essex Street.

He held the useless instrument for effect. It was a prop for his character. He had a lot of character, Tom said. And the banjo helped that.

Tom said he was hanging at the station once and a small group of college-age kids were gathered around him while he stood there, just holding the unplayable banjo. Tom said it was unsettling. They were just staring at a silent, motionless man, filming him with their phones and snickering to each other in a condescending manner. Tom thought they were insensitive brats, but he stood there too. Like a kettle.

They finally prodded the man to talk and he told them about his father. He brought up his father often, according to Tom.

He said his father was from Des Moines, Iowa and owned a sour cream company. It was called Ibzan Valley Cream and they did very well in the midwest, circa 1950s.

So, Tom surmised that Phineas Q. Butterscotch or Billy, Grover, Lester, etc., was raised in affluence.

If any of that sour cream business were true. Tom also expressed his doubts from time to time.

He went on to tell the college kids (and Tom) about his family's butler, a Swiss immigrant named Adolfus who cried when they got the dog spayed. The dog's name was Chimney (for unknown reasons) and Adolphus took the loss of her ovaries hard, sobbing into his *Älplermagronen*. Chimney was an Icelandic sheepdog and Adolphus fell for her friendly, agreeable nature. He felt she understood him on an almost human level, far beyond the typical canine display of empathic comprehension. It seemed Chimney was what we now might call a "therapy dog." That was Tom's observation.

Tom once witnessed the banjo man drink an entire half-pint of Yukon Jack in one long burning swallow and he never even made a face or

took a stabilizing breath. As far as Tom knew, he didn't puke either and he theorized that the facts of his personal history weren't really facts at all but fond illusions catalyzed by wet-brain dementia. It was a convincing theory, he said, with a degree of conceit. And Tom knew him better than anyone. Tom said he drank a hell of a lot yet never appeared drunk, indicating a bear-trap tolerance for alcohol. Yukon Jack was 100 proof. The honeyed liquor didn't fuck around.

Larry Pym III once told Tom about spotting Bigfoot at a Grateful Dead concert. It was at the Red Rocks Amphitheatre in the Colorado Mountains. He wasn't a Dead fan and didn't trust Jerry Garcia but he attended the show anyway, tagging along with his witchy friend, Lenora and their mutual confidant, Marcus "Mac" Truck. Lenora had ingested frightening, massive doses of LSD in her storied career as a hippie chick and had damaged her chromosomes, passing on the aberrations to her newborn daughter, Cassandra, who was delivered with scoliosis, low-set ears and webbed fingers. She also had onyx eyes and nascent second-sight. Lenora predicted great paranormal fame for Cassandra once she started talking and justified her fresh existence. Her gnomish little Nostradamus baby. Lenora also claimed that Cassandra could make the fuzzy-bunny mobile above her crib dance just by looking at it. As "proof" she shared Polaroids of the telekinesis in action, which, being still pictures, didn't exactly make for compelling evidence. She showed those photos to everyone and everyone pretended they depicted something uncanny. Most just told Lenora, "Wow," and then handed them back.

Anyway, Tom told about how the banjo guy (who was Marmaduke Anchovy for the day) wandered away from the pot-embalmed crowd and wound up on the outskirts of the venue. He was urinating into the bushes when a Sasquatch suddenly confronted him. It happened out of nowhere, as unexpected as a UFO abduction.

He described it as approximately eight feet tall and four hundred pounds and it was carrying a carved Victorian table leg as a club (for some nebulous reason). The two bipedal creatures found themselves locked in a staring contest while "Sugar Magnolia" piddled in the distance.

They stood facing each other for several minutes, neither daring to look away, until the Sasquatch held out its huge hand. It was holding a piece of sticky, hexagonal honeycomb, offering it to him (Marmaduke Anchovy, ostensibly) as a sign of peace and respect.

The astonished human tucked away his penis and then accepted the gift. He tasted the honey to demonstrate trust and the Sasquatch nodded approval with its massive, shaggy head and receded back into the evergreens.

He carried the honeycomb in his pocket for the rest of his life and showed it to Tom on occasion. By then it was an unrecognizable twist of mummified black wax.

It didn't look like much, but Tom vouched for its authenticity.

Tom went back and forth on matters of veracity. He had a lot to say to anyone who listened. His sincerity seemed genuine. And he kept his eager audience rapt. He collected Edwin's, Karl's, Bob's tall tales like a scribe. He had genuine value as a dedicated urban anthropologist.

But this is about Benjamin Early Day.

That was the man's final name. The pseudonym he assumed on the day he disappeared.

It happened like this:

He was holding his banjo, whistling Classical Gas to a scatter of passengers that had just disembarked from the Essex St. subway, when the entire station was suddenly flooded under an abrupt and unanticipated torrential downpour. Within mere moments the tiled, cement track-troughs had transformed into whitewater rapids. The escalator was a waterfall.

The trains were halted at once, the power cut to prevent electrocution from the submerged third rail. The rich minerals in the water would've made it dangerously conductive.

And Benjamin Early Day stood on the platform with his blank banjo in hand, witnessing what he must have thought was another Biblical flood. The sudden current wrapped itself around his ankles and he tumbled into the water. Tom said he was slightly off-balance even under stable conditions, so the instant river toppled him with relative ease.

Then, Banjo Benjamin noticed the boy. A little kid had fallen into the roaring current that sluiced through the tunnel and Ben rolled into the river to rescue him. He acted without a hint of hesitation. Presumably, the fact that the river's current might also carry an *electrical* current didn't occur to him. Or he didn't care and responded with bravery and selfless compassion. Tom preferred the latter explanation.

There was a bit of hero-worship in Tom's accounts of the man.

The man (Benjamin) and the kid (Danny, they'd learn) were whisked like driftwood into the tunnel. Tom said that the two were borne by the rolling flow for a good half-mile, blind in the darkness, until they reached the Beaver Boulevard line and his flailing limbs made miraculous contact with the kid. He grabbed him like a Hasselhoffian lifeguard and once the boy was locked in a secure hold, his head safely above the rapids, he scrambled to safety with the aquatic strength of the Sub-Mariner, lifting him gingerly to the solid surface of the Pond Avenue platform, where he administered CPR.

The boy vomited gritty gray liquid and gasped in a life-sustaining breath. He would survive.

But then, the man (Benjamin, remember) snap-decided that he was satisfied with the length of his long, strenuous existence and leaped back into the river, wiggling like a pollywog under the churning, polluted surface of the spill-stream and he floated away, disappearing back into the dark tunnel, never to be seen or heard from again.

He was presumed dead. His body was never recovered. There were no real obituaries.

When Tom breathlessly told us this final, outrageous story, I realized that he was just making it all up. It was too outlandish to be true. Plus, the Sub-Mariner reference gave it away. Tom had gone too far.

I felt like a dewy-eyed dupe. Like a credulous child eagerly eating whatever silly fantasies were spooned to him.

None of it ever actually occurred and the sweater-wearing, banjo-holding, whisky-swigging, Bigfoot-meeting, child-rescuing, sour-cream heir—the esteemed and inexplicable Mr. Phineas Q. Butterscotch, etc., etc.—never actually existed.

But I couldn't really get mad at good 'ol Tom.

Because he isn't real either.

Kyle Coma-Thompson

Strays

The old man had been a killer in a previous life, the nurses knew, and for this he had been made a national hero. That was over half a century ago. When admitted to the home, he had expressed a willingness to accept visitors. People would travel the world over for the opportunity to sit bedside or next to him at one of the large tables in the community room. Not a few were retired military, many of whom had seen combat. This the nurses gathered from overhearing their conversations with Pär, the translator the old man's family had hired and kept on retainer for just these sorts of visits. The old man, who had a name, one which was famous among circles who still valued and nurtured a knowledge of history, famous or infamous the nurses couldn't decide, it depended on who they asked, he would sit crumpled in his wheelchair, oxygen tubes inserted into his nostrils, listening to the foreigners talk. Pär, who'd spent a few years of his youth in compulsory service and found a future there, picking up a knack for languages during that time, would watch the foreigners with his antifreeze blue eyes and listen. Occasionally he would brush the table with the palm of his hand, clearing it of imaginary crumbs. After the foreigner had finished explaining the reason for their visit, he would watch them smilelessly for a moment, as if waiting for more. Once the foreigner confirmed that, yes, this was the end of their turn in the conversation, Pär would pat the tabletop with his hand, lightly, soundless except for his wedding ring's tap against wood. The nurses were unsure Pär was aware of his habit but it was one they derived some shared amusement noticing.

After this little pat of the tabletop, he would then turn to the old man to translate. Not all the nurses knew English, a couple knew German, one or two were moderately conversant in French, so both halves of the conversation were not always understandable to them. They would hear the original and watch the foreigner talk and Pär listen nodlessly, smilelessly, then wait to hear Pär's version. He was shy by nature it seemed, soft-spoken during their greetings to him at the front door, in the community room, in the hallways. A half inch from the bottom right-hand corner of his left eye was a growth of some sort, a skin tag or mole or wart. During their earliest interactions he had caught them noticing the growth and lowered his eyes to the floor. In the months and years since, his eyes fell to the floor and stayed there as they passed and greeted him.

Pär's translation voice was calm and slow-spoken and loud but not too loud, firm. The old man had many health concerns, faulty hearing one of the more benign among them. He wore hearing aids in both ears and spoke with more volume than was necessary, but usually only to the nurses or visiting family. When taking audience with these non-native-speakers, he seemed to luxuriate in a lowered voice, relieved of having to be heard for his own sake. Having worked with the old man for a while now, Pär had become skilled at decoding the exact phrasing of wheezes and whispers and mumbles. The old man spoke his own language of a sort, in the dialect of old age, and Pär appeared fluent in this tongue also. Discussions between the old man and his visitors might have been wholly obscure to them, lost beyond the reach of nurses' gossip, but for Pär's clear enunciation and careful repetition of each utterance the old man presented for translation. The old man, having heard Pär's translation of a visitor's comment or question, would pause, often a long while, perhaps considering whether the comment or question required or deserved a response or was worthy of a portion of his increasingly valuable breath, then would speak in a dry, crackly proto-croak to Pär; listening with fixed concentration, the translator would pause, tap table with a hand, then repeat the old man's response back not to the visitor but to the old man, in the language they were birthed by and raised within. If the old man was pleased, he would weakly nod, granting his consent. If he was dissatisfied for some reason, vexed by the absence of a certain explicitly expressed detail, he would say so, pointing out the flaw in Pär's version before describing how the phrasing should be corrected. This painstaking process, which the translator appeared to take in stride, annoyed and exhausted the nurses, testing the limits of their abilities at eavesdropping. Easygoing almost always with the details of his care, in conversation with strangers the old man insisted on strict meticulousness. The nurses knew him as a resident and an old man, and it could be these versions of him held little value. These strangers brought a different version of him through the doors, checked in with it at the front desk, sat down with it in the community room, at the usual table in the quietest corner set aside for such conversations, then when the nurses rolled him to the table, these strangers rose with effusive smiles, eager to shake his hand and in doing so, would gift it to him. He was no longer an old man, but a rarity, a hero, a glamorous killer. A sniper who had for half a century retained a record for most confirmed kills, most of which were committed in a two-month period in the wilderness borderland between Russia and Finland.

On first learning this, the nurses viewed the old man differently. They brought the news home to husbands and brothers and friends and, if old enough to bear such knowledge, children. This old withered self of a grandfather who played cards with other such versions of himself in the community room, who preferred lingonberry jam on his toast most mornings, who watched sentimental movies and sitcoms on television without so much as a faint throat-clearing to express amusement, was a murderer, a prolific reaper of lives. In his dotage he was no less the murderer than he had been, his many intermittent visitors proof of this. There was an endless supply of old men across the world but few, the nurses imagined, commanded such pilgrimages. He attracted aspirants like a holy man, but his holiness was unwholesome. He was a dangerous figure rendered harmless by infirmity. They helped him shower, sanitized his bedthings when he soiled himself. Did their care for such a person make them complicit, they asked each other, uncertain they could do otherwise. They had considered catching the translator in the hallways, to pull him aside and ask how

he felt serving the needs of such a history. Doubtlessly the translator would bashfully excuse himself and walk to the community room to take his appointed chair at his appointed table. Instead they were resolved to earn back their good consciences through careful listening and gossip. They had done so these past four years, wondering where this left them. The old man slept better than most of the home's residents and they considered this revealing; but of what, they couldn't tell.

Having pleased the old man, having confirmed the message to relate, the translator would turn to the waiting visitor and switch languages. It was the subtlest of shifts to witness, the translator turning in his seat thirty degrees, hand planted in its usual spot on the tabletop, the axis it seemed on which he pivoted. Expressionless, he would change his nature, not outwardly but inwardly, the way chromatophoric cells receive directives from an octopus' instinct for self-preservation and change color in unison almost instantly, conforming to the hue of rock or sand around it. He would become a speaker of English or German or Spanish or French, and from this new version of self would offer the old man's reply by proxy. Monoglots among the nurses would lose the old man's words along the way, as they were absorbed by the translator, then transformed into a different species of speaking and hearing. The visitors would sit with tempered excitement, receiving utterances, no matter how secondary, from their idol. This man was a significant figure, had accomplished extraordinary things, had been feared by his enemies and revered by his countrymen. In a short time he had buried more Russian souls than could have been birthed annually by sturdy Russian women in a large village. The Russians had hated him so specifically they had named him "The White Death"; if they'd known his actual name they would have cursed it until the name itself became infused with curse-energy. The visitors brought a great deal of romantic anticipation to the table, which the old man both appreciated and seemingly didn't notice. He had been a deer hunter in his youth, the visitors would state, repeating facts of his own life back to him. He had preferred a glassless sight to his rifle, to avoid glints of reflected sunlight. To chill his breath so it didn't appear as breath-puffs and so give away his hiding place, he would stuff his mouth with snow. He was a patriot and hunter of men and killed several hundred before taking an exploding bullet to the face. Jaw shattered, he had been dragged back to camp by his compatriots and judged dead. But he had lived. He had healed and lived half a century and longer with this broken face he now tendered as evidence of his greatness and his sacrifice. This news was received among the nurses as a revelation. They had been too polite to ask about his face; though they had checked his medical records for an explanation, none had been offered there.

Exchanges between visitor and translator, translator and old man, were usually composed of two intertwining strands of inquiry, and the purpose of their conversation, as far as the nurses could tell, was to twist these against one another until they were bound together into a length of rope. The rope could then serve as a lifeline cast from the present moment into the distant past, where the old man in his younger, more heroic days might reach out a hand and, critically wounded and bleeding out on the snow, grasp it. If the young soldier held onto it tightly long enough, he might be dragged across the wastes and decades to join them in the very room where they sat talking. What had it been like, the war, lying belly-flat among snowbanks, camouflaged in white and taking aim at Russian targets and popping them open like bottles of champagne, blood spurting from head-wounds after bits of skull had taken flight like corks? Versions of the first strand to be bound into a conversation all boiled down to basic curiosity, what had it been like? The second strand, its tension-bearing strength and quality, depended on the visitor's level of knowledge regarding the sniper's art. For some the techniques involved were objects of worship, rendered awesome by their own lack of lived familiarity with disassembling, cleaning, then reassembling a weapon, for the specific explicit purpose of taking a human life. Most who requested time with the old man were surely gun owners, but practiced the art of life-taking during carefully regulated hunting seasons. Aligning sighted crosshairs with distant targets, they saw deer or ducks or turkeys. They were self-aware enough to not assume the hunter's art was readily comparable to the sniper's, so posed their questions to the translator and old man with the utmost humility. These were the majority of the second-stranders, but there were a few who brought into the room and to the table an intimate familiarity with the topic. These were veterans of later, less admirable wars, wars that often did not end with a clearly identified victor or loser but which instead petered out into a protracted stalemate. For all the nurses knew these wars were still ongoing and these visitors had taken leave to consult the old man on how to perfect their craft. A few who visited the old man had been in active service and made a point of stating so at the outset. Active service members, veterans, civilians, the old man welcomed each the same. What had it been like, they asked, what are the secrets of the trade? With Pär as their intermediary, these two lines of inquiry were braided into a tight, lean tow line and could be tested with a tug. The past was sitting at the table with them but they would need to pull evenly and carefully on their end of the line to tease it fully into the present, so they might share a little of its glory. They had met the old man, they would tell their friends, their peers online, and were honored to occupy with him a few minutes at the end of his life. What had ended as an old man in a wheelchair in a nursing home's community room had begun as a country boy with a rare skill honed during a childhood hunting deer. The call of history intervened, disrupted that life, and drew him into the wilderness as a soldier. There he had accomplished the unthinkable without conscious effort, had killed to survive and in defense of his country. The Russians had been sent to meet him but hadn't known yet, had gained awareness only after it was too late and the boy's bullets had flashed from nowhere and cut into them, maiming or killing them. The fools had been sent into the snow like so many deer, improperly camouflaged for the weather and landscape, brown uniforms against the white all around. Recounting their meeting with the legend, they would skip past the old-manness of his current shape and gush to their envious friends of the greatness that still resided in his right eye and right pointer finger. The very eye that was gifted with perfect vision, that peered down the stock and sight and barrel to find little figures advancing through snow; the very finger that rested snug against the trigger and skillfully applied pressure, to fell those figures before the echoes of a rifle shot reached them. Those very eyes watched as they spoke, that very hand shook their own. The afternoon they shared with the man would be recounted eagerly for the rest of their lives, even after they had become old men who pushed themselves around in wheelchairs. There still existed quality of character and greatness in the world, and they had met its acquaintance. They had met a stone-cold killer and had lived to tell of it. They would hope, for even a brief moment, he had considered them a friend.

The translator Pär would not exaggerate the old man's responses to flatter the *ulkomaalaiset*, the foreigners. Maintaining the temper and manner of an undisturbed glass of lukewarm water, he would relate the old man's simple, direct responses in unadorned fashion, tinged around the edges with boredom. The earliest visitors had been a pleasant surprise, and perhaps the old man had derived genuine enjoyment from the conversations, but through sheer repetition and the unvarying trajectories of such exchanges, the visitations had quickly become predictable, tedious, a chore, and for a while the old man had refused requests when they arrived to the home by phone call or email. Having refused several he was soon reminded of the sheer repetition and unvarying trajectories of his days in his room and the common room and dining room, so rescinded his rejections and arranged for the translator to arrive and wait in the community room for now-welcome visitors. Given a choice between two tediums, the old man had chosen both. Similar to the visitors and their strands of inquiry, he chose to twist the two against each until they were bonded by tension into a single, stronger string. It was a way to pass the time, which never seemed to tire of arriving.

Should the old man die, would there be a state funeral? Would these strangers travel to honor the official end of a life they admired and perhaps envied? Greatness was rare in the world, their visits seemed to suggest, so was well worth the cost and trouble. They would tell to anyone who would listen, I met him once, spent an afternoon revisiting the past with him. And now the past would be gone, leaving them to treasure it as a conversation once held in the company of other tables and other elderly residents and one or two nurses and orderlies standing by. Thanks to old men such as he, who had once been younger and more lethal, Finland had not been conquered, had resisted annexation by Russia. They became murderers so the country could live; and here lies the most prolific savior of them all.

The conversations ended the same each time. The old man, tiring of the moment, savoring little of its occasion, would raise a hand to put a stop to the questions. Not a brusque gesture, but a feeble one, a request to be spared further translation and answering. The translator would translate the exhaustion and feebleness to the visitor, who, sensitive to already having asked more than they could have reasonably expected from the old man, would thank both old man and translator politely and profusely or politely and stoically, before shaking the hands of both and excusing themselves. The old man and translator would have a word or two afterwards and, sensing a conclusion, one of the nurses would walk over to take hold of the wheelchair's handles, waiting for signal from the old man to roll him from the community area, down the eastern wing hallway back to his room. The translator, hands in pockets, would watch them go before lowering his eyes to the floor to walk towards the front doors. Sunlight and the parking lot would be waiting for him, a life unburdened by community rooms and visitors-in-translation. He could be his own person and raise his eyes again to the level of wherever he was walking.

There were other witnesses to these meetings and the nurses, exquisitely attuned to passive-aggressive feuds and intrigues among the residents, watched whenever these visitors would enter, to see how they changed the room. Many would be sitting around their usual tables, often in the company of a nurse or orderly or social worker, playing Paskahousu or Ristiseiska or poker, nurse or social worker serving as dealer and, if needed, referee, should there arise a disagreement or if a certain outcome was contested. At less popular tables there would be others who preferred their own company, The Watchers as the nurses called them, playing solitaire or knitting wool scarves or crocheting. The Watchers seemed to enjoy the tempered liveliness of the room, but from a distance. They could absorb relevant news about other residents and the goings-on of the outside world, its economic vagaries and geopolitics, through stealth and curious osmosis, much the way the nurses did. In general they kept their opinions to themselves and were often thwarted by bad hearing, so the information gleaned from larger tables retained its secrecy by default. There were cliques and hierarchies and petty grudges and these the nurses both endured and half-enjoyed, laughing amongst each other at the dearth of wisdom on display among the elderly. One such loner was a gentlemen who had been admitted to the home a short while before the famous old sniper; a squat, still muscular man with an odd accent. He had arrived with his wife from Rovaniemi but the wife had fallen ill not long after; transferred to intensive care, then hospice, she had disappeared quickly into her body, which had withered without a full woman to inhabit it. For a few weeks the man's children had attended to his grief, which he did not show except by remaining silent, then had consented to his wish to be left alone. They were two, a man and woman, and both had spouses, but neither had children; so there were no grandchildren to welcome should they visit; they were busy people, with careers and pets and lively social lives and partners; he would rather not be an imposition. There was no requirement to visit, so they didn't, believing this was what he wanted. One or the other would email occasionally to check in with the staff about his health and his mood, and the staff would respond that, while he largely kept apart from social activities around the home, he did not seem particularly unhappy with the arrangement. He would talk with the nurses when they made conversation; but they gathered he did so for their sake, not his. He seemed content. If he grieved his wife, he did so in private.

In one such email exchange between staffer and child, it had been mentioned that the old man had been born in Russia and spent the first half of his life in Moscow. He had slipped across the border by foot as an emigrant, hitchhiked to Lapland; there he worked first as a laborer then as a chef, and at the restaurant where he worked he had met their mother. Don't call him a dissident, the staffers were advised, their father tended to bristle at the term. He didn't leave for political reasons but for the opportunity to live an actual life. He was a quiet Muscovite, and preferred not to be reminded where he came from.

Learning this, the nurses wondered whether the man was privy to the conferences held across the room from him, days when visitors would sit with the old war hero and his translator. Surely he had gathered awareness of the old man's reputation, hearing the revisions of statement between old man and translator, in their common language. What did he make of these visitors, their fawning effusions, and of the old man who had killed so many like him? The nurses would watch the Muscovite at his table near the window, cards arranged in rows before him. Flipping over a fresh card, he would take a long pause to consider where to place it. Paced to the rhythm of a thoroughly aged nervous system, the hand seemed to move slower than the mind that directed it; at times the hand would even disconnect briefly from its mind and roam the table's surface, card in tow, until the mind reoriented and the eyes blinked and hand was caught mid-roam and brought back to order. After which the card would be laid face-up on the table.

Was he listening, was he thinking? The man seemed to have been born with a poker face, there was no hope he might suddenly outgrow it. None of the nurses could attest to having ever seen either share a table or conversation. One had aged into fame and the other into a manageable obscurity, but there appeared no difference between them. To a nurse's eye they were similar because they were old, and the assistances they required were indistinguishable. The Muscovite entered and left the room with aid of a walker, whereas the old man came and went in a wheelchair. This was the sole discrepancy between them. Both entertained the nurses' attempts at small talk politely, with an attitude of soft resistance. Both watched late night talk shows when they couldn't sleep. Both were widowers. Both seemed accepting of bodily weakness. They both enjoyed sopping runny egg yolks with toast and, with magnanimous relish, eating it.

During one such visit, one of the nurses, determined to take measure of the man's awareness of the conversation and its translation about to take place several tables away, invited herself to sit with him. The man, too polite to tell her he preferred to be alone, had accepted the intrusion by allowing her to gather and reshuffle his deck of cards. She asked whether he was familiar with the game Rummy and he said no. She asked if he would mind if she taught him how to play and after a soft pause he agreed. She didn't mean to disturb him if he would rather sit alone, she explained, but she was tired and her shift was already feeling long, so she could use for a good game to pass the time. Such was the conversational ninjutsu of nurses; how could he say no?

Across the room a guest with an American accent spoke words beyond her understanding, not because she didn't speak English but because her handle on what an accent could do to certain words was spotty. He appeared young, no older than forty, and sat with another guest equally young. From the translator's rephrased introduction, she gathered they were military officers stationed in Berlin and had travelled on their weekend leave for the expressed purpose of meeting him. The conversation unfolded from there, hitched with revisions and recalibrations and pauses. The translator Pär's hand tapped the table and tapped again, every two pats catching tabletop against wedding ring. The nurse had taken a seat that afforded a view of the Muscovite's profile and beyond it, the conference of officers with war hero. Between offering instructions about how many cards to draw, how to discard, where and when to play threes of a kind or straights, she would ask the man what he thought the strangers at the table nearby were discussing. The old man and the translator, she said, they seemed to entertain guests quite of-

ten, and often these guests seemed to travel from faraway places. She wondered who the old man had been in his life, to warrant such attention. The Muscovite watched the cards while she spoke and, out of politeness, took up his part of the conversation, aware that leaving his part silent might be taken as rude, unaware this was just how she had intended it. I don't know, the man replied. I have seen many of them come and go, and can't say what it is they usually talk about. They seem to come more often during the summer, he said. They were almost always men, though on one occasion there had been a pair of women, one older than the other but both young compared to him.

Your accent, she said, it's interesting. Where was he from, originally? As soon as she'd asked it, she'd regretted it, thinking this might have tipped her hand too much, too quickly. The man seemed unbothered by the directness. I am from Moscow. I came here forty years ago. Really, the nurse exclaimed, feigning surprise. Have you been back since the changes to the country? No, the man told her. I was old by then and didn't have the interest, didn't miss it. He had married a woman from her country and had children and on the whole enjoyed his life much more here than there. Did he have family still in Russia, she asked. He did at one time, he replied, but it had been so long since he'd last spoken with them, now he wasn't sure. Just some cousins and their children, no one close as a sibling. He'd been an only child, so leaving had been easier, and his parents had died before he left. He'd left after they'd died, freed because there was no longer anyone he would need to keep company or look after. He could leave freely, with full blessing from his conscience. A bold move, the nurse said, to which the Muscovite responded with a hum of benign disagreement deep in his throat. Not so much, he told her. Though for someone who had never been impelled to flee a country, it might seem so.

Do you still have memories of the city, the nurse said, drawing a card from the deck, I've never been to Moscow. The man lifted his eyes from the cards and slowly rolled back his head to view the ceiling, as if memories of the city might be found there. Snow in the winter, sunshine in the summer, he said. Buildings and streets and buildings. And dogs. Many, many dogs.

Dogs? the nurse asked. Yes, the man said, eyes lowering from ceiling back to cards. Dogs.

They were everywhere, he told her, even rode the subways without much intervention. Quite a population, some thirty-thousand and feral, many descended from lineages of strays going back to the nineteenth century. He had read an article about it once in a magazine and it had reminded him of what he'd seen day-in day-out about the place without conscious awareness of what he was seeing. His youth was followed by dogs, and his early middle years. He'd abandoned the place to dogs, you could say. Good riddance. The article had told him, though, something he didn't know and which even in old age he considered exemplary of the place. These groups of dogs, they'd remained feral for so long, they'd evolved beyond their dogness; roamed in unique pack structures, like wolves, avoided humans, no longer wagged their tails. They were a living phenomenon, evolution in reverse, there for anyone to witness, if they could look upon them and realize what they were seeing. Stray dogs cultivating a civilization of their own, surviving on scraps and trash; devolving back into the wolfishness they'd originally come from. Actual hybrids, half-dog, half-wolf, both and neither. That is what he remembered about the place when he'd lived there, and largely the reason he'd left it. It was a place where dogs were free to un-domesticate themselves and hunt in packs. No, he didn't miss it. He was happy to sit at this table with her, playing cards, free of such cares.

The nurse agreed this was a bizarre development and that, while she'd never heard of it, believed it was something happening still, in the city he had left behind, so he could leave behind a whole country. There were differences among their people, she said, fully aware of the banality being released from her in the moment, wincing to herself, hoping the comment didn't sour the man's willingness to continue talking. Finns, Russians, there was a border but the land continued between the two countries and shaped the people in ways more similar than different. This was an opinion stated for the sake of keep-

ing the conversation going, and she hoped he wouldn't take offense at it or challenge it. The man selected three cards from his hand, a three and four and five of diamonds, and laid them on the table. From the cards left in his hand he discarded a queen of spades. This reminded the nurse of her own hand, its gaps between straights, its twos of a kind. A jack and king of spades waited in her hand. She slipped the discarded queen from the table and dragged it to her side, laid the jack and king either side of it. These she translated into points won through the pairing. Each face card was worth ten points, so this made thirty. If he had the ten of spades, he could play off her pairing for ten points of his own. If he had the ace, he could win fifteen, since aces were fifteen, the highest amount of points for a card. He could add to her play for his own advantage, but only after she'd discarded. The man watched her hands and her face as she explained this, and while his eyes were on her she failed to notice the translator and guest rise from the table across from them. Then movement at the other end of the room caught her attention, as another nurse was in the process of taking hold of the wheelchair's handles to turn the old man in the direction of the hallway, to roll him back to his room. The translator shook hands with the guests and the guests left. He did not follow them out into the parking lot, never having once done so after a visit, but stood with hands in pockets watching the television in the upper corner of the room, nearest the windows and above their heads. At a glance it might have appeared the translator was looking at them, but knowing the man's shyness and aversion to eye contact, she assumed otherwise. The television volume was on mute but nonetheless he was watching. What was playing there? Once the translator had turned on his heel, shuffled and left, she'd excuse herself from the table to look. Her companion was looking in the same direction; how long, she couldn't say, because she hadn't noticed until he'd folded the cards in his hands and laid them on the table. He was watching the translator stand with hands in his pockets, his blue eyes vivid against the unremarkable simplicity of his face. Subtly, the translator shifted weight from one foot to other, this she saw and would swear by later when telling the other nurses about it; discomfited at populating a stranger's gaze, the translator removed hands from pockets, wiped one downwards across his beard and mouth, then rolling out of a slight sway walked to the double glass doors, pushed one open, and left. The man sitting beside her lifted the cards again off the table, apologized. He was sorry, he said, he was old, as if she needed reminding, and sometimes old things happened to him. He would drop into a daze and not realize it. When he snapped free of it, it'd often take him a minute to remember why he was sitting there, what he was doing. All of which was to say he was sorry, could she remind him whose turn was it to discard? If it was his, and the game lasted another round, he just might have a chance at winning. She had to think about it. It was her turn. She was sorry to disappoint him, but as her hand stood, she thought they might reach another round, no problem. Not a problem, he told her. It was his first round. No expectations. He hadn't earned the right to disappointment yet. *Häviäminen on oppimista.* Losing was learning.

ALEX TRETBAR

BAD SPEED

When there was a lot of money around, Slim would turn gray, and I would agree with him that yes, he looked like an alien. He would abduct himself from a nimbus of Sterno heat, probing and probing until a kind of answer was reckoned up from the question of his body. And when he inevitably came back down, he tucked himself into that body.

Slim believed in aliens. Told me about them during our nights in the warrens and sewers of Portland. He became most rabid when speaking about the Grays. Claimed to have waylaid one in a vast and ancient waterworks under the northwest quadrant of the city. When the Gray refused to answer his questions in English, he bashed its head in with a blackjack. To his horror, wires and sheafs of motherboard spilled out. "That explained everything," Slim said darkly.

Slim believed in a scientific spirit, thought himself a ghost when his sores wept ectoplasm, an android when he survived a three-story fall. When he spoke he spoke twice. There was an undervoice, an astral body pitched many basements below. When I listened I listened twice, and I heard myself listening.

His stories moved into my mind, shared rent with the bad speed going around that summer. Ghosts became synonymous with aliens. Death became synonymous with a life distant and suspected but yet unproven. Deep in Washington Park one night, I encountered a woman with a robe of chainmail and bramble. We were traveling in opposite directions, and I stepped aside to make room for her on the narrow path. Her staff was a wonder of mechanical ingenuity. I thought about going to rehab.

But there was so much money around, and I was enjoying the stories—mine and Slim's. In most corners of this empire, people flock to money when they smell it. That was not the case with those around us. Friends stayed away when Slim and I had money. Money rode us into the sunset. Rode us through hell and holler. At dawn we loaded black powder into six shooters. We aimed them at our necks and sang for joy.

Stephen Baily

The Lost Chord

Mrs. Shulman, at the lectern, cleared her throat into the microphone and nodded at Mrs. Cox, at the upright piano.

Mrs. Cox nodded back and, with a flourish of her plump arms, sent a mighty chord—a G seventh—ricocheting off the walls of the auditorium.

—How do you know it was a G seventh?

I had a good ear back then.

—Not anymore?

Today I'm lucky if I can tell one note from another.

—I understand.

Maybe you do and maybe you don't, but—if you'll allow me to continue with a minimum of interruptions—while the G seventh was still reverberating, Mrs. Cox followed it up with a decisive C major. This was our cue to stand up, clap our right hands over our hearts, and join Mrs. Shulman in pledging allegiance to the flag that hung from the ceiling above her silver-gray head like a bedsheet from a clothesline on a breezeless day.

We hadn't gotten to the republic for which it stood when we were distracted by a commotion behind us. A cop had burst through the swinging doors of the auditorium and was tramping down the aisle that divided it in two. As he mounted the four steps to the stage, Mrs. Shulman—mystified by this unprecedented intrusion—hurried out from behind the lectern to intercept him. What he said to her we couldn't make out, but her jaw dropped as she turned and pointed at the dozen or so teachers facing us from the back of the stage, most with their palms still over their hearts.

"That's Mr. Pocus, in the short-sleeve shirt."

Her mention of the shirt, though spot-on, was superfluous, since Mr. Pocus was the only male teacher, not just in sight, but in the whole of P.S. 98.6.

—The whole of it? You exaggerate.

Not a bit. Surely you remember how uncommon it was—and may still be, for all I know—to run across males teaching elementary school.

—Come to think of it, you could be right. That I can recall, I never had a male teacher till I got to junior high school.

Neither did I, with the exception of Mr. Pocus—or Hokey Pokey, as we used to call him when he wasn't in earshot.

—You didn't like him?

On the contrary, he was a jolly roly-poly little man who endeared himself to us by insisting we call him by his first name—Marvin—and by bringing his pet canary to school to perch on his head and warble for our entertainment. He was also always ready to drop whatever he was doing and mix it up with us in our stickball games in the schoolyard.

—How old was he?

Probably a lot younger than we thought, but, at eleven or twelve, we had a natural tendency to confuse a receding hairline with old age.

—He was prematurely bald?

To the point where, whenever he passed by, one or another of us would be sure to start singing—to the tune of "My Old Kentucky Home"—

> O the sun shines green
> On Hokey Pokey's baldy bean

and so forth. That wasn't very nice of us, I admit, but, if he happened to overhear us, he invariably took it in good part and ended up joining in our laughter. He was shorter than many of us, too, which further strengthened our identification with him. So that we couldn't help breaking into cheers when he suddenly darted from the line of female teachers, leaped from the stage, and—with the startled cop in pursuit—bolted up the aisle toward the exit. He might even have made good his escape, if backup hadn't been stationed by the swinging doors, in the form of a second cop who quickly subdued him and, together with his colleague, frog-marched him out of the auditorium.

"I tell you I didn't do anything! You're making a mistake!"

His protests were still sounding in our ears when Mrs. Shulman returned to the microphone.

"Everyone! Back in your seats!"

From the edge of mine, I waited for her to make sense of the bizarre event we'd just witnessed, but—not a word. As though nothing had happened, she proceeded to announce that the sixth-grade talent show we'd been assembled to watch would now get under way.

"First on the program, Tod Toder will play for us an old favorite, 'Humoresque,' by Dvorak."

To titters touched off by the sight of his cello, which was almost as big as he was, Toder, a classmate of mine, stiffly emerged from the wings and settled down on a chair adjacent to the piano bench on which Mrs. Cox sat poised to accompany him.

Not ten seconds later, he was laughed off the stage when he couldn't keep the spike of his cello from slipping on the acrylic finish of the floor.

—That's all very interesting, but I'm still waiting to hear why they came for Pocus.

How would I know, when Mrs. Shulman refused to discuss it? And not only Mrs. Shulman. Mrs. Odgers, the substitute they sent from the office to take over his classroom—permanently, as it turned out—brusquely cut us off when we pressed her for an explanation.

"That's nothing to do with you."

—So you're telling me you never learned what Pocus was accused of?

There was a rumor, but I don't like to repeat it.

—Why not?

Nobody knew where it originated, or if it had any basis in reality.

—Repeat it anyway.

Let's just say it involved Mr. Pocus, a nine-year-old girl, and her skirt.

—I see. And you don't believe rumors like that can be trusted?

It depends. There may well have been something to this one. Only, in the absence of proof, I prefer to proceed with caution.

—Out of concern for Pocus's reputation?

Out of concern for my own.

—In any case, I gather from what you've just said that Pocus never returned to the classroom.

Not to my knowledge.

—So what became of him?

Don't ask me. All I can tell you is photos of every teacher in the school used to be pinned to a corkboard on the wall outside Mrs. Shulman's office.

—His picture was removed from this place of honor?

Right after his arrest, and replaced with that of Mrs. Odgers.

—And you heard nothing at all about his eventual fate?

Not even a rumor—though, some weeks after his disappearance, Tod Toder reported seeing him duck into a neighborhood pet shop that specialized in canaries, parakeets, and cockatiels.

—So?

So Toder told me he'd stopped buying birdseed for his parakeet there because, the last time he'd bought some, the proprietor, on the pretext of showing him a rare u-mac bird, had lured him into the back room and exposed himself to him.

—I'm not sure I follow you.

Toder thought—you know—birds of a feather . . .

—And that's it?

Afraid so.

—What about the newspapers from those days? Wasn't there any notice of the scandal in them?

If there was, I never saw it. Years later, I had occasion to visit the offices of the East Bronx Weekly Bullhorn, but, in the pertinent bound volume of back numbers in its morgue, I uncovered not so much as a trace of Mr. Pocus. Either the story fell through the cracks, or—what was just as likely—it was killed so as not to undermine confidence in the public schools.

—I can understand your frustration.

Frustration's not the word for it. It doesn't begin to do justice to what I feel.

—And what do you feel?

Let me see. How can I put it? ... It's as if Mrs. Cox had struck a resounding G seventh on the keyboard, then got up from the piano and walked away, never to come back.

Lawn Jockey

I had these neatly trimmed hedges in my front yard.
Hell, they weren't just neat, they were exact. I used an electric hedge trimmer to make them perfectly square.
Maddy appeared on the porch with a cold beer.
She walked into the yard, gave me the beer, then turned around and walked back inside the house, the screen door slamming shut behind her.
Good woman.

It was a hot day and humid. Black thunderclouds loomed in the distance.
A slight breeze cooled the sweat on the back of my neck and blew through the wisteria.
I inspected the hedges with a critical eye and noticed that the third one on the left was slightly asymmetrical.

I wasn't going to live with that! Why should I?
Was I pissed off? Hell yeah I was pissed off!
Wielding the hedge trimmer with surgical precision I corrected the offending oblique.
My lawn was one hundred percent St. Augustine seed that I carefully tended and kept mowed at 6.35 centimeters.

Now what the fuck!
A daisy! Where in God's name did that weed come from?
My neighbor was jealous of my yard. Might he have blown a daisy pod in my direction?
My temples throbbed with agitation.
I worked my jaw to keep it from seizing.
The offending interloper was extracted using a steel trowel that I had machine grinded to razor sharpness.
Son of a bitch—that asshole!
I'll catch him. I'll catch him in the act. Thinks he can get away with it? Not on my watch.

I heard the screen door slam. There was Maddy with another cold beer.
I took it without a word and watched her walk back across the yard. She opened the screen door and disappeared into the black vertical rectangle. A disembodied white ankle flashed for a millisecond then went dark.
The thunderclouds had crept closer. I regarded them with suspicion.
They moved when I wasn't paying attention.
Everything in my life moved when I wasn't paying attention.
Which was why I remained hyper-vigilant.
A man had to be, otherwise the world would take advantage when he was sleeping on the job. Quick as a whip cut him in half. Your legs would still be standing when your top half hit the dirt.
You know it's true! Everyone knows it's true, even if they pretend not to know.
But still, it wasn't easy. I didn't have eyes in the back of my head.
Wish I did.

I had to keep my head on a swivel.

What else could I do? How else could I do it? What would *you* do?

I could be calculating millimeter differentials on my hedges while the world was just standing there behind me, laughing and set to strike.

I knew people who had dropped their guard.

I had an uncle who did that and never saw it coming when it dropped out of the sky like a hawk snatching a rabbit

That's the way the world operates. It's patient. It can easily out-wait you.

Like those clouds milling around in the sky acting all innocent when I was watching them.

Then moving closer when I was busy with the daisy.

I know what deception is. I've seen it up close, goddamnit!

Now the breeze was picking up. The sun disappeared, the trees began to sway and the birds flew with urgency while the thunderclouds drifted toward my yard no longer caring if I was watching them.

Maddy appeared in front of me, her arm extended, holding a beer.

I hadn't seen her coming. I hadn't heard the slamming of the screen door.

Her face was deathly white. An oval light against the black sky, alabaster smooth and expressionless.

I took the beer from her outstretched hand.

She vanished.

My neighbor appeared standing on the border of our front yards holding a bag in one hand.

I watched him reach into the bag and pull out a handful of daisy pods.

He blew on the pods, sending them floating over my lawn where they landed in silence.

Something was amiss.

The St. Augustine was now nearing 12.7 centimeters.

How could that be?

I looked at the arm extended in front of me. It was wearing a long sleeved white cotton shirt.

The hand was clutching a lantern.

Maddy and my neighbor walked out onto my front porch, drinks in hand, smoking cigarettes.

I heard them laughing.

The sun was blazing in a cloudless sky as they strolled along the stone pathway, walking past me . . . as if I didn't exist . . .

Jake La Botz

The Old Lady

Jim's friends, bandmates, and even Nick the roofer who hated music, cautioned him not to take a side gig working with his hands. "Have a tough time rockin' out with this," Nick would say, flashing a wedding-ringed stump—the remains of a circular saw mangling.

But no words of warning could stop Jim from joining the roofing crew. For one thing, he needed the money. Music paid in drink and pussy, as Jim would often brag, and in that, it was one of the highest-wage jobs around. Nonetheless, he had to pay rent and eat like everyone else and unlike many of his musician pals, Jim refused to rely on women for financial support. It wasn't that he was a particularly scrupulous person. No one would accuse Jim of that. But given that his father, grandfather, and uncles had all been tradesmen—mostly carpenters and electricians— handy work was in his bones. More than anything, though, it was one of his dad's old sayings that caused Jim to exchange guitar and picks for hammer and nails when he was back from the road.

"If it was work they wouldn't call it *playin'* the guitar," James Sr. would lecture young Jim when he was "fiddle-fartin' around with that gizmo" instead of looking for a job.

From his dad's constant haranguing, Jim grew his own disregard for the instrument. Over time, the guitar became useful to him only in satiating his strong desires for sex and booze—things any construction worker, including James Sr., could understand.

Nick and the guys envied Jim nearly to the point of resentment. He had screwed more women than all six of them combined, even when you added in their tall tales, stretchers, and total fabrications. From morning til sundown, the laborers leaned into the gory details of Jim's every pickup line, unzip, and hip thrust as they tore off roofs and nailed down new ones, imagining themselves in the lucky lad's place.

Although he never explained his carnal philosophy to his coworkers, and they never thought to ask, Jim took care to have sex only once with any particular woman in any particular town, and within the encounter to have only one type of sex. This approach, which Jim developed early in his touring career, prevented the messiness of emotional entanglements and kept the memories clear in his body and mind. But Jim didn't rely on memories alone. In his apartment, he kept a highly organized log of names, dates, and cities with headers for each type of intercourse: BJ, Vaginal, Anal, and Pussy Eating. "The four foundations of fornication" as Jim called them—a title he thought would make a great band name too. Though Jim also enjoyed handjobs and had received many in his life, he'd decided early on not to include them on his lusty list. To his thinking, they were only a half-step above masturbation. And while he enjoyed masturbation as well, and engaged in it more often than most, Jim considered that to be a mere bodily function—on par with eating, sleeping, and shitting—bearing almost no relationship to sex at all.

On the day it happened, Jim had just gotten back from tour with the New Wave retro act Neon and the Signs. It wasn't Jim's usual type of tour. He was more of a black t-shirt and blue jeans rock n' roller. Still, the "waver gig" gave him his fill of free drink and pussy, same as any tour. On their Midwest run, Neon and the Signs played twelve shows in twelve cities and Jim had a different woman in every one. As per usual, he couldn't wait to get home and add the recent conquests to his long catalog of sexual encounters. And so he did.

At his desk, Jim pulled out various colored pens—blue for BJ, pink for vaginal, brown for anal, red for pussy eating—and got to work filling in the names, dates, and cities of each session. After the new additions, Jim counted the full tally. Two hundred and twenty-seven BJs. A hundred and thirty-two vaginals. Twenty-eight anals. And the rest pussy eating. Three hundred ninety-nine total. For Jim, the four hundred mark had been an important milestone to pass and he was positive that Sarah—the woman he went down on in the hotel breakfast room in Cleveland—was in fact number four hundred. Though he counted and recounted, she was only three hundred and ninety-nine. Her place in Jim's chronicle of copulating suddenly seemed much less significant.

It was devastating to Jim. He'd been running the details through his mind more diligently than ever, readying himself to tell the roofers every moment and movement of number four hundred. How he watched her before the show. How he figured out her personality type based on the color and style of her clothes. How he pretended to like her friend better at first. How he shot glances her way every time he finished a solo. How he told her he needed a ride to the hotel afterward because the band left without him. How he pretended to like every cheesy song she played in the car on the drive over. And, ultimately, how he ate Fruit Loops out of her pussy in the breakfast room of a two and half star hotel near the Cleveland airport where her orgasmic screams were so loud someone called the cops. But none of that mattered anymore. Sarah would only ever be number three hundred and ninety-nine. Frustratedly, Jim grabbed his tool belt and left to meet Nick and the guys at the job site.

As he tacked toe board jacks onto a pitched roof that chilly, early morning, Jim contemplated when and where he might complete his four hundredth sex session. He'd learned the hard way how much chaos it brought to sleep with women who lived in or around Cincinnati. They'd show up at a local gig or even find out where he lived. Better to restrict his womanizing to the road, he thought. Only problem was, his next tour wasn't for two weeks.

As he pondered the problem, Tommy, another laborer on the crew, humped a seventy-pound bag of shingles up a forty-foot ladder and flopped them off his shoulder onto the board Jim was standing on. One of the rusty metal jacks that held the toe board, and Jim on top of it, snapped with the sudden extra weight, sending Jim and the shingles skidding along the roof and sixteen feet down to a concrete driveway where Nick stood sipping coffee.

"Fuckin' A Jim. Y'alright?" Nick asked, bending over the fallen crew member.

Jim rolled off his right hand with a groan. To his horror, one of his fingers was bent in an unnatural direction.

"Told you 'bout those hands," Nick said matter-of-factly, loading Jim into his pickup.

After X-rays, it was determined Jim not only had two badly broken fingers but also a wrist fracture.

At home, Jim sat staring at the cast, worrying that he'd never play guitar again. Though music had become ever less important to him over his ten years of performing, he knew without it he didn't stand a chance of boinking all those beauties in all those towns. It was the guitar that brought them in. That and Jim's sixth sense about which women to pursue. But the guitar was part of that too. It gave him the confidence to approach women in the first place. Without the guitar, he'd be the same as Nick and Tommy. Just another chump hanging his nuts off the edge of a roof, waiting for payday to blow his wad at the bar. Maybe he'd never even cross the four-hundred mark. Stuck at three-ninety-nine for the rest of his miserable life.

Lying around the house all day, Jim got hornier than hell. Though he tried masturbating with his left, Jim was a solid right-hander. Every time he tried yanking it with his southpaw it felt creepily like a child was touching his dick, or, at best, an extremely awkward stranger. Unfortunately for Jim, there was nothing in his persona that was ambidextrous. His left only accomplished the small things in life, like scratching his head or holding nails for his hammer hand. He didn't so much as pick his nose with the left. In the few brawls he'd ever been in, Jim's right did all the punching while his left hung low, merely threatening to join in the fight. And when it came to guitar playing, the left only made simple chords and fingerings. All smoke and mirrors. His fast-picking right hand did all the real work.

No guitar, no pussy, and not even able to pull his own pud, all Jim could do was drink—and that wasn't free anymore.

A few days after the accident, Nick came by with groceries and a bottle of Old Crow. Jim figured his boss was extending the kindness in an attempt to prevent a potential lawsuit, but he was glad for the company just the same. Hungover and self-pitiful, Jim joked drearily about his sexual deprivation, waving his heavily plastered right hand over his crotch.

"Dude, I got just the place for you," Nick said. "A little handjob hut off'a Route 27 . . ."

Jim started to protest. Though he didn't say it out loud, paying for it was for chumps and losers, and it took a particular type of loser—someone like Nick—to pay for a handjob.

"It's on me, bro," Nick said, sensing Jim's hangup.

Jim knew he couldn't drive with his left, so Nick took the day off and drove Jim himself. The whole way over Nick went on and on about an old lady at the massage place who gave "great hand." Jim didn't engage with the banter, figuring his boss was setting him up to be the butt of a dumb joke.

Nick pulled into a strip mall and drove past a liquor store, a vaping store, a pizza parlor, a pawn shop, and a Tai Kwon Do studio, finally parking in a far corner of the lot across from a payday advance place.

"Ask for the Ol' Lady. Trust me," Nick whispered as they walked through a tinted door below a small sign for Diamond Star Massage.

A cute Asian woman at the counter welcomed them. Jim checked out her tits and wished he could play guitar for her. She'd probably do him in the bathroom for free, he thought.

Nick piped up, "He wants the Ol' . . ."

Jim interrupted, "I want the hottest youngest chick you got."

Jim was led to a small undecorated room with a massage table in the center. He disrobed and lay down, covering himself with the thin sheet provided, wondering how often they were cleaned. More often than his own, he decided, staring at a vulva-shaped stain on the popcorn ceiling that gave him a stiffy.

The hottest youngest woman at Diamond Star walked into Jim's room looking at her phone. She chewed gum and squirted something in her hand from a plastic pump bottle near the door, never once averting her eyes from the device. The lotion-filled hand found Jim's penis under the sheet and fondled it noncommittally while she remained fixated on her phone. Though she had earbuds in, Jim could tell she was deep into a TV show by the way she stopped stroking every

time something interesting happened. Unfortunately for Jim, something interesting happened every time he was about to ejaculate.

Fifteen minutes after she began, an alarm went off on Diamond Star's hottest youngest woman's phone.

"Time's up," she said, walking out, eyes still glued to her screen.

"I told you," Nick said on the drive home. "The Ol' Lady."

Two days later, still unable to wank and more frustrated than ever, Jim decided to go back to the massage parlor on his own. When the cab dropped him off, Jim clumsily paid the driver with his left hand and then clumsily let himself in the door to Diamond Star.

"I'd like to see the Old Lady," Jim said sheepishly as he entered.

"Ole Lady not available now," the receptionist informed him. "Medium-old, ok?"

Jim agreed to see the medium-old lady and waited for her on another massage table in another undecorated room.

The medium-old lady announced herself with a door slam, causing Jim to jump.

"I gotcha babe," she said, reaching under the sheet with a hand already dripping with lotion. At least Jim hoped it was lotion.

"Oooh. You're SO big . . ."

Everything about her—her blonde wig, heavily painted face, and large enhanced breasts—looked a little lopsided to Jim.

". . . oooh, dontcha wanna cum all over these big tiddies? OOOH . . ."

Her brash style and the way she fist-pumped Jim's cock like she was trying to yank it off his body made it impossible for him to cum. While he struggled to pry her fingers off his dong, the medium-old lady put her mouth close to Jim's ear and whispered loudly that she was willing to "try something else." He wasn't.

In the lobby, Jim asked when the Old Lady would be available. The receptionist checked her calendar.

"Only opening tomorrow 10 AM. Pay now, ok? Ole Lady don't touch money."

Jim took the slot and paid in advance.

Unable to sleep that night, Jim stared at reruns on an out-of-whack TV that, like everything else in his tiny apartment, was furnished by a shady offsite slumlord. He ruminated about the crappy couch, the crappy bed, the crappy three-channel TV, the crappy building, and the crappy neighborhood it all sat in. He lamented the worthlessness of his right hand and the near-worthlessness of his left. He considered that the whole situation was made worse by the fact that his bank account was empty, the Workmans comp checks he received for the accident barely covered his needs, and he was nearly out of beer. To top it all off, the only thing he had to look forward to in his entire lousy life was paying for a handjob from some old lady that occasionally jerked off his stupid boss. He flipped back and forth between cheesy sitcoms on the TV's three grainy channels, wondering how it had come to this.

Jim called a cab at 9:30 AM the next morning and arrived at Diamond Star five minutes early, eagerly awaiting release. When he walked in, the receptionist handed him an N-95 mask.

"Before see Ole Lady, put mask," the receptionist said.

Jim looked curiously at the N-95 before snapping it on his face. He followed the receptionist's directions—first left then all the way down. When he came to a fuzzy welcome mat at the end of the hall, he knocked.

"This is it," he heard from within.

Inside the room, Jim found the Old Lady sitting in a recliner watching The Price is Right with her own N-95 on. She grabbed the remote from a TV tray and clicked off the show. Jim watched silently as she folded down the foot support and stood up, placing a frilly-edged baking apron over her clothes. She motioned for Jim to sit in the La-Z Boy, and then flipped the lever, popping up his legs.

"Mouth, vaj, or ass?" She asked.

Jim's face belied his horror at the thought of entering any of the Old Lady's orifices.

"*Pretend time* big guy," she said. "Which hole you wanna do? Or you a kinker . . . pussy eater?"

Jim wasn't sure what to make of the situation but didn't think eating pussy was a kink.

"I like . . . BJs, I guess," he answered.

"You and the rest of 'em," she said flatly.

The Old Lady clicked the remote again and pulled out a laptop. The TV came to life with a video of a blonde woman sucking a large pink penis.

"Work for you?" The Old Lady asked. "Color preference, dick size?"

"No, this is fine," Jim said.

The Old Lady jimmied his jeans off and flung a beach towel over his chest.

He heard the squishy sound of lotion coming from a pump and then felt the Old Lady's hands gently touch his genitals—one on the penis, one on the testes.

As he watched the video, it was uncanny how the Old Lady followed each movement of the actress's mouth with her hands—even using her thumb to flick under the head of his dick like a tongue. It was good. In fact, Jim thought, it was better than the real thing. It was so good that Jim didn't want it to end. In an attempt to avoid premature ejaculation, he looked away from the screen and turned his gaze toward the Old Lady.

"Nothing for you up here, sweetie," she said.

But the more Jim looked, the more he did find something up there. Though he couldn't see much of her face, there was something about her gray-blue eyes. They seemed loving. Caring. Forgiving of Jim's indiscretions, including the one he was engaged in at that moment. Her eyes were putting him at peace with his less-than-peaceful existence.

The Old Lady allowed Jim to stare a bit but stopped fondling him while he did so. When he finally returned his gaze to the screen, Jim climaxed quickly, and for the first time in his life, he cried while he came.

"No need to cry over spilt milk," the Old Lady said, giving his head a comforting pat while humming an old tin pan alley tune.

When he returned home that afternoon, Jim pulled out his long list of sexual exploits. He'd been thinking to add the Old Lady, to make her number four hundred, but it just didn't seem right. Not because it was only a handjob—though it was so much more than that—but because of how it left him feeling. Raw. Tender. More awake to the world. Awake to the fact that his previous three hundred and ninety-nine sexual encounters meant nothing after what he'd just been through. And unlike the other women he'd been with, Jim wanted to see the Old Lady again.

After considering it awhile, Jim opened a fresh notebook with his clumsy left hand and scrawled the title "The Old Lady" listing number one under the header Hand-BJ.

With the small Workmans comp checks as his only source of income, Jim couldn't afford to see the Old Lady as often as he liked. But, he figured, if he cut back on drinking he could at least go once a week. And so he did.

As Jim became a regular at Diamond Star, he tried the Old Lady's other offerings—first vaj and then anal. Somehow she was able to replicate the exact velvetiness of a vagina and the precise sausage-casing-tightness of an anus with her talented palms, fingers, and thumbs. As with the hand-BJ, they were better than the real thing. But more than the simple sexual pleasure, it was the heart-opening experience of feeling seen and cared for by the Old Lady that moved Jim to return week after week.

After a month of visits, Jim asked the Old Lady to choose whichever type of digital manipulation she would employ during a given session, leaving him to enjoy the surprise of "dealer's choice." Though she no longer allowed him to look at her during the jerk-offs, Jim found another way to feel close to her. Rather than watch the videos, he kept his eyes closed while she touched him, allowing himself to be at one with the tender care of her hands.

Week after week, Jim returned from the encounters feeling refreshed and alive. He marked each type of handjob down under its appropriate header in the new list: Hand-BJ, Hand-Vaj, Hand-Anus. But his catalog was missing a category and the lack had become bothersome to Jim. *What would she do? What would I do?*—he wondered—a little nervously, a little excitedly—once he'd decided to move on from dealer's choice and tell the Old Lady he wanted to try pussy eating.

On his next cab ride to Diamond Star, Jim was so anxious he almost threw up in the car. He was so lost in his own excitement that he didn't notice the frown on the receptionist's face when he walked in the door.

"Ole Lady not here. Ole Lady sick today," she said.

The words stopped Jim in his tracks. He stood staring at the receptionist, trying to understand what her mouth was doing.

"Ole Lady . . . sick today . . . not here." She repeated louder and slower.

When the receptionist added hand gestures to her words for emphasis, Jim began shaking his head side to side like he'd suddenly come down with a nervous tic.

"SICK?" He finally blurted out.

"You come next week," the receptionist said, opening the door and ushering Jim out.

The next few days were tough ones for Jim. Worrying about the Old Lady and her sickness. Feeling lonely for lack of seeing her. Blowing his money on booze again. The only good news was that his cast was coming off that week.

When Jim went to the hospital on the morning of his appointment, he had the idea to snoop around various floors to see if the Old Lady might be there somewhere.

"May I help you?" A charge nurse in the intensive care unit asked.

"I'm looking for . . ." Jim stopped, realizing he didn't know the Old Lady's name or even how to describe her, other than by her kind gray-blue eyes and supple hands.

". . . the place where they take off casts," he said at last, waving his heavy right hand.

After waiting in the orthopedic center for some time, a pretty young nurse called for Jim to follow her down a corridor—first left and then all the way to the end—just like visiting the Old Lady at Diamond Star. He couldn't help but get horny thinking about it. The nurse removed the cast swiftly with a small oscillating saw and scissors. She cleaned up Jim's pale hand, had him flex his fingers, and gave him a tube of ointment to put on later.

Before leaving the hospital, Jim found a private bathroom, unzipped his pants, and opened the slippy salve just given him. He squirted some into the palm of his newly freed hand and stroked himself, imagining sex with the cast-cutting nurse. He tried and tried, but no matter which way he pictured her—sitting on the toilet giving a BJ, sitting on his lap for vaginal penetration, or bent over the sink for anal—he couldn't keep an erection. It wasn't until he imagined the N-95 mask-wearing Old Lady lifting her frilly baking apron and exposing her gray-haired pussy that Jim was able to complete masturbation for the first time in nearly two months. He yelled so loud after the climax that someone knocked on the door and asked if Jim was alright.

When he got home, Jim tried other right hand activities—eating, writing, TV remote clicking. Eventually, he even picked up a guitar and played a little. It was comforting to know he could do all the right-handed things again if he wanted to. But he didn't care about those things. Not like he used to. More than anything, he wanted his healed hand to touch the Old Lady. He realized suddenly and happily that with the cast off he could drive himself over to Diamond Star and check on her. And so he did.

"Ole Lady still sick. Maybe . . . don't come back," the receptionist said cagily when Jim came in.

"What do you mean?" Jim asked.

"Have nice young lady. New one," the receptionist offered with a smile.

Jim asked for the Old Lady's whereabouts repeatedly but could get no answer. As his frustration mounted, so did the volume of his voice. The noise caused a leather-jacket-wearing goon to come out from behind a beaded curtain and flex his shoulders menacingly. When Jim's hollering grew even louder, the big man moved in sluggishly to do his duty. Almost imperceptibly, Jim shifted his feet and drew his newly available right fist behind him. The unexpected face punch landed hard on the bouncer's nose and mouth. He hit the floor with a resounding whump followed by a horrible wheeze from the wind getting knocked out of him.

"Ole Lady at Peaceful Garden!" The panicked receptionist hollered.

As he drove away, Jim realized his right hand was hurt badly from the one-hit KO. He'd have to go back to the hospital, and he knew it, but not before driving himself to Peaceful Gardens, Inc.—an old folk's home off Route 27 whose sign he'd passed many times on the way to and from Diamond Star.

Jim searched Peaceful Garden's dayroom, moving quickly past residents and staff as he did so. Not spotting her, he took his first right and followed the hall to the end as he'd always done at Diamond Star. When he didn't find her there, Jim combed every corridor of the facility until, on the fourth floor, he finally came upon the Old Lady's fuzzy welcome mat.

After knocking, Jim walked through the unlocked door and found an old lady in a recliner watching The Price is Right. But he wasn't sure it was his old lady.

"Oh . . . you," the old lady said.

Jim sat on a kitchen chair across from her and studied her unmasked face. It was hard to say if she was pretty or not. She looked serious. The oxygen tubes running up her nostrils made her appear frail. Her thin lips, bulbous nose, and weathered sagging cheeks took attention away from her kind eyes. He almost asked her to put a mask on. Unable to look directly at the Old Lady, Jim started reading labels on the dozen or so pill bottles that sat atop her kitchen table. Jim noted that they were mostly heart medications, many of the same ones his mother had taken before her untimely death when he was six.

"Don't you have your own people to worry about?" the Old Lady asked.

Jim thought about it a minute. When his mother died, James Sr. sent him to live with his grandparents. For eight years Jim enjoyed the attention and care of the older relatives, but when his grandfather was moved into hospice and his grandmother became too feeble to take care of him anymore, teenage Jim was sent back to his dad.

"Some. But none of 'em ever touched my pecker," Jim answered, defensively.

"Aw crap. You're a kinker," the Old Lady sighed. "Madame Pearl, my first boss, always said 'Kinkers'll come after ya'.' Tell you what, I give you a quick wank, you get outta here and don't come back. Ok?"

Jim rubbed his swollen right paw with his left, unsure what to do.

"What the hell did you do?" The Old Lady asked, taking Jim's hurt hand into her soft ones.

Jim lost himself in the Old Lady's eyes as tears fell from his own.

"You got one wish kid. Make it a good one, then let me be," she said.

"I want . . ." Jim sniffled, "I want to go down on you."

Jim's request caused the Old Lady to let out a belly-laugh-turned-coughing-fit that lasted through two TV commercials—one for term life insurance, the other for dentures. As The Price is Right came back on, she turned the TV volume up, put the La-Z Boy footer down, and lifted her skirt to expose a pair of large beige undies covering a diaper.

"Get those off and it's all yours, kid," she said.

The diaper and smell of stale urine didn't phase Jim. He took the outer coverings off carefully and lowered his face upon her privates. The Old Lady stroked his head gently, humming the same old tin pan alley tune she always did during their encounters.

Jim was down there a long time, licking and nibbling, sucking and dribbling, waiting for the tell-tale vaginal pulsing—excited to share in the Old Lady's post-coital bliss. But no pulsing came. After a while, he realized there was no more head stroking or humming either. In fact, there was no pulse at all. Jim jumped up, hoping she had simply fallen asleep. He shook her and shook her but she wouldn't budge.

No one seemed to notice when Jim left the Old Lady's room, or when he walked hurriedly through the lobby, or when he peeled out of the parking lot. Nonetheless, he looked over his shoulder incessantly as he knee-drove away from Peaceful Gardens, narrowly avoiding accidents.

Jim parked away from the hospital entrance and stared into the rearview, worriedly replaying the scene. He considered turning himself in but that seemed ridiculous—he hadn't forced his way in or forced himself upon her. He considered calling Peaceful Gardens anonymously to tell them the Old Lady was dead but figured somebody was bound to check on her when she didn't show for a meal or a bridge game or something. Then he told himself that, after all, it wasn't such a bad way to go. And anyway, she would've died soon enough judging by the pills she was taking.

As his thoughts ping-ponged, Jim finagled a grey pube from between his lower front teeth with his unwieldy left hand, barely noticing his throbbing, melon-sized right. The Old Lady's voice came back to him then, saying "kinker"—first in an accusatory tone, then in a friendly familiar one as if calling a pet by its special nickname.

"Here kinker. Feeding time . . ."

Jim bolted from the car and ran into the hospital. The doctor who patched him up the first time happened to be on duty when he dragged his giant fist into the examination room. After looking at X-rays, the doctor frowned at Jim and his disfigured duke and said,

"Somehow you managed to double the size of your fracture. All we can do is put another cast on, my friend. I'm sorry to say, your right wrist will likely not function as it used to."

Jim's thoughts and feelings, like his hand and wrist, were once again stuck in a hard place. There was not one thing, including alcohol, that could take away the pain in his throbbing limb or the ever-present memories of the Old Lady—particularly her haunting humming song which played on repeat in his heavy head.

Workmans compensation wouldn't cover the re-injury. As a result, Jim sold off his guitars one by one to stay afloat. With the money from his first sale, he ordered a recliner and had it delivered to his living room so he could at least sit comfortably while staring at the half-broken TV day and night. In the late mornings, when The Price is Right came on, he got hornier than hell but was unable to do anything about it. At least, he thought, the hard-on was proof he was still alive—even if he sometimes wished he wasn't.

A couple months later, when the second cast came off, Jim's right wrist was so stiff he was unable to turn it in any direction. It looked as if it were glued to his arm. He could use the hand, more or less, to drive, to feed himself, and to wipe his ass, but masturbation was definitely out of the question. More than anything, though, it was his inability to play guitar that weighed heavy on him. Without that Jim knew there was no chance for any more free booze or pussy.

A former bandmate named Pat stopped by one day to dig through the last of Jim's music gear. He noticed that though Jim's wrist was inflexible, his fingers still moved freely. Pat asked if Jim had considered playing keyboard, suggesting that it required less wrist dexterity than guitar. He also mentioned that he had one he'd be willing to trade. Though Jim balked at first, knowing that piano proficiency requires a great deal of left hand ability, he eventually agreed to a trade, handing over a decent Les Paul knockoff in exchange for a well-worn eighty-eight-key electric piano.

The keyboard sat in a corner collecting dust for a couple weeks before, out of sheer boredom, Jim began plunking on it. It was easy enough to tinkle out simple melodies with his right fingers, but it took Jim some time to add in the left. Oddly, when he began using both hands, it was as if his left had been waiting—like a neglected child craving attention, routine, and discipline—to be brought into the fold. From chopsticks, to simple boogie-woogies, to more complicated arrangements, Jim's left hand came ever more to life.

When he was finally able to play through entire songs with both hands, Jim began searching for the tin pan alley tune that ran incessantly through his mind. After several days scouring libraries and record stores, whistling the melody to anyone who'd listen, he found it: "All Alone" by Irving Berlin.

Jim rehearsed "All Alone" day and night. He tried it in various keys and tempos and infused with different emotions and levels of intensity. As he worked through it, a sense of ease came over him. It seemed to Jim that as he mastered the Old Lady's song, he transcended the haunting of her humming. She was no longer in his head, but in his fingers—just as he had once been in hers.

As he grew more proficient at the piano, new qualities developed in Jim—or at least in his left hand. From the playfulness of his pinky to the thoughtfulness of his thumb, the left struck major, minor, and diminished chords in the most heartfelt and joyful ways. Similarly, when Jim patted a friend's back or shook their hand, genuine care and appreciation came through his loving left. Beyond that, his left had begun opening doors for the elderly, offering change to pan-

handlers, and flashing the peace sign at aggressive drivers. Where his right hand had always been on the take, grasping at the world for his own selfish needs, Jim's left developed in the exact opposite direction. It became his giving hand.

The more Jim played the keys, the more his left dominated everything he did. It was his guide to music and his guide to the world. When he searched for new songs to learn on piano, his left led the way, pointing him to composers like Gershwin, Ellington, and Strayhorn. He dug into the Jazz standards with a childlike fervor and soon realized he was heading toward a new career path.

It was clear that Jazz piano wouldn't get him work with his former bands, but Jim figured there were other audiences for the old-timey music—namely, old people. It wasn't long before he picked up gigs in piano bars and hotel lobbies. From those experiences, Jim realized he liked performing alone—following his own rhythm, choosing songs that best fit his mood—but it wasn't until he started playing in the "nursing home circuit" that he landed a steady, stable income to support his solo endeavor.

With his left hand leading the way, Jim landed weekly spots playing happy hours, ice cream socials, and other "mixers" at the best assisted living centers in the tri-state area—including three locations of the Peaceful Gardens, Inc. franchise.

Though Jim knew piano would never earn him fortune or fame, it paid far better than the dive bars and clubs he'd previously played in the Rock scene. Booze didn't flow freely in Jim's new work environment, but that was no problem—he'd lost his taste for the stuff anyway. One thing there was plenty of, and Jim certainly got his fill, was pussy. In that, he still had one of the highest-wage jobs around.

Marvin Cohen

Stone Versus Cloud: The Bout of the Ages

(Two men sitting at a picnic spread in a park with trees, etc. No building seen. They're in a clearing, with a view that sweeps up from the horizon high in the air. But the foreground they occupy is solidly the ground.)

Here we are, at a picnic. Us two alone, and the ants as luncheon guests. I'm hefting a stone *(does so:)* in the palm of my hand. A stone, whose home is the in the land.

But *I* have a *higher* awareness. My contemplation is on that *cloud* over there.

That's the sky for you! It's always marred by clouds.

I don't regard clouds as blotches or impediments, or as negations of a pure sky's clarity. I regard them as positive ornaments, things-in-themselves.

How high-fallutin can you get? A stone *(hefting it:)* has more solid merit, any day!

It may *seem* real, *here*: but a cloud *is* real, *there*.

You're a *dreamer*, is what you are! Your head is where the clouds are. But I'd rather palm this stone. *(Palms it.)*

You think I'm balmy? You're merely palmy. If you need *weight* for assurance, any stone will do. A stone is merely the slave of gravity. And gravity's kingdom, democratically unselective, lacks the taste of discrimination. Whereas a *cloud* is a real connoisseur's delight! It makes us soar above our station. It *raises* us out of the dust. We're *with it*. But a stone—a stone, like a parasite, is only *with us*.

A stone *clings* to us. But a cloud's *above* such petty dependency. *Truly*, we may call it *liberated*. Its destiny is unlimited. A stone *is* only what it *is*.

That's a lot of hot air! Your vapor rises and dissolves in meaningless spirals of inconsequential ascent. Your words drift. And I've lost the drift of them.

A *stone*'s destiny is in its *density*. Compare what's merely a stone's-throw away, with what *(gazes high, deep, far:)* surpasses forever, in its lonely day.

The spirit is a puncturable balloon. But it takes *some doing (admiringly:)* to split a *stone*!

Splitting a stone merely divides it into halves, a bigger half and a smaller half, but they weigh the same as before, (And what's weight?—it's merely dross.) But a split *cloud* will multiply!, and feed our dreams eternally.

You've got your atoms all wrong. You've got to start with *elements*/ Now, take a *stone (admiringly:)* for *solidity*!

Solidity?! it *crushes* me with its weight. A cloud vessels our travelling infinitely, and skips us lightly on the sun's multidirectional ray.

Our argument finds us too opposed to go anywhere. I'm really *earth*bound, and you're *high-up-there*!

We can reconcile these two factors of our dispute, by regarding a stone as a puny *symbol* for a cloud, a *dormant* cloud that hasn't gotten off the ground yet and by considering a *cloud* to be a graduated, liberated *stone*, having shaken off its earth-captivity and been promoted to the deep reward of a metamorphosis and transcendental uplift. It has sloughed its *earthly* skin, and found heaven pragmatically laden with welcome, and nearer to reach than supposed. Nature is the lowest layer in a hierarchy astronomically monumental. A stone is a puny thing. It's only stage one. It doesn't move until pushed, or scooped up to be hurled. A *cloud*'s momentum is its own. Its soft sibilants caress the gods in language.

Pretty words! But they're not worth a stone! They sit dreaming on the air! What do *ideas* matter? *Matter* is the best idea!

Your matter-of-fact materialism is finitely bound to one dimension. And it gets you nowhere.

Everything I need is only a stone's-throw away. I'm content.

That brave declaration is insincere. *Aspirations* give our minds airy room, where talent is free to be marvelous.

Is your talking nonsense?—Or is your nonsense talk? I fail to grip the difference.

You needn't *grip* anything. Trust the clouds.

I wouldn't trust them within an inch of my life! All they do is rain on me.

(*Solemnly:*) Clouds reign an imperial dynasty. Each cloud is an idea's materialization, and ideas are our spirit.

(*Rudely:*) What good will all your sublime visions get you? If you're such a visionary, why ain't you *rich*?

My *mental* wealth is jewelled infinite. Clouds rove with their treasures. An angel's economy requires no more than wings.

You're violating the simplicity of this (*showing it:*) stone. Your language inflates all the non-stones, whereas modesty should give you the stone's-measure of proportion, in restraint of your exaggeration. Your mind runs wild. It's a child of irresponsibility, in its unbroken course.

Which is better than being *coarse*! Cloud-dwelling is an imponderable refinement, and diets our coarse thickness in rarity and aesthetics. If you were asked to locate beauty, then you must raise your eyes.

No; to praise the *stone*, is to show *concrete* beauty. Concrete beauty is the only beauty we know.

There's no hope for you. I dwell (*eyes skyward:*) on the blue!

You bore me, with no sign of fatigue. Your wonders have no value, for you ponder the intangible. The precious will soon evaporate. The *enduring* is hard, like this (*shows it:*) stone.

Oh, go stone yourself! We dwell apart—obviously.

So do these tokens of our championing: here, the stone (*shows it, looking down*), and (*searching up, in vain:*)—where's the cloud!?

(*With composure and serenity:*) It'll be back. It's roamed elsewhere. Is the earth so sacred, or so exclusive, that it must confine itself *there*? No: its voyages transparently vacate space, with outward-bound excursions into the inner mind. Clouds are poetry's source. Stones are what buildings are raised from. In poetic myth, our *souls* dwell. The buildings only *physically* house us. Our priorities are separate. You can *have* the earth. But my soul's growth has no flimsy *stone* in it: its satisfaction has less definition. (*With finality:*) Go. I stay.

As a stone will stay. Hard put to do otherwise. But wither blows the soul's companion-in-one, the cloud? No knowing goal can trace it. Myths are not what you can pin facts on, or hang stones from as a beady necklace. God reserves a cloud for His visit. Stones are for humans to touch. I think a stone is a punished cloud, having fallen into disgrace. But the sentenced angel resolves to rise again. He's jailed for a term in the hard stone's core. He learns how not to err, that way. Earth is very practical, with him.

(*Stonelover remains sitting, with tailor's crossed knees, contemplating his precious stone. Cloudlover roves away, with a light indeterminateness of direction, on a slightly rising angle. A stone curtain falls. A cloud curtain rises. They embracingly meet in tender caressing, then push on past each other. Between them, they've covered the total stage. All is symbolically accounted for: nothing is left over.*)

MIKE SILVERTON

Some Poems and Other Poems

Some Poems

Some poems require torque, others, punctures.
Fingers and a keyboard are a promising start,
also baskets, air horns, popcorn and cigars.

Examples

Empathy's least reliable measure
lies in what one's threshold can bear. For example,
one's heart goes out to victims till they vomit on house pets,
only to discover, alas, too late,
that this never happened. For example,
a set-upon bearded lady escapes through a rent in a circus tent,
but when? I thought you were talking about heaven
or suave policemen or, for example, a nihilist with psoriasis,
for whom, for example, we weep briefly, actually
more for sad children sitting in water
up to their noses.

A Belovèd, First Sighting

She was hanging off the eaves. "I have drifted
down from the stars," she said,
and lost her grip.

Poets

The poet who squints at the dawn
through his belovèd's toes
is emphatically spiritual and
likewise sentimental.
The poet who questions poetry's fungibility
is properly pragmatic.
The poet who kidnaps a rival's belovèd,
were he a cork, would sooner disintegrate
than allow the fizz to escape.
Two pink lights under a freshly laundered guayabera
hang off a poet whose interests lie elsewhere. The poet
who stirs cauldrons with teaspoons . . ..

The Poet as a Lieutenant-Colonel

I led a battalion past halved potatoes,
their placid white faces here and there gazing.
I led a battalion into barrels of brine
where, in time, I harvested pickles.

The Morning Begins

The morning begins. Daylight frames the room's draperies
in silver-grey. The poet lies beneath his robes in thick gurgling sleep.
A loud rapping pops the (flimsily attached) house rules
off the door. The poet, alarmed, leaps from his bed,
winds his robes about his hips (he sleeps in the nude) and
stumbles toward the door against which some insolent fool is
bruising his knuckles—a messenger in livery. "I have a message."
The poet acknowledges, running his tongue across his mossy teeth.
"It's to be spoken." The poet acknowledges, running his tongue
across his mossy teeth. The light in the messenger's eyes,
as it had been those years ago, shades to pale pewter,
like nacreous shirt buttons. "Your slide talk slid me off my seat.
How can I thank you?"

The poet pauses. He finds himself standing before an excrescence
he takes to be Chopin's tomb (actually, Chopin's tomb's in
the Père-Lachaise Cemetery, Paris, France). The poet removes a stylus
and etches esses on the excrescence. A stranger shuffles his feet
in a way that speaks to a need for attention.
The poet looks up from his task. "Mister, tell me what you think.
An old gentleman with hair in his ears and enameled pins in his lapels
left only moments ago. I'm at a loss. I cough, I sniffle,
I make small talk, but mostly I wonder."

"Since you loathe us, please be good enough to explain."
A strange interruption! We return to our story.

The old gentleman hands the poet a small envelope similar to those
announcing weddings, births and deaths. He departs.
In the envelope, a smaller envelope, in it a card in raised lettering:

$C_6H_7[CH]_4CO_2H$

This is quite possibly the formula in which one soaks rocks to produce
a Philosopher's Stone! The poet hears something, also possibly.
Or possibly not, yet there can be no question
that he is standing at a shop window.

Kafka's Bad Day

He oversleeps. He awakens in the middle
of an afternoon he doesn't recognize.
He finds hair in a pocket.
There's a towel in his shoe.
His cuticles are out of control.
He stands, confused, at the center of a ring
of shattered orange manicure sticks.

A Woman at a Window

A window opens.
A woman leans over the sill.
She peers so intently that the poet's
hands are suddenly helpless and damp.
She hits a pot with a spoon
and shouts "It's you!"
A man jumps out of his car. "It is you!"
A wizened tailor runs from his shop,
index finger out like a lance,
stopping when it dimples the poet's cheek.
Squinting, he agrees, "Yes, it's you!"
The mayor waddles over.
Loiterers draw near.
The mayor nods and smiles,
his teeth glistening like wet Chiclets.
"Welcome home!"
(The poet smokes stinky French cigarettes.)

The Ideal Poem

The ideal poem resembles iridescent karp in a pond
they don't recognize, or better, choose not to.
The ideal poem need not be statuesque, nor a statue
on which ravens perch, so long as, nearby,
we find a bronze plaque.
The ideal poem, were it kissed, would
bite the lover's lip, gently.
The ideal poem resembles vistas
upon which dangerous eggs have been strewn
by partisan ornithologists.
The ideal poem, tho sometimes absurd,
is sometimes less intentionally so,
which is to say, sometimes disarrayed.
Certain aspects look like ice cubes,
with or without decals, or like arrow shafts of
Port Orford cedar, but this is optional.
The ideal poem serves no purpose, least of all
as a to cushion to transitions.
Here, perhaps, the ideal poem goes too far.
To remedy that, the ideal poem,
face to the wall, tries on several expressions of concern
when dealing with serious questions
(stone, plaster, sheetrock, makes no difference).

Murder Mysteries

"The fit's upon me!
I have to smash eggs!"
"How many?"
"One."

"I am dying, literally, to kiss your lips."
"Literally? How so?"
"I misspoke. I mean I would die, literally."
"Again, how so?"
"Your gears would grind up my face."

"I find this bludgeon unreliable."
"Oh?"
"It feels like fog.
It feels like mush.
It feels too friendly."

"Blut und Boden? That's our motto?
You think it's easy, peeling
a homeland?"

A miniscule fanatic lurks in a stucco dimple.
Leaping forward, he bellows "Eternity forever, and
I'll settle for less!"

Operating from his nest
of a thousand dim lights, Sticky Eddy,
the noiseless pro, plunges a stiletto into a roll
of Calypso baloney.

Such are the field marshal's gifts,
he convinces the enemy that landmines are
potato latkes ready for harvest, yet
he cannot spell enigmatic.

Joseph Ignace Guillotine:
"The condemned, his neck as one with my device,
could wish the blade a skittish bird."

Magic trousers remove themselves from a victim.
Quips regarding décolletage seem
inappropriate.
A message in a time capsule:
Better a masterpiece locked in a vault
than a football in a dead bishop's mouth.

A Parable

I happened upon a bindlestiff essaying to fell an out-of-towner,
whom he likely mistook for a tree owing to the visitor's demeanor
and shrubbery trilby. I took the would-be forrester aside
and spoke to him, concluding with a parable:

An elephant had escaped from its traveling circus, taking shelter
in my back yard. I called my town's animal-control officer. "What
is the elephant doing?" he asked. "It's picking cabbages and,
God forgive me, you'll find this difficult to believe,
pushing them through a crack in the sky." Eyes and ears,
and as lagniappe, a bulge.

A Man's Body

A man's body is more intricate than any machine!
Yes, his body! Have a tissue!
A man's body is a factory where one worker's an ulna,
another, a follicle. A man's scapula often looks like a snow shovel.
His breastbone often looks like a necktie.
If a man sits down too hard he is likely to injure his coccyx,
a small bone resembling a bent finger, which protects his sad sack.
Nerve endings in a man's skin detect pain, anguish, love, mirth,
insincerity and fraud. A man knows not to touch hot things.
The tiny hairs in his nose tell him something's burning.
A man's skin prevents organs from leaving his body.
When the skin is broken a man is said
to be spilling.

This Young Poem

I arise, dress, breakfast and go,
and shake hands with the manager of the parts department,
and his hand comes off in mine,
and a word comes to mind. Poise.

If you were to brandish a cucumber,
if you were to pop a balloon,
if you were to chew at a certain rate,
if this were 1921.

Faith, some distance above the scalp,
descends. One wants to scratch it
behind the ear (if you were to wave
a cucumber).

Young legs carry one wherever one wants to go.
Young heads grow hair. Like a jewel that took a million years
to develop, this young poem is its own reason for being.
This young poem is a jewel.

Performance

Stuffing one's sporran with Gaelic pride
is the point and fruit of its own performance.
In draping oneself in cucumber vines
one's performance bears the promise of salad.
Early evening. The glancing sunbeams
bathe the soapstone just so—
bubbles!

It Doesn't Matter

"Surely not me," the poet cried,
"who craves no more than garbage to eat,
as soon as is convenient, of course.
It doesn't matter, I am crazy.
Also the loneliest man in the world. And
I don't want to be in this poem!"
(Palaces spit out viceroys,
Poems spit out poets.)

A viceroy rolls over and drops into a bay. It is evening.
Questioned, he says, "I like to write poems.
Is it the same where you come from?"

And, as an afterthought,
"I want you to have an immaculate future."

Early Morning

The sun creeps up the window.
From across the pond, thup thup thup!
It is a goddess laundering a thunder cloud.
Her daughter's buttocks glisten.
The goddess's hair is grey. In a bun.
The man of the house,
his necktie is a tapeworm.
An odor of cigar.
The goddess is preparing a German potato salad.

Weeping Commissars

In a Marxist-Leninist state
the economy comes first. No sooner turned off,
hordes of weeping commissars slog through the suds.
The least among them whispers,
"I like that you sleep with your eyes open,
keeping tabs on the potatoes."

Lucian Staiano-Daniels

The longue durée as a great sturgeon, thinking of time beneath the river Detroit

Behold the river breaker: her outlook scans the ebb and flow of the longtime. Her long eyes fare forth from the smallness of swiftly shifting samenesses. Her widespread witness takes in the bigwork of deeptime spans. It lays bare the unseen and bulksome grounds that underbed swift happenings. Still searowunder unhides these longstanding and standhearted beds, the swift silts whereon shortcoming ripplewinds drift and are gone.

Her drawnout watching maps the longwork betweentides of forthshifting lifeways. It outsheds the landmarks which shortspell seers take for earth's unwon backbone. She has wormed through sandy loam, fine loam of buried earth: under regollic masses of rusted iron the illshaped fish outlasts the enddeed, the brook and warmaker, rippling insmall-hither, and outweighs them in evermore weight of laiddown holdings.

In an eavelong outwatch her gaze innerholds the standshape evenworks, wherefrom fortfaring men wax and overwear their earthspan.

Richard Dinges

Two Poems

Survival

Trapped in this mass
of flesh and fluids,
I wait out another
viral intrusion,
listen to my bones
rattle and rub eyes
raw, wipe away
my leaks and odors,
avoid contact with
anyone who might
stare back long
enough to recognize
my slow erosion
and act to cull
my weakness
from the herd.

Chickens

With a talent
for indifference,
chickens ignore
me until I bring
a bow of scraps
to scatter across
their piece of land,
and then they charge,
a feathered phalanx
of anxiety
that they will not
get their portion
before I deliver
their just desserts.

Four Poems

Wise Owl

Forego clamshells of triple-washed power greens in lieu of something out back from a friend who says it's enough to intuit and everything else is academic. That it's fine to be academic as long as you give people a break except polluters who are doing enough breaking. In fact, they're taking naps on your pillows of organic greens because plastic film is stretched around the clock but seldom reinvented to wake them up. I can't get any city back from time. That's a constant transformation of pedestrians into crosshairs and sciatica in the shape of car seats whipping roundabouts. Whipping children into strong neck muscles and gummy strawberry Dramamine. If you buy a used car there is breakfast in the backseat. If you buy a new bible it comes wrapped in hot plastic. But if you buy new poetry you'll contribute to a superfund cleanup site of love not money. Line broadsides like a litter box under owl trees to catch the necklace teeth of deep-pocket gophers. These absorbent papers—where would you like them burned, New Gadsden? Tallahassee? We blow out those candles with a sincere wish for your many strange years of undiagnosed syphilis.

Enfant terrible

I turned my laptop upside and shook. Dear email, is anybody out there? Does anybody think of me on Sundays at 11:26 am Pacific? The answer: Big Skies Country Store, The Home Network Sweepstakes, IBS Insights, Bay Cities Morning Report, Wolverton's Bakery, James Taylor Concert Alerts. That's a decent cross-section, I said. It winked at me and its power went out. My bedroom, my house, the valley below, the hill above. The outage kept spreading. I'd seen this same thing before in my lame duck with staph foot. It won't stop 'til it reaches a knee. Power gets stumped these days. Oh, my grandmother with a blackening leg. They told her, amputate or die. The deterioration took out my view of Los Angeles, then all of Southern California. Really put a damper on Vegas. You will never take my leg, she said, I would sooner croak. She sooner did. The laptop battery sustained awhile, gave off blue light, but there were no servers left to circulate validation. Outside a rabbit harvesting the last strands of sunset. It was a delight because I'd known her before. Named her Zelda Fitzgerald and dabbed her nose with salve. With burns like that, I could only assume she'd escaped a wildfire. Later, she tried ballet but ran off. Left one slipper behind. Once all the electronics were good and dead, the city, the grid, I looped that slipper on my keychain and hiked up to San Francisco. There was sourdough spilling all over the place. The main arteries of town were receiving a hell of an angioplasty, its humans squeezed to raisins like diamonds. Yeast is the start of something good. We love the smell of baking bread. Well, we asked for it.

Red Tape

People adore being correct, precise, about wild flowers, exotic pharmaceuticals, corresponding diagnoses, coffee tasting notes, all sorts of distinctions and antique valuations. I know the best cider mill. No, not the one with the water wheel. You'd think so, with all the people, but you need to focus on the orchard, not the distracting folk trio. You start to notice that everything requiring precision is a real hike. Take the best waterfall, for example. The travel guide recommended a lovely well-traveled path about a half mile from the parking lot. Good for families of all ages, a charming pool filled by a spritely forty-foot descent. I'd say accessible, in the sense of broad popularity, but accessibility, it seems, is the torment of sophistication and rigor. Tom knew a back route, a real ankle twister, to the upper falls that was only frequented by adventure seekers donning specially certified backpacks dangling with rainbows of unused metallic carabiners. You'll need all sorts of carabiners if you're going to take matters seriously. Tom promised a hundred-foot drop, and he may have been accurate, except the trail dumped you out right at the slated crest of the river's jaw. You couldn't see the majesty of its veil, the terminus below, without plugging yourself in a barrel and shoving off the cliff. You'd probably have to sign a waiver with the parks department and I'm just so tired of fine print, and Tom.

Population Wise

The hummingbirds have gone mad for my purple sage! Get over here all of you. I have room for eight billion. Shush your folding chairs and surrender your phones. Don't make another sound. Listen to them sillying up this place with their tweets! I have enough openland for all. Look beyond their flits of ruby and gold, it's rolling out like a fresh palace rug. Purple sage brushing up the entire planet. Hummingbirds sticking landings like a branch's pandemic. Miniature vortices taking down airplanes that were absolutely itching for a herd of fleas. I saw a hummingbird chiseling at the World Bank like a woodpecker. Help it get through! It just wants a bit of nectar for all its occupation. Just enough for its children nesting silently beneath a plump nectarine. Silence? I spoke too soon. Some little scoundrel just squeaked his chair leg and it sounded like a big idea. What an afternoon this turned out to be. I didn't get anything done.

Nate Logan

Six Poems

On the Banks of the Wabash, Far Away

I don't need to see another Internet video on how to cook perfect eggs.

That doesn't mean I don't love you.

Sneezing-on-demand.

In a field somewhere, state history is taking a turn for the superstitious.

The psyche of someone who commissions a painting of a sword-wielding naked woman on the side of their van.

It's the wine talking indoors.

One bullet point: the dreary wilderness.

Or DW if you don't have a lot of time.

No more discussion necessary.

I can't imagine myself wizened and interested in pottery on the banks of the Wabash, far away.

I Thought We Were Friends

A Frenchman and a Scotsman race on the beach.

When asked, you couldn't describe the sea that day except to say it was "completely normal."

The short history of carrying a blowtorch for you.

The audacity of a wolfman mailbox.

Everyone's getting diagnosed this year.

I'm going to be late to the dog show and that's what really kills me.

I can't tell you anything you don't already know.

Catherine Persian Rug

Get the fries, you'll need energy in the coming days.

If offered the key to the city, I would simply refuse.

Maybe one of us is too laid back.

Whee.

The made-for-TV blues all over your face.

My penchant for starting and abandoning a list of enemies.

Maybe tomorrow, maybe the next day.

You can name your catamaran whatever you want.

If you really love me, you'll do me this one favor.

Duck, Duck, Gray Duck

You phone tag me, so I'm it.
Taking a stroll down to the thunderdome.
Some jackass falls from a rock-climbing wall.
He's interviewed, that's how we know he's a jackass.
Nate lights up the room with a catacomb torch.
The production value's not here either.
Something is rotten in the city of Duluth.

Many People Were Scandalized, Some Still Are

Search terms: evil jazz?? / speed jazz / most fucked-up free jazz album.
I don't eat oats I just want answers.
Back on a hill in the south of France with an American accent.
Leaning over, hands on your knees, really looking.
Your monocle hits me in the forehead.
We have a good laugh.
Punks spitting wishes in a well.
You're breaking up, the train is going through a tunnel.
Later, we shared a brief moment of worry: a dog marionette chased the garbage truck into a roundabout.

There's That Grin

Someone shampooed the neighborhood pets in the night.

Amber Isaac

Readying a Bath

While I pop the bathtub mat loose, you
brush stray hairs away from the drain.
I thought the world was ending, too,

so we lit candles and moved the shampoo
bottles to the side, our bottoms aimed
exactly where the bathtub mat was. You

toss hot into cold, true
to our needs. To cook and eat ourselves again.
You thought the world was ending too

soon because who didn't or doesn't stew
over rollover minutes. Each grain
of dirt caught under the mat hints at a new

and stable life, one snapped in two
to distribute the weight of a strain
like learning the world must end, cruel

but predictable. Life under our shoes
and the bodies will not wash away with the rain,
so give in, pop the bathmat all of you.
Soak the world and begin anew.

Three Poems

The 1971 Skydog Calculus Poem

after Jan Beatty/in memory of David Scott Graham/gratitude
for guitar wizards Dickey Betts & Duane "Skydog" Allman

Back when youngsters could say without irony *"In Memory*
    of Elizabeth Reed" is better than Jesus a Penn State
calculus teacher was Dickey Betts' doppelgänger. The planet

    has always been midden & music, irony ferric
as blood. Just ask Louis Armstrong or any Cistercian
    inking neumes in Brittany. Betts' tone spits razors,

Skydog's makes weather. Nittany Dickey oozed love
    of calculus. None of us knew or would've cared
if we did he was a graduate student, which one of us

    realized seven years later when "seven years" still meant
"a really long time." Other than Calc Betts, the oldest student
    had a potbelly, a German accent, Robert Plant ringlets,

a slick, pustule-ridden face, some kind of thing for me
    & I think a yen for heroin, but maybe I'm muddling
what a dorm mate confessed while cueing the claymation

    short he'd shot. We did smoke hashish once after Calc—
I'm guessing the Lebanese Blonde miraculously everywhere then—
    from the chillum Dieter had pit-fired back in Frankfurt.

The hash compelled me to whisper *My gramps lived there!*
    at which Lena (Nico's doppelgänger) giggled *Deet!*
You must keep ziss one! He is zo sweet! The War was everywhere

    (though mostly bloodless there)—asshole-deep terror,
howled, grunted, sobbed-out rage, flag-snapping psychopathy,
    it's-my-turn duty, friends, cousins, brothers, fathers

vanishing into C-7s or schlepped across the tarmac into pointless
    ambulances at Fort Dix or materializing at softball games
& anthropology lectures & teach-ins, jungle hats screwed down,

    dog tags jingling. A welter of candles burned in Dieter's
punky apartment, Lena lounging willowy & impassive on the couch,
    In the Court of the Crimson King draping us in aural velvet,

Dieter gargling *Zuch a beard, mein Liebchen* as he tapped my knee,
    Lena performing history's most fetching French inhale,
then a lot of wine & my first hit of schnapps, thick, damp

    cigarettes plucked from a green box, vast thirst, Lena gliding
to the bathroom, Dieter gleaming beside me on the brown carpet
    then Lena draped on the couch & could she really have lain

in billowing smoke wearing only red boxers, eyelids smudged black?
        Back in Calc, blotto Dickey inscribed a mirror-image integral,
pondered it, rubbed it with the heel of his hand, chalked the backward

        thing again, rubbed, chalked, hand caked yellow, oily, blond,
center-parted hair swinging, mustache squirming as he muttered
        while thirty hirsute scholars slid lower at the farcical desks

till he freed us. I just verified acing Calc I & remain convinced
        I earned it. Last week, I discovered a friend's draft number
was 69. Mine was 11, so my crumpled despair in the dorm hallway,

        the pre-induction physical in Newark & my father's
If you gotta go, you gotta go beats David's retrospective stoicism,
        but he's dying & not as we all are, but breath by breath.

Lissome Nico kept whispering *herrroeen,* though I don't think heroin
        ever appeared, but Dieter did spread the mimeographed pages
of his novel on the rug so we could *rrread zem togezer* & gently drew

        the hand I'd curled around Lena's ankle back to the chillum.
Thus went my best chance at a threesome, tying-off (etc.) & a blowjob
        (etc.) from a German or Dutch or any man. Decades before

being tethered to a tank, David crammed a Chicago summer full
        of Slice-of-Life Weekends that made my Calc Afternoon
an episode of *Romper Room*, but I could & did brag I had mine

        at nineteen, so there! The War is permanent. My friend died
as I worked on this poem, but within it he'll always live & die
        as we all do. I miss him. May I live long enough to know

what that means. Making-believe those slices would've been right
        in character, bless him. I want Paco to wave me into his room
& drop the needle on "In Memory of Elizabeth Reed" so we lean

        in bliss against green cinderblocks as Skydog—months dead
as the platter spins—conjures wonder. Is that too much? Very well then.
        I've just verified (never mind how) David did live those weekends,

the living more vivid than the telling. Last I knew, Paco was a diplomat
        in Chile. Permanence is mist, names fundamental. Dickey Betts
carves the air in my ears this second & Skydog will soon sluice rapture

for the 3,498th time. So there.

THIS IS an ELEGY FOR Dean YOUNG

& a prospective elegy for Neil Young,
who makes hood ornaments profound
by singing in that cracked-porcelain
falsetto while Dean writes *Never will we*
be sealed in the necropolis again & 482 other
galactic assertions seemingly at whim,
so how come I'm far from the only one
sealed in a self-crocheted necropolis?
After all, the present day is the most
self-conscious epoch of organic burial,
so on a sylvan Tuesday at least 205 years
from now, please nestle whatever's left
of me beneath a dwarf pine uprooted
from Lebanon State Forest so my aromatic
fat can enrich it endlessly. The stiles
in the grove a blue kissing-close-to-apex-
Vermeer, the holy precinct will forever
generate its own weather. *Oh Oh Alabama*
mourns naively from the plastic speakers
my girl props in her bedroom window
each time her guy pulls up, so I pull up,
slip from the Jeep, wave & goddamn it,
Neil should roll Dean another number
for the road as he stirs three teaspoons
of sugar & a glug of condensed milk
into a mug of asphalt-black coffee
while they each ponder the fuming urn
here in the Ship Bottom Grange.
Fresh Asphalt & a Robust Spliff
Aroma of fresh asphalt & a robust spliff—
enough to rubber-band the Corvair to Lebanon
now that the shattered jar of pickled peaches
glitters atop the midden where Scotty—
that twelve-year-old, albino hoodlum—
pisses as the yellow bus shudders alongside
the Texaco sign signifying fill-'er-up-bonus,
insulated mugs of hot joe, so Magda's first
out of the rain, scarfing a cherry snack pie
& doing the Mashed Potato down the aisle
on these outskirts of *Le Paris des élevages de poulets*,
sumptuous gladiolas, fifteen newspapers

& ubiquitous porkpies all the Dexter Gordon
necessary to cheer the camels, surplus British
Expeditionary Force ammo satchels & surprise
Renaults schlepping from picturesque Nepal
the communion wafers soon to guarantee
Current Events Assembly Day's wonder.
Alex's Apollonian shoulders deserve all
the contemplation we can devote, as do
Darlene's bracelets & that Roman coif
she rocks so insouciantly. Though new specs
brighten the widow's walks here in Bath, Maine,
the tanks remain invisible as the Cornwall coast
in January, Turkish coffee ridiculously chewy,
an Armed Services Edition *Tom Sawyer* spread
beneath my left hand, Sartre having just doffed
his trench coat forty-seven days since smiling
in Addis Ababa, where shattered curbing can still
be sat on, splinters of winter in spring's bright
midnight precincts, three rusted bolts beside
his demitasse of steaming chocolate, the nave
of a cathedral now rubble raccoons & kids
scrabble over, so this can't be Addis Ababa
nor that Jean-Paul. Time to find the atlas
(even this almanac won't suffice) sprawling
multi-hued nations across two-page spreads.
What benevolent sovereign, what ancient
fermentations, what chief export, hieratic dance,
epoch of sculptural flourishing? So fun to stroll
tarpaper & corrugated-tin cities creaking atop
mosaics because here lie the galaxy's first coal pits,
six lost empires become metamorphic rock.
Contentment lounges in a sling chair at the misty
trolley stop right over there. *Yum yum* says
the first pull on a damp cigarette, this thought
not quite having given way to this.

Ode to Pie

I miss the peach snack pies
I'd sometimes call lunch & think
healthy for the fruit, the lack
of icing & the brown jacket
speckled with the carbon
a century of heat had baked
into the vast ovens long ago
razed in three cities. Strolling past
the awning shop before breakfast,
I contemplate blueberry mouthfuls
spooned from the wedge Audrey
dished up soon as I slid into the booth
at Cascarelli's, where Steve mulled
The Eumenides or muttered vacuum-
sealed sentences from *The Grammar
of Motives*—ponytail undone, a pencil
in his beard, mug of tea cold. I ponder
the milk frigid as the wind sluicing
down Sixth Street that made Maxine's
mince edible, the tears a cherry slab
loosened down my cheeks as thunder
rolled over the heart wing & the two
circus-tent apple pies one grandmother
(the pebbly-voiced, mothball Methodist
who bunked with my sister from March
to May) baked first thing so we'd make
the early service. Pie has soothed emboli,
heartbreak, Charles Ives, Chuck Melini
beaning me, lice, haggis, linear algebra,
mother's death, infestations of fleas,
gophers & woodworms, Albert Ayler,
colic's treeless, cloudless, windless,
basalt-shard steppe, cost accounting,
father's death, four types of fungus,
one friend's suicide, another's murder,
the implacable fact of *pi*. Who wouldn't
miss Robert Kocik's buckwheat-crust
wild raspberry, the Clock's pear,
the Village House's blackberry
that warmed the winter I feasted
on Pound, Levertov & what little

I could make of Zukofsky?
Jim & Larry's sweet potato,
Mary Headrick's pecan festooned
with scoops of Richman's vanilla
after a repast of crabs & spaghetti,
my *gemütlich* grandmother's quivering
lemon meringue? Only the luckiest
of men by forsaking such as these
could know the luxuriant yearning
that soaks his morning walk,
body no longer fit for pie fried,
baked, or set up cold in life's first
Frigidaire, whether forked, fingered,
or broken in the hand & wolfed.

Matt Dennison

The Winter That He Aged

I wonder which room I'll expire in, he mulled,
wandering down the hall. This would be nice,
he thought, entering a dust vault, the youthful

Hymen still framed on the wall—for there is
no pleasure but in copulation with the moon,
he reminded himself, sensing the light. I hope

we are encusped by a claimed face, for a timely
capture calmed taut in the endless vagina of time
would be a good room in which to grow timeless

—his parents in the autopsy theater not so much.
Gossips populating the dark called to him by name,
their shadows cast large, their chorus grey-moaned

as burdensome discards—as was his own, falling,
once, over a pile of ghost cats. Resumed, his search
glanced comfort up the stairs he could not ascend.

A warm of robins swallowing the stove's one kind
mirror, though quaint, was to be avoided at all costs,
for one might get burnt. But is it truly the house,

that throb-laden brute, that drives us here? Or is it
there I must go, glancing the cabinet's stashed trove
of old letters unspread. O Shame, thou art most

welcome indeed, for my hands are gathering snakes
as the sudden birds gypsy their way into this world,
pulsating the air between our legs—the glands of a

sick man's calling. *No beds, no beds . . .* he swore,
having risen at last from his. Lead your hands with
your other hands, then, unroomed, for children,

once fever-struck, wandering the night, must look
elsewhere for the door. Study the memory hounds,
their whimpers of discretion, those curious creatures

who gnawed when the only means of going was upon
a horse—but neither hounds nor stallions remain.
Maybe the coal bin beneath the house, that abysmal

room he once knew through feeding the mesmerizer
blasphemous lumps. Or perhaps the since-abandoned
washroom—could slip toward the cold, break the lock

off this rummage prayer's clasp, the sodden easily hosed.
He placed his hand upon his brother's hands in passing.
I'd thank you, my Voyager, for this call to arms seeking

angels en masse, only my ferry's but a vessel of ruin,
a pencil sketch of bed sheets, half-mast. More to show
than a lungful a' mushrooms, he hoped, though we fix

one moon in the softness of our lunacy as the earth spits
weeds up through our lawns—by the time our mothers
have weakened down to us: the bleak winter of finally.

Spite the poison! It's all sniff-talk! O take my hand,
remove this agitated flurry unto your foreign demise—
I'll drop my corpse in the living room, and smile.

GREY WALL WITH THE SCRAGGLY BARBED WIRE

Martin Ritt's *The Spy Who Came in from the Cold* (1965) after
John Le Carré's *The Spy Who Came in from the Cold* (1963)

Not following the robust wall that fell
but an uneven grey wall
an almost paper-maché wall
with scraggly barbed wire
sweeping over pavement
with puddles of recent rain
until the first spoken words,
coffee, sir, are uttered
not as question but as gesture
to the back of Richard Burton's head.

Ritt turned to black and white
not to capture black and white
but to capture grey in all its variations.
We don't need the browns of Le Carré.
We don't need Control's shabby brown cardigan.
We don't need Leamas's apartment with its brown paint.
Nor his brown eyes.
Nor even the shilling's worth of
the yellow, crumbling geyser of hot water.

With all its grey ambiguities
its reversals,
betrayals and deceits,
chess moves played out in secret
and in open,
in this Cold War
of the blacklisted director.
Which friend is projected onto
the young librarian
with her earnest Communist phrases?
And how poignant the line
We have to live without sympathy, don't we?
voiced with soft-spoken brutality.

The ever-present black bottle of whisky
with its white diamond label,
the label always facing out
the identical bottle
appearing and re-appearing
handed to Leamas across the pub counter
to slip into an overcoat
appearing on desks and tables,
even in Holland waiting interrogation
with all sides drinking the same drink,
engaging in the same cruel
aimlessness.

when a poet dies
language dies
to the extent that poetry
perpetuates language
to the extent
that what the poet
does to language
lives beyond
the small but conscious
life
the poet lives
as poetry makes
innovations,
makes
deep resonant sounds
that echo
in its listeners
in their deep hearts
and actions

FOR Iván

*"He had a very difficult life which he accepted. The steady
soft glow of your friendship for him was a balm and your
understanding insightful and frequent reviews were a gift to
the community."*
　　　　　　—Malcolm Margolin

isn't it just like you to die *a las cinco de la tarde!*
Bang ! Bang ! la vida la pinche vida, hombre !
　　　　　　　　and the deserts rolling
like futile seas towards Las Vegas and points east
"You're not American, you're an Indian."
I met you something like forty years ago.
I knew Marilla from Park School
and I had told her that I knew Ishmael Reed a little:
"Oh. Ivan"—not *Iván* in those days—"would like to meet him."
And so it began. you gave me a book, I wrote you back.
"What you wrote was closer to what I think I'm doing than
anything else I've seen. You say you write poetry. Listen.
I'm doing a reading at Larry Blake's. Why don't you read with me.
If your poetry is half as good as your criticism, I'm sure
you'll be fine." and so it began and so it began.
I was completely unknown. had done no readings
except for one that Iván attended at CCAC. there, Adelle and I did
one of the choral pieces I was writing:
that the hummingbird's wings are of a remarkable rapidity
he had noted often—nothing could be done—the
shift of his breathing—

and hearing it you grew excited. then the reading at Larry Blake's.
I wanted to write something special for it—
something elegant & long—
and as I wrote it bit by bit I phoned you and read you
what I'd done.
"Is it all right?"
"Yes, yes, it is. Keep it coming." your beautiful voice
assured me. I was amazed. no one, literally no one
had ever even liked my verse. yet I had continued,
if no one else was subject to its power, at least I was.
and then there was Iván. we were a great success
at Larry Blake's. someone had made a poster
and there we were. a young woman
came up to me afterwards and singled out the long, special poem
I had written, "Sweeney Adrift."
"What a poem!" she kept repeating. "What a poem!"
Nancy Peters and Phillip Lamantia were there to hear Iván
but they heard Adelle and me as well.
"Something original," said Nancy about my choral piece.
"welcome to the house of failure," I had written in "Sweeney Adrift,"
"see these are the structural bases of the house
its beams and arteries
its artificial light its hands its vast appendices
who is
not here?
the range of things
delights us welcome welcome

see there is the door it opens for us
welcome"
yes.
suddenly that door of poetry opened
and it was all Iván's doing.
everything I have ever done
was in that moment
which I shared
with a man
who would be my lifelong
friend.
dear man,
do you remember our many
times in Saul's Restaurant and Jewish Delicatessen
in Berkeley?
"Are you going to say it again?" you asked.
"Yes, I am," I answered.
and when the waitress served me
my matzoh ball soup, I asked her, deadpan,
as I did every time a waitress
served me such soup,

"And what do they do
with the rest of the Matzoh?"
"ARGH," said Iván.
will you tell me in a dream
if there is matzoh ball soup
in Poet Heaven?
our times together
flood over me,
there was so much
and so much richness
in them.
"Do you want to hear a poem?" you asked.
"Of course," I answered
and you read me
something beautiful.
"THIS IS DEDICATED TO THE ONE *I LOVE*
on earth to say there are couples that don't match
and flames of equidistant breath their smoke release
the sign is higher than summer and the cipher
cannot be discerned all sites and directions weathered
and grasses of twilight lift weary shadows to a god
whose nature is as unknown as death and what's
to sacrifice if not the soul's plagiarized copy afloat
in clouds where sleep is buried and poetry too
descant and folio of vast unremembered lines"
your lines will be remembered
and because of you perhaps some of mine as well
and perhaps our friendship.
goodbye, my loving, wonderful friend.
I'll go to Saul's and order matzoh ball soup
and I will say, as I always do,
"What do they do
with the rest of the Matzoh?"
and I will hear your laughter
and your moan
and I will know
some things survive
even the dark, dark hand
of Death.

Iván Argüelles, January 24, 1939–April 28, 2024

The Beginning of Scene One of a Famous Molière Play In a Translation Into English Rhyme

PHILINTE: What happened? Is something wrong?

ALCESTE: Go away.

PHILINTE: Something's surely bugging you. That's easy to say.

ALCESTE: Get lost! How can I be alone if you're still here?

PHILINTE: I implore you to listen! But you'll get angry, I fear.

ALCESTE: I refuse to listen! But obediently *will* get angry.

PHILINTE: Your sullen moods stink! But as friends, we . . .

ALCESTE: Friends!? Only so far! But now I'm not so sure.
For what I've seen of you lately—you're just not pure.
So cross me off your list. We're through.

PHILINTE: what's the bad blame I'm guilty of for you?

ALCESTE: Your shame is enough to commit you to death.
It's unpardonable. Any man of honor who draws breath
condemns you instinctively. I just saw you smother
a man like a hot and holy mother
with loving vows and eternal devotion,
offering friendship with profuse commotion.
Then I ask you who he could be, and you
can't remember his name or merit, once he's out of view.
His back turned, he suddenly has no importance left!
You're base and treacherous, and of honor bereft,
to turn your heart around and wear its false coat.
I'd hang myself in remorse, if *my* oath should so dote!

PHILINTE: But this is no hanging matter, I plead.
By your leave please let me live, for what's the need
for self-hanging, however horrendous the deed?

ALCESTE: You joke, after your crime shows the life you lead?

PHILINTE: Crime?! Be serious. How else can anyone behave?

ALCESTE: To sincerely utter only what his heart feels, you knave!

PHILINTE: Then a man warmly greets you, of course
you return his loving vows with equal cordial force
and politely match his showiest display.

ALCESTE: Your false formula is all the rage today,
but I despise that hollow society fashion
of giving cheap lip service to an inflated passion
with pretentious embraces and all the courtesies of fawn
to flatter alike both noble worth and any fool I'd scorn.

(This translation was discontinued at this early point, due to a case of translatorial laziness inspired in great measure by translatorial difficulty. Other than that, the rest of the play should have been translatorially consistent with the above translatorial beginning fragment. Meanwhile, the translator's apology to the living original for daring to slice a sliver off the top, sparing for posterity and its heirs forever the bulging untouched bulk that followed in its pure shapeliness of merciless French wit.)

Not in Translation

LANGUAGE, MEMORY, LITERATURE, FICTION, AND IDENTITY

A Conversation Between Giorgio Ferretti and Andrea Scrima

A.S.: Giorgio, the last time we spoke in person, late this past summer, it was about the state of vulnerability that arises when we remove ourselves from our ordinary environment. You were on the tail end of a two-month residency in Graz and about to return to Leipzig, I was at the end of a year-long fellowship and planning to stay longer. I remember you saying that being uprooted, being forced to adapt and improvise, to live without your books and other possessions, called many things into question, and ultimately your own identity.

We've both spent a good part of our lives living out "other" parts of ourselves, the parts that take place in languages other than our native tongue. I've written extensively for German-language newspapers and journals, but you've gone a step further and made German the language of your literary work. How does this affect your relationship to your past, or to memory?

G.F.: I get asked this a lot: what does it feel like to write in another language, or why do I even do it? But you're asking me how it affects the past and memory, which is something I actually think about a lot. Sometimes I think the whole point of literature is to erase the difference between present and past, that its goal is to eliminate time, that a good work of literature is one where you lose yourself and everything seems so real—so *timeless*. Somehow, you have to trick the reader into thinking that time is not passing. I am interested in this temporal threshold, where the present and past seem not to exist. Language plays a big role in it for me. Primarily because I see language as a way to describe time, more than reality or space. I cannot really explain what that means, but I've been realizing more and more that I translate my memory: some-

times I find myself remembering situations with persons whom I couldn't possibly have been speaking German with, because they don't speak German at all, and yet in my memory we are speaking fluent German until I realize what is happening and I try to remember the situation in the language in which it happened. And yet, as you beautifully put it, I am living "'other' parts of myself" in another language when I speak in German or English. Writing is basically not letting things go, a kind of stubbornness about the fact that things have to carry on. I know my texts almost always begin with spiraling in on something, mostly something that happened to me. But why am I not letting go in German, then? When I think about this fact that I translate the memory, I always think about the person (it's almost always one person) I am talking to, but until now I never thought about what I do with these memories. Why is it that the "other part of myself" that is not letting go is in German? I think I am more distant, a bit condescending, but also aware that while I have gained this skill (speaking German), I have lost something else. We think of learning a new language as a major skill-gain, but I am pretty sure that we think this way because we don't realize that we are losing something else. I cannot really put my fingers on what *it* is—in German I would say "Selbstverständlichkeit," some self-evident quality of being, but even that doesn't really come close to whatever *it* is. Do you know, maybe? Do you have the same experience? Someone (maybe you?) told me that it's probably like this because German has also become the language in which I began to reflect on what is happening or what has happened. I wanted to know if this resonated with you in some way.

A.S.: Perhaps your "not letting go" has to take place in German because the feelings attached to the memories are too intense? What you say about how memory reconstructs the language of an occurrence in retrospect is puzzling and unnerving, and it's happened to me many times as well. I have often distinctly remembered entire conversations in German, with my sister, for instance, who doesn't speak a word of the language. Perhaps it's a subconscious need to insert your more mature self, the one who moved away and experienced various stages of emotional and intellectual awakening in this new language. It's like you want to take this more aware, more adult part of yourself back into the past and rectify certain things, set things straight. Maybe. But it also has to do with the timelessness you speak about, with this layering of identities we're all made of. It's all there, every part of us, simultaneously: the problem is one of access, of figuring out what's standing in the way.

G.F.: I think what you say about the *rectifying* of memory might be very true for me too. Maybe that was exactly what I meant when I was saying that writing is not being able to let things go. In some way it makes me think that this is where writing begins: in the way one is accustomed to work with memory. But then again, does the way memory works lead you to writing or does the impulse to write lead you to a particular way of working with memory? I remember when I was twenty or twenty-one and obsessed with the concept of memory and this being strictly connected with writing: I failed at almost all the short stories I was writing at that time because my goal was to write exactly how things factually went down. Obviously, it frustrated me that there was no way to know if what I wanted to write really *did* happen or was just in my head, was just my perception of things. When I started inventing things, I thought I was actively betraying the way things went—as if there was one way which things go, one narration, one side of history (somehow it seems really Catholic of me to think this). I emancipated myself almost completely from this way of thinking, I know now that it's the effect of reality that has to be true and that you can also tell "real" things through fiction. It's the text itself that decides what the facts are—because facts are not real in literature, but the general mood of a text can be real if you don't betray the text. Which sounds really simple, but to me, of all a writer's jobs it seems to be the most complex: to really understand what a text needs. And exactly as you say, the problem is *access,* also to the text.

A.S.: Yes, the truth, if there is such a thing, lies in the text. When I published my last book, I had to answer the question of authorship and autobiography so many times that I was almost angry. I thought it was a given that everything we write—and yes, even when we think we're sticking to the facts—is fiction. The very fact that we're trying to take this tangle of lived experience and translate it into language is already a first step towards abstraction, towards changing the "story." Even trying to take what you "think" and convert it into words requires a fundamental transformation. We often tell our deepest truths through fiction, because there is no other way to do it. I thought this was a known thing, but as it turns out, we have to explain it again and again that a first-person narrator or protagonist is not one and the same as the author's person—that a book requires a feat of organization and structure, it's an architecture, really, and that the form of the text dictates a lot of what we write. I've come to bristle at the word "autofiction," as though writing from lived experience were some kind of automatic process: all you need to do is sit at the computer and it all comes pouring out, in coherent sentences.

Maybe writing in several languages sets all this into sharper relief, I don't know.

But there's also another aspect to all this. As a foreigner, an outsider, you can always stand on the sidelines and observe from afar, with the benefit of a multipolar perspective. This makes us very good cultural critics: we see things that have grown invisible to others through habit. We're often able to recognize and name things that otherwise escape attention; we register cultural change with a kind of internal seismograph. But there is also a slippery, opportunistic side to this—I become an American when it's inconvenient to be German and vice-versa. It's the mindset of a professional diplomat or spy, and there is something very suspicious about it.

G.F.: It's funny to compare our situation to that of a diplomat or a spy because I've been thinking a lot about the concept of the double and its implications when you live and write in another language. The concept is at the same time ludic and frightening, there is a truly funny aspect of being two, but it's also a strange feeling, like being part of a scam. The (in)famous *imposter syndrome* is a major part of an artist's life, and also of a foreigner's life. And writing in another language also brings a responsibility with it. You're sort representing your other language and culture, and so you basically carry two weights, two traditions. But that is also why I've been so interested in the concept of the error over the last few years. It too can be a laughing matter, but then again it can be a serious and suffered experience, since there is so much power in grammar, in the decision of who is saying something right or wrong and for what reason. I thought that questioning grammar was also a way of questioning power structures and I was interested in what kind of dynamics would appear if I actually showed the errors, which I obviously do as a person who doesn't speak and write in their mother tongue.

A.S.: It's interesting to think about error, grammar, and the power dynamics of being a foreigner. I have painful memories of my first year or two in Berlin, struggling to learn German, when I longed to tell people that I am normally a very articulate person. Because when you're learning a new language, you always sound like an idiot at first, and it's frustrating. This was before the ubiquity of English became commonplace. The fact is, we've worked hard to achieve fluency in this startlingly complicated language, and yet I've felt the loss very strongly at times; I have literally felt injured by it on some level. I've found myself wondering who I would have become if I'd allowed myself to simply stay in the US as a young woman, if I'd retained that "natural," "self-evident" identity (there's that word "Selbstverständlichkeit," which is so hard to translate) that is now forever lost. I spent four months in the US last year and it was surprisingly easy to let go of German, and, later, surprisingly difficult to return to Germany. I remember wishing I could have stayed. I recall being unable to speak at all for the first few weeks; it was as though the muscles required to pronounce all these harsh consonants had grown lax, had eased back into the American slur. I recall telling my friends that it didn't matter that I was fluent: I'd discovered that I was and would forever remain "monolingual." I know that sounds nonsensical, but I think it had something to do with the fact that my oldest layers had formed in English, and I had finally been allowed to fully occupy that space again. I actually experienced the return to German as a kind of injury. Sometimes, in the middle of a conversation, I would suddenly switch to English. I think it came from a subconscious need to emotionally "know" whether or not what I was saying was even true. It's often abrupt and somewhat embarrassing, but it happens: an affliction as opposed to an affectation. Day-to-day living in German means suspending my access to these deeper parts of myself—and sometimes a reconfiguring, a rewriting, as you've observed.

G.F.: Your experience in the US last year and returning to German is fascinating, as if the linguistic environment made you come back into contact with a primal place. While I was reading this, I was wondering if that is one of the reasons why I live and write in German. Because I "subconsciously" don't want to have contact with that original layer? As if there were an original layer that cannot be influenced by all the experiences we've had in life. I find it extremely interesting what you said about needing to emotionally "know" if it's true. For me it's the same, but with the "tools" of writing—I learned this in literary theory but also in creative writing in German. And to me it speaks a lot to something else that is typical of writing as I see it: writing is for me a way of tidying up the chaos in my mind but also, in reality, it's the first thing I do when I'm trying to understand something, anything: I take a piece of paper and write stuff, not even necessarily the things I want to understand, but random words—I grasp onto words trying to make *it* make sense. I use German as a way to see clearly through the mess. And the mess can be beautiful, but also overwhelming sometimes.

A.S.: Yes, writing can be a way of untangling the threads, of trying to make sense of a terrible inner noise. But for me it works a bit differently: I write quite a lot in German—I've had to crank out a regular column here in Austria this past year—because it's easier than trying to translate myself into English, as every time I translate something of mine back into English, I discover that I am a very different author in German. Which is unsettling and sometimes weird and another topic altogether. But when it comes to my fiction and essays, I write in English because, for me, the initial digging into memory and the process of transferring that whatever-it-is into language has to be in English. Perhaps it's different when you learn several languages simultaneously as a child and they all become mother-tongue bubbles of time, with varying degrees of proficiency. A friend of mine who grew up in Queens and whose parents moved the family back to Germany when he was 11 or 12 speaks English perfectly, but as an 11 or 12-year-old. It's funny to hear him talk about current events.

G.F.: This is connected to the interest in errors I was talking about, but what I found out a couple of months ago was that showing the errors and working with them also shows that I've never completely left where I come from. The errors I make are part of my identity, if not the most significant part of it, because it's where all the layers meet.

AS.: Showing the errors requires a kind of bravery I might have now, but didn't used to have. When I think about how hard I worked towards *not* making errors, it really makes me stop and think. It's like a form of self-erasure, isn't it? I also love what you said earlier about writing being a way of not letting go, of trying to abolish time. I feel this too, and suddenly I see the paradox in these two different things being equally true—because insisting on the past is also a way of *resisting* erasure. I think it's a fate that many writers share, particularly writers who have left where they're from. This impulse to remain true to memory and to one's origins is an impulse that probably requires exile in some form. And it didn't begin with Joyce, of course. Ironically, the black sheep of the family are usually the most loyal: we never let go. I've been writing about my family for years; right now, for instance, in my writing I'm back in Italy, in the mountaintop village my grandfather lived in more than 120 years ago before he emigrated and wound up in the Bronx. I'm the only one in my family who really cares on this level.

G.F.: It's so true that the black sheep of the family are usually the most loyal. I think my family thinks I don't care a lot about them, but I don't think there is a text I've written in which some memories with them didn't play an important role. That is also what interests me in your case: 120 years seems like a long time ago, but it's actually approximately two generations. And yet I am assuming that the language of your village, probably a wonderful dialect of Southern Italy, is not something you come into contact with that easily. I am sure it's one of those things that endures through the generations, but I don't know how accessible it is. How are you dealing or working with this absence?

A.S.: The language is Arbërisht, a medieval form of Albanian. The Arbëresh are a UNESCO-protected minority that has been living in the southern part of the peninsula for over 600 years, but of course the language is dying out as the younger generation leaves in search of employment opportunities elsewhere. I'm actually trying to write a book about my grandfather's village and his and his mother's emigration; it's also about poverty and racism and eugenics and working-class labor laws in early-twentieth-century America and anarchism and rebellion. I was in my grandfather's village a few years ago staying with a lovely elderly couple and heard the dialect for the first time "live." The wife, Rita, is the only person in the village who speaks English. Every time her husband Pino spoke Arbërisht, he grew a lot louder, to the point of shouting, although he never looked angry—he was actually a sweetheart. Then he'd switch back to Italian and simmer down again. And that's how it went the four days I spent with them: from Arbërisht to Italian and back to Arbërisht, shouting in a harsher-sounding dialect, then Italian, then the shouting again, often mid-sentence. It was music to me. I have no plans to learn Arbërisht, but I'm relearning Italian, or trying to, which I spoke to some degree as a schoolkid until it was buried under the heavy weight of German. Again, another topic altogether. I've already written so much and there's been so much spill-off in all sorts of directions that I've had to take a lot out, and so I have a growing essay collection parallel to this book that has to do with displacement in a more general sense. I am obsessed with the theme, and I suppose it's quite likely the reason I have willingly displaced myself again and again—as though some force were inducing me to relive their experience, even if symbolically. But it's emotional somehow, and so tied into a layer that feels like my naked skin that it's taking me forever to write this. My father was the youngest of nine siblings, and I'm pretty sure he didn't even know that the dialect his father spoke with the other people from the "old country" wasn't Italian. It hurts me just to think about it.

G.F.: The Arbërisht language is a mystery and has a lot to do with absence. There is (was?) also an Arbërisht-speaking community near where my family comes from, in Pescara—I just looked it up. Of course, I think it has to do a lot with the heritage we have: in my family many people had to move to other places, it's just how things are. It's something that I am obsessed with too, the heritage we don't see. We often think we're the only ones going through this, but we are most probably not, and the people who did experience it first-hand are most probably in our own family. And I think it's simply because we inherit the same struggles and the same way of seeing the world.

A.S.: Displacement is universal, it's the way of the world. But there are families that seem more affected than others. Sometimes the roots seem to blend into the background but sometimes there are echoes that get passed down, although those born later have no idea there's a connection.

In my father's family, where eleven people lived in two rooms and the kids had to sleep in shifts, there was a lot of mental illness—it affected at least four of the nine children, with two of them winding up schizophrenic. My uncle, one of the oldest, was institutionalized. I've done a lot of reading on the prevalence of schizophrenia in migrant communities. I remember my Aunt Emma reciting a rhyme her father taught her when she was a child. I didn't write it down and forgot it—but it was supposed to ensure that she wouldn't forget where he came from. No one else in my family remembers it, not even her sons. Evidently, it was up to me to retain this, but I only remember Via Orientale, and there is no Via Orientale in Greci, and so I'm wondering if it goes back further. These things really affect me for some reason; the rest of my family is indifferent.

G.F.: I'm sorry for that lost rhyme, and yes, it's a reminder to my own memory, too. I hope I'll find the time to write things down. But as I was reading what you wrote, I had to think about Anne Carson's translation of Sappho, where she leaves space for what's not there, because it was either not transmitted, or was not decipherable from the manuscripts. I love this book of translation, *If Not, Winter*, which I'm sure you know. It's one of those books I come back to often. I love Sappho and Anne Carson, but most of all I love the book because it reminds me how even from the absence of things, art can be possible.

A.S.: Yes, I love it too, but it suddenly occurs to me that maybe that's why we write, in the end: to enter into those absences. But on another note: Giorgio, you won a German literary award for *America*, a piece for the stage that traces the beginnings of a young man's sexuality and his growing awareness that he's gay—and you performed two feats: you wrote this in a German that's easy and natural, and in a way that really universalizes the experience of sexual shame, in other words—and this is going to sound ironic—is "inclusive" to people outside this particular coming-of-age experience. I really loved reading *America*. What was it like to write this? Did writing it in German give you enough of a distancing effect to deal with something that might have been harder to approach in Italian, the language of your upbringing, your family, the teachers at school, the Catholic Church, and so on? Shame is like a black box for most of us, I think—we repress, deflect, go deaf and dumb, and we'll do anything not to "go there"—and so it seems that switching languages can be used as a psychological strategy to face the Thing. It occurs to me that we might be getting at the core of something here.

G.F.: I wrote *America* approximately four years ago in a period where I was actively trying to figure out what the "Thing" for me was, as you wonderfully put it. I was writing frantically, trying every possible type of text, and I had a lot of ideas. I was eager to find something that would define me as a writer but also as a person (as if it were possible to separate the two). I know this last bit sounds very egoistic, as almost everything concerning writing does, but actually the goal is basically to be honest with whoever is reading the thing you are writing. And in order to do that, you have to interrogate what it is with you. That's why most of the time you go and look for what you're most ashamed of, because you want to bond with others through writing and to do that you need to develop an honesty pact. You sort of have to say to the reader, "all right, that's the worst of me, we cannot go lower than this, let's begin," but the craziest thing to me is that every text is a new beginning of this process. Somehow, you find new things each time that define your honesty. And so in every text, to begin the conversation, I try to find the worst thing about me.

During the time I was writing *America*, it had a lot to do with errors: most of the time I feel that my sexuality is an error, or the way I live it—even if I don't live it, or probably precisely because I don't or didn't live it. This is a peculiar experience of homosexuality, of course, but then again, who hasn't felt weird or like a freak or simply ashamed because of their desire? I think everybody has! Society might be better at transforming heterosexual shame into something better, or into a "phase," while the shame of homosexuality or being queer—and generally of all marginalized people—lingers on like a permanent stain. But it's in all of us, and that's the reason why *America* works on another level than

94

"just" for queer people (I would hope at least!), but it does connect a lot with queer people and people who have to move places to find their way.

The other thing I was really interested in is how to translate orality in texts, especially in performative texts. Writers learn very soon that things you say in a natural environment don't work on paper. It's a strange phenomenon, but somehow you get used to it. In this phase, though, I was really obsessed with trying to be as faithful as possible to an actual way of speaking. That is why there are grammatical errors in the play: the errors in my texts are somehow proof that I cannot or should not be writing, and they both define me and shame me. I tried to hide them for a long time, asking various people to proofread my German before sending my texts out. But during the period I was writing *America*, I focused my attention on the errors themselves and instead of hiding them I put them at the center of my literary attention.

Also, I wanted the main character to be someone who is not "finished yet," somebody who comes from somewhere and is going somewhere—and that is why he hasn't mastered the language he's speaking in.

I am curious, what is your relationship to errors? For me it used to be the very core of shame somehow, I don't know if it's ever changed, but I look at it in a different way right now.

A.S.: My relationship to errors? It's still kind of complicated. For a time, I was fascinated by Hannah Shygulla in *The Marriage of Maria Braun*, and as I've mentioned, I had this weird fantasy of being a spy. We're all, in a sense, spies when we master a foreign language, because we get an "in" on a world that we wouldn't ordinarily be part of—but in my mind it was more literal: I wanted to know if I could *really pass* as a German, in other words, if my life depended on it. There have been many situations in which I was able to keep up the masquerade, and it really makes me wonder a bit about myself—what's interesting is that a small amount of alcohol made it easier to eradicate the traces of an accent. Maybe because of the disinhibition—as we know, learning a language also requires a kind of roleplaying, a willingness to take on another identity—but I've lost interest in it, almost completely.

G.F.: Oh, I can very much relate to what you say about "passing as a German!" But I gave up way before you did and decided to embrace it. Probably because of my interest in "errors" in a literary or artistic sense—but of course embracing it came from the fact that I could never be "one of them," so it seemed necessary if I wanted to continue living there. Sometimes people said they thought I was German, but I think they were saying it out of politeness, or they thought it was my goal, since knowing German is basically my only skill.

A.S.: That's so funny—it's like we're demanding someone give us a medal for going through all this torture! Seriously, though: I've grown indifferent, I allow the English accent to creep in, I interject English words and even sentences, there is this insistence now of being foreign that maybe wasn't there before, in the "assimilation phase." The question of error always seems to bring us back to the question of identity. I make very few mistakes in written German, but when I speak, people understand that I'm from somewhere else, I actively signalize this, although they can't always place it. I prefer to expose myself now.

I'm wondering, though—we're both editors of literary magazines and have both worked with translated writing—how does all this factor into the editing process for you?

G.F.: I'm not really sure how any of this ties into the editing. I guess knowing what it's like to be an author writing for a literary magazine, I try to communicate with the authors as I would like people to communicate with me. Sometimes I think that writing is basically making a series of choices in written form, and curating a literary magazine is much the same. But most of all, I think that, although the job seems very similar to writing, it's actually very different because it comes from a different place. Writing comes from the impulse to create something, while editing comes from the impulse to observe something, to read. I've only been an editor for the magazine, so I don't know how it would feel to work in a publishing house, but with every issue I feel a certain responsibility and I want to make sure we do a good job. This means that the texts we choose are thought through and edited, and when we edit, we always try and communicate to the author what we think the best outcome would be, and what the text still needs. Sometimes, or most of the time, the texts are very good but they don't harmonize with the other texts, and so we decide against them, but even then, it's not a choice against a text or an author. The ultimate goal is always to make good literature and good authors visible, because good literature is one of the things I love the most.

But you know, I wanted to really ask how you are—I mean, we can pretend we're speaking in a vacuum without time and space, but it is very much the 15th of January 2025, with less than a week to inauguration.So I want to know how you are and if you're okay. I could understand if writing feels different for you now. It feels a bit like the bad guys are winning.

A.S.: Yes, the bad guys are winning. I have one positive experience to report on that front: right before the election, on the way back from Vienna, I got a call from a young journalist asking me if I'd take part in a three-way pre-election panel. I almost said no: I've been desperate to write and to stop filling my schedule with things that take up all my time. And yet, as you say, we're not living or writing in a vacuum, and so I agreed. I'm glad I did—it turns out they're two very young, alert, passionate journalists trying to hold up their side of reality at a paper known for its reactionary editorials, and we quickly formed a bond. A few days later, they asked me to write an editorial for a pro and contra format. Essentially, faced with a "sanesplaining" piece on Trump by one of their renowned elder editors (who, in all seriousness, quoted FDR: "the only thing we have to fear is fear itself"), they needed me to confirm their take on reality by providing an argument for why we do, indeed, need to be afraid of a second Trump presidency. I suddenly understood the degree of gaslighting they had to deal with every day, and that they were hoping I'd kick ass. These are unexpected moments of grace, and we have to learn to recognize and be humble and grateful for them when they happen. I see it as a survival strategy: focus on each thing as it comes and try to be as clear and honest as possible, as though the future depended on it. Because, as it turns out, it does.

Jennifer M. Phillips

Road Trip

Memory drives all over the road
though the eyes are dull and bones
no longer willing, holding the crook
of the seat like a protest sign.
Harder to get to you, feeling
along the ribbons of love, following
the crumbs left by desire that passed
this way before. Just when this inclination
to gather you all in subsides into a tarpit
of solitude, I'm kindled hotter
like a coal seam burning underground.

My clock dashes forward and back
in a clumsy time-lapse graphic
as I remind myself this life was born to be consumed—
a consommé of bone and song,
the sweet meaty smell of skin
I was moored in once before the fray.
You seemed to be born without selvage,
always trying to bind up against fear—
but don't we all unravel?
I trust there at the last knot
something more will be gleaming.

The Poet Wolfgang Berends: "a piece of passing in my hand"

It may be an invented story—I heard it long ago: When Wallace Stevens, Vice-President of the Hartford Accident and Indemnity Company, won a Pulitzer Prize for his *Collected Poems* in 1955, some employees at Hartford commented: "What? I didn't know old Wally wrote!" If Dr. Franz Kafka, a jurist in the Legal Department of the Arbeiter-Unfallsversicherungs-Anstalt, an insurance company in Prague, hadn't retired early due to his incapacitating tuberculosis and had he achieved a literary reputation during his lifetime, his colleagues might have someday reacted similarly . . .

And now to the German poet Wolfgang Berends. He is not in the word business in the contemporary sense, by which I mean a product of a "creative writing" program at some college or university with a degree in "poetry" as are many writers today—especially in the United States. An equivalent academic track doesn't exist in the university system in Germany—at least not yet—the closest being a degree in German literature—which Wolfgang Berends does not have. On the contrary: he studied Electro Engineering and Precision Mechanics. You might say he slipped into the literary world through a side door.

> On the slope
> I climbed.
> In my cold hand
> grass lies down.
> Atop
> in the sea wind,
> I wrote as person
> a black song
> onto your skin,
> on earth.

The above is the opening poem of his first book, *Erdabstossung* (something like "Blasting Off From Earth" or maybe "Earth Repulsion") in a section entitled "The Oldest Reports". Attempting to render a text from one language into another, even under the best of circumstances, is always a thankless task. Translation can only be an approximation, better said, a matter of opinion, because no two languages are ever alike. This is especially the case when translating poetry that aims at being a true distillation of human language: a juncture between earth and eternity. Which brings us back to Wolfgang Berends and the title of his first book. His blast-off or repulsion of gravity is nothing less than an expression of that struggle between heaven and earth that takes place in all of us—even if we ignore it. He doesn't.

Otherland

> The senses elongate
> into frayed worlds,
> so that paths grow out of the earth,
> when we step on them.
> In the wordless silence of nature
> all forces unify belief
> and the cherry blossom locks me
> into its prison of winter
> with a helpless language.

(From "Erdabstossung")

Tight poems, musical language, words that you can read on multiple levels. Nearly impossible, alas, to render justly in a translation.

Wolfgang Berends has published three books of poems—so far. All at Stadtlichter Presse, a German "Indie". *Erdabstossung* appeared in 2010, followed by *Nach Durchsicht der Wolken* (something like "After a Review of Clouds") in 2016. His most recent book is *Manchmal um uns Glas* ("Sometimes Glass Around Us") in 2021.

He has a talent for using words compactly. In German the word for "word", "Wort", has two plurals, "Wörter", referring to individual words. Hence, a "dictionary" in German is a "Wörterbuch", i.e., "words book". The second plural is "Worte" and is used to define a group of words that together yield meaning. A Berends book of poems is in the true sense a "Wortebuch". His word combinations have a transformative power.

Better said, his poems are metaphysical, which is to say, his words poke into the ineffable. A risky place to set up camp now that in recent years finding words for the things behind the things has fallen out of favor in literary circles, replaced by banal expressions of satisfaction or dissatisfaction in relationships and of course self-centered identity tantrums revolving around an emphasis on "me me me!". Bold explorations into hidden realities interest few editors and writers. Rilke's *Duino Elegies* wouldn't stand a chance in today's "lit market".

No wonder esoteric poet Wolfgang Berends is an outsider in the business of poetry. His lack of an academic degree in the field of what Ezra Pound identified as "Kulchur" doesn't make it any easier for him to find his audience or his editors—at least currently. Take note: today's five-year-olds may one day be his readers!

Frankly, I can think of no German poet who is presently as courageous as he is. Granted, there are a number of predecessors who have (or may have) influenced him along the journey of finding his poetic voice. Johannes Angelus Silesius, a name most definitely unknown in the Anglo-Saxon world, comes to mind. In fact, I don't know if even Berends ever read his works. I do know however that he is an admirer of Paul Fleming (1609–1640). Here a poem by Fleming:

When They Were Having Fun in the Snow

Keep on playing but think of this,
    beneath the fun there's something serious!
    You transcend, my dear, bright snow's rule:
    The whiter you get, the colder too.

Hölderlin comes to mind as well. Especially in his late poems where he departs radically from the formality of his era. In those poems, form explodes into meaning. I'm sure that Wolfgang Berends has also read Novalis, Ludwig Greve, Georg Trakl, Rilke, Stefan Georg and most certainly Paul Celan. In my opinion, the two poets, Celan and Berends, two parsimonious wordsmiths who reach into their word purses and pick out the absolute minimum of phonemes needed to assuage the muse, both succeed in transforming verbal communication into word magic. Personally, I consider Berends' poems warmer, more inviting than Celan's.

Berends himself mentions Johannes Bobrowski (another poet most certainly unknown in the Anglo-Saxon world) as a salient influence. That may be, but in my opinion, the influence is superficial. When you read a Bobrowski poem, it is easy to "get the message". In Wolfgang Berends' poems there is nothing to "get" because nobody "gets" the mystery of existence—at least not in words.

A Berends poem is a realm of spirited word images, a No-Platitude-Zone, where you may participate in an alchemical transformation.

Birch Leaf

Air, wingsplit; barely heard
the geese that passed on
by the holy mount.

In the land where stones grow
from tundra and bog,
wind drips, yellow,
a piece of passing in my hand.
It is time to build
a nest from it.

Once again I wish
    to feel your heartbeat,
wind, on me.

Wolfgang Berends is no snob. He never plays the know-it-all. He is acutely aware that the Mystery can never be explained. And most important: he is never interested in feeding his readers some humdrum ideology. I fear there is too much poetry "out there" these days that is mainly interested in communicating some "message".

Berends feels free to trawl his memory in search of events, places (concrete and abstract), and inner landscapes—in search of the words that might describe them. He harvests his crop from the tree of the knowledge of good and evil (as all humans do) and provides them with a unique form in time and space. He seems always to be on the lookout for words imbued with magic and meant to serve as a compass in the kingdom of mystery.

In other words: Wolfgang Berends is one of us—at least one of us when we recall how small we are in this world—someone we can trust with our time and attention. "Now words hang there in the landscape, on trees, mountains, streams". With these as his tools he practices the lonesome calling of the Poet.

Fed on forgetfulness,
    I want to grow so light
    that I need no language
    anymore, then I shall bring
    the light to the

waves of the stream. There
    language will
    end . . .
    (from: "Stony Order" in "Manchmal in uns Glas")

Contract with the Dead: Adventures in Chinese Horror

Introduction

When we think of adventure films like *Indiana Jones* or *Tomb Raider*, we picture heart-pounding action, ancient mysteries, and daring escapes. The thrill of exploring long-lost civilizations has captivated audiences worldwide. But in China, the allure of ancient tombs isn't just about adventure—it's about crossing the boundary between the living and the dead, a theme deeply embedded in Chinese folklore and mythology. While supernatural tales have existed in China for centuries, it was *Ghost Blows Out the Light* (鬼吹灯, *Gui Chui Deng*) that opened the door to modern Chinese horror, bringing with it a revival of interest in ancient beliefs, superstitions, and ghostly encounters. Since its publication, a wave of novels, games, and comics has flourished, marking the rise of Chinese horror in popular culture.

Lighting Candles, Awakening the Dead

"A person lights a candle, a ghost blows it out; when the rooster crows or the candle is out, the treasure remains untouched." This ancient saying might evoke memories of the Basilisk from *Harry Potter*, which feared the crowing of a rooster. In a similar vein, deep underground and facing mysterious dangers, this proverb serves as a crucial survival rule for tomb raiders in China. The phrase comes from the traditions of the Gold-Touching Captain, tomb raiders who carefully followed specific rituals when plundering graves. According to custom, a candle was lit in the tomb's southeastern corner before they began looting, where the most valuable treasures were often found on the bodies of the deceased—pearls in their mouths, jade in their hands, and even jewels placed in orifices.

If the candle flickered out, it was a warning that spirits were present, and the raiders were to return the treasures, bow respectfully, and leave the tomb. The belief was that some spirits, bound by their attachment to wealth, refused to reincarnate, guarding their treasures for centuries. Scientifically, of course, the candle going out could be attributed to a lack of oxygen in the tomb, and the rooster's crow simply signaled daylight—hardly the ideal time to rob graves!

The Ancient Profession of Tomb Raiders

The Gold-Touching Captain were originally military officers, dating back to the Three Kingdoms period (220-280 CE) when the warlord Cao Cao authorized them to fund his campaigns by raiding tombs. Tomb raiding, however, is a practice as old as Chinese civilization itself. Evidence of grave robbing can be traced to the Neolithic era, and one of the earliest recorded instances being the plundering of the tomb of Shang Dynasty's first king, over 3,600 years ago.

The rampant tomb-raiding in Chinese history is closely tied to the traditional practice of extravagant burials, which dating back to the Xia and Shang dynasties (2070-1050 BCE), and reaching its peak during the Qin and Han periods (221 BCE–220 CE). For example, in the Han Dynasty, it was customary for the emperor, one year after ascending the throne, to allocate one-third of the nation's tribute to build his imperial tomb. The practice of lavish burials is rooted in traditional Chinese ideas of ritual propriety and is closely connected to the ancient belief in the immortality of the soul. The *Annals of Lü Buwei*[1] notes that

国弥大，家弥富，葬弥厚。含珠鳞施，夫玩好货宝，钟鼎壶滥，舆马衣被戈剑，不可胜其数。诸养生之具，无不从者。题凑之室，棺椁数袭，积石积炭，以环其外。奸人闻之，传以相告。上虽以严威重罪禁之，犹不可止。

The greater the nation, the wealthier the families, the more extravagant the burials. Pearls are placed in the mouth of the deceased, and countless precious goods such as jewelry,

---

[1] Lü, Buwei. Lüshi Chunqiu 吕氏春秋 [*Annals of Lü Buwei*], 239 BCE. Taiji Library. Accessed September 18, 2024. https://www.8bei8.com/book/lvshichunqiu_47.html.

bronze vessels, chariots, horses, clothing, and weapons are buried with them. All items used in life follow the deceased into the grave. The burial chambers are adorned with layers of coffins, surrounded by piles of stones and charcoal. Yet, when evil people hear of this, they pass on the information to each other. Although the authorities impose severe punishments with strict prohibitions, the practice cannot be stopped.

The treasures buried within ancient tombs have long attracted tomb raiders in droves, but the owners of these tombs were no fools. Aware that their final resting places would become targets, they hired skilled craftsmen and designers to fortify their tombs with elaborate defenses. Poisonous snakes, scorpions, and bees, toxic gases, deadly arrows, giant stones, and even mythical beasts—these were just some of the traps laid to protect their graves. Layers of locks, intricate puzzles, and lethal surprises turned tomb raiding into a battle of wits between the living and the dead, spanning across time and life itself. These high-stakes confrontations have given rise to countless stories and legends, leaving a rich legacy for future generations of artistic and literary creations.

Reviving the Genre: Ghost Blows Out the Light

For centuries, tomb raiders and their superstitions were whispered about, but it was Tian Xia Ba Chang's novel series *Ghost Blows Out the Light* that brought this ancient tradition back into the spotlight. By weaving together folklore, adventure, and horror, the novel captivated modern readers and paved the way for an entire genre of Chinese supernatural thrillers. Today, the legend of the Gold-Touching Captain continues to inspire novels, games, comics, and films, highlighting an enduring fascination with the mysteries of connecting life and death.

First serialized on Tianya Forum in 2006, the series spans eight volumes. The initial four books follow three protagonists cursed in the Lost City of Jingjue as they journey across China's ancient tombs, seeking a way to break the curse. The latter half focuses on their quest to collect mystical relics to destroy the undead corpse deity, culminating in their discovery of the elusive

Underground Immortal Village. But more than just an exciting tale, *Ghost Blows Out the Light* sets the groundwork for the tomb-raiding and supernatural genres that followed.

Drawing inspiration from the ghost stories of the Wei, Jin, and Northern-Southern Dynasties (420–589 CE), the novel goes beyond its abundance of imaginative and curiosity-piquing descriptions, as well as the engaging, fast-paced narrative typical of web literature. It delves into China's traditional culture, reimagining elements of mythology, folklore, Taoist practices, and ancient alchemy. Rich with references to yin-yang, the five elements, ghost exorcism, and other Taoist concepts, Tian Xia masterfully blends fantasy with historical and cultural themes, making ancient tombs and shamanic traditions accessible to modern readers.

Tian Xia himself admits that much of the tomb-raiding lore and terminology in the series is a mix of hearsay and imagination. He has been weaving together folklore and his own wild ideas, with even the central concept of "ghost blowing out the light" and the jargon used by tomb raiders being his own creations. It's precisely this blend of history and daring creativity that made *Ghost Blows Out the Light* a sensation. From ancient graves and imperial mausoleums to supernatural creatures and wandering spirits, from fox spirits and mystical snakes to mountain spirits resembling ginseng roots, the series offers a world that is at once terrifying, strange, and tantalizingly close to believable.

Blending Ancient Wisdom and Folklore

Here are some fascinating examples of how Tian Xia draws inspiration from Chinese classics and folklore in his works. Take *luopan* (罗盘, compass), for instance. It's a tool commonly used in feng shui to detect energy patterns. This instrument consists of a central magnetic needle surrounded by a series of concentric circles, each representing a different level of cosmic understanding according to ancient Chinese philosophy. The protagonist Hu Ba Yi frequently uses a luopan, reciting an incantation from the fictional scripture "Sixteen-Character Yin-Yang Feng Shui

Secret Technique": "Search for the dragon, check the wrapped hills; each layer is a barrier. If there are eight dangerous passes, it forms the shape of yin-yang and the Eight Trigrams."

This incantation is actually a creative adaptation of a passage from the *Dragon-Shaking Classic* (撼龙经, *Han Long Jing*), a seminal work in traditional feng shui. The original text reads: "Search for the dragon, check the wrapped hills; each layer is a barrier. If there are a thousand locks on the gate, there's a prince or marquis buried here." This classic is considered the most authoritative text on dragon vein feng shui and has been hailed as the pinnacle of ancient Chinese surveying. Its author, Yang Yunsong (834-900 CE), served as the Imperial Geomancer during the reign of Emperor Xizong of Tang. He was famous for his ability to use geomantic techniques to help the poor improve their fortunes, earning him the nickname "Poverty Relief Master."

Tian Xia not only obtains insights from ancient Chinese classics but also incorporates diverse regional folklore and legends into his work. This blend of sources adds depth and authenticity to his fictional world. One particularly interesting aspect he explores is the spiritual practices of tomb raiders. Given the secretive and psychologically demanding nature of their work, which involves constant interaction with burial sites and the deceased, tomb raiders often seek spiritual comfort and protection. In northern China, particularly in regions like Henan, Hebei, and Beijing, tomb raiders traditionally worship entities known as "Great Immortal Lords."

These "Great Immortal Lords" are not typical deities worshiped by the general population. Instead, they are specific animals believed to possess spiritual significance. The choice of animal varies depending on geographical location and local beliefs. In the tradition Tian Xia draws upon, there are five primary "Great Immortal Lords," each represented by a different animal: the Fox, Weasel, Hedgehog, Snake, and Rat. Each of these animal spirits is believed to offer unique forms of protection and guidance to tomb raiders in their perilous profession.

Fox Spirit: Respectfully called "Hu San Ye" (Lord Hu Third), the fox is revered for its cunning and ability to remain undetected. Tomb raiders, operating in secrecy, pray to the fox spirit for stealth and cleverness in their illicit activities.

Yellow Weasel: Known as "Huang San Ye" (Lord Yellow Third), the weasel is often found near tombs. Working in the oppressive atmosphere of tombs, these robbers often become mentally ill, mistakenly believing it to be the work of the weasel spirit. Offering respect to "Lord Yellow Third" is a way to protect oneself from such misfortunes.

White Hedgehog: Referred to as "Bai Lao Tai Tai" (Old Lady White), the hedgehog's quills are likened to acupuncture needles, symbolizing health and safety. Tomb raiders seek its protection against the physical dangers of their work, such as toxic gasses and bacteria in sealed tombs.

Snake Spirit: Called "Liu Qi Ye" (Lord Willow Seventh), snakes are sometimes considered "small dragons" in folklore. Their presence in tombs is seen as auspicious, linked to the concept of dragon veins in feng shui. Alternatively, tomb raiders worship snakes to avoid being harmed by them during their expeditions.

Rat Spirit: Known as "Hui Ba Ye" (Lord Grey Eighth), rats are seen as kindred spirits to tomb raiders. Both are nocturnal, skilled at burrowing, and considered "underground workers." In the raiders' belief system, the rat is a god of wealth, assisting in finding valuable treasures.

The use of respectful titles and homophones for these animal spirits (e.g., "Hu" for fox, which sounds like a surname) demonstrates the deep-rooted Chinese cultural practice of showing reverence through indirect naming. This blend of supernatural belief and the harsh realities of tomb raiding creates a unique atmosphere where superstition and necessity blur, adding tension and mystique to the stories. It's a testament to how contemporary fiction can serve as a vehicle for exploring traditional cultural elements while crafting compelling narratives.

BUILDING THE TOMB-RAIDING UNIVERSE

Tian Xia's *Ghost Blows Out the Light* series pioneered the tomb-raiding genre in Chinese web novels by creating a rich and intricate world of underground treasure hunting. This universe is populated with various factions, specialized terminology, and unique tools, all of which contribute to a mingling of historical lore, supernatural elements, and imagination.

For example, the story introduces specific jargon unique to the world of tomb raiding. Terms like "Dao Dou" (倒斗), which literally means "overturning the dipper," refer to the act of tomb raiding itself, inspired by the reverse pyramid-like shape of ancient tombs. "Zong Zi" (粽子) is a colloquial term for corpses, drawing a comparison to wrapped rice dumplings. Variants include "Big Zong Zi" (powerful zombies), "Old Zong Zi" (dangerous, reanimating zombies), "Dry Zong Zi" (skeletal remains), and "Meaty Zong Zi" (corpses laden with treasures). The series also introduces tools like the Luo Yang Shovel, a specialized instrument used to analyze soil composition, allowing raiders to detect the presence and age of tombs without extensive excavation.

Crucially, Tian Xia establishes four main factions of tomb raiders, each with distinct specialties and characteristics, creating a comprehensive system that serves as the foundation for the genre.

The Mo Jin (Gold-Touching Captain) Faction: Known for their expertise in locating tombs, they excel at locating tombs using feng shui and astronomical calculations. They hold a deep respect for traditional tomb raiding rules passed down through generations, always ensuring they leave a way out and never push their luck too far.

The Ban Shan (Mountain-Moving Taoist) Faction: Masters of traps and mechanisms, they are skilled in dismantling complex tomb defenses. Often disguised as Taoist priests, they're less concerned with traditional ethics and more focused on using brute force when necessary.

The Xie Ling (Unloading-Ridge Hercules) Faction: Straddling the line between bandits and tomb raiders, they're known for their immense strength and keen sense of smell. They avoid spicy foods and alcohol to maintain their olfactory abilities and are skilled in traditional martial arts.

The Fa Qiu (Hill-Opening General) Faction: Similar to the Gold-Touching faction but with a greater emphasis on teamwork. They often disguise themselves as pawnbrokers or antique dealers and are the only faction willing to cooperate with official authorities.

By creating this detailed world of tomb raiding, complete with its own history, factions, terminology, and tools, Tian Xia has not only crafted an engaging narrative but also established a new subgenre in Chinese popular literature. This rich backdrop allows for exploration of themes like the tension between preservation and plunder, the allure of ancient mysteries, and the dangers of disturbing the past. It's a framework allows later works to branch out and variously evolve.

The Lost Tomb: Turning Fiction into a Cultural Phenomenon

While the novel *Ghost Blows Out the Light* carved out a niche in Chinese horror and supernatural fiction, its rich references to ancient texts and its Ming-Qing vernacular writing style make it a little daunting for readers to go wild. It wasn't until *The Lost Tomb* (盗墓笔记, *Dao Mu Bi Ji*) emerged that the tomb-raiding genre truly captured the mainstream cultural market.

Building upon the world established by Tian Xia, *The Lost Tomb*, serialized online between 2007 and 2011, reached extraordinary commercial success, with over 20 million copies of the print version sold. It spawned a plethora of spin-offs, including comics, games, radio dramas, and TV series, igniting a cultural phenomenon where fiction crossed into the real world. For instance, the "Ten-Year Promise" at Changbai Mountain in Northeast China, inspired by the protagonist Zhang Qi Ling's departure into the Bronze Gate on August 17, 2005, became a fan pilgrimage. Believing that August 17 would mark Zhang's return, thousands of fans and tourists flocked to Changbai Mountain on that date in 2015, turning the already busy tourist season into a full-blown spectacle. Adding to the frenzy, the author released a new final chapter on Weibo at midnight, where the main characters reunited at Changbai Mountain, further heightening the sense that the characters exist alongside the readers.

Comparatively, *Ghost Blows Out the Light* leans towards a more logical structure. Even when dealing with supernatural phenomena, it strives to explain events using folklore and modern science, carefully avoiding crossover between fiction and reality. On the other hand, *The Lost Tomb* delivers a more cinematic "spectacle effect." From the mysterious tomb chambers to underwater adventures, from the mimicking Cockscomb Snake to the symbiotic centipede, and from the terrifying bronze tree to the mythical Candle Dragon, the novel creates a fantastical world far removed from everyday life. This allows readers to escape their mundane routines, offering temporary relief and entertainment. Despite - or perhaps because of - its more exaggerated and unrealistic narrative, *The Lost Tomb* garnered an unprecedented level of reader devotion, demonstrating the powerful allure of fusing fantasy with reality in modern Chinese literature.

Unearthing a Treasure Trove: The Rise of Chinese Horror Fiction

As I mentioned earlier, *Ghost Blows Out the Light* cracked open a rich vein in Chinese horror fiction, bringing the genre to the forefront. Following in its wake, *The Lost Tomb* further proved the immense popularity of supernatural and tomb-raiding stories, leading to a flood of creative works exploring every possible angle of the theme. Within the tomb-raiding genre alone, we've seen the emergence of concepts like grave-cloth artisans, corpse shrouds, or river coffins. Beyond tombs, other elements of traditional Chinese folklore have also found their way into popular culture.

For instance, tomb-raiding naturally brings to mind the ancient relics buried within. Ma Bo Yong's *Mystery of Antiques* dives into this world, highlighting the saying, "Appraising antiques is easy, appraising people is hard." Each artifact carries a historical and cultural legacy, while each forgery is a maze of cunning deceptions and unfathomable traps. In this story, the protagonist, Xu Yuan, armed with a half-complete family manuscript on antique appraisal, a collection of fragmented photos, and two suspicious partners, meticulously unravels the mysteries of relics, exposing the true enemies hidden within forgeries.

Besides tomb raiders, the communication between life and death is often navigated by Taoist practitioners, who are revered as masters of the unseen realm. Stories like *Part-Time Half-Immortal*, *The Last Taoist*, and *The Years I Worked as a Yin-Yang Master* draw deeply from Chinese folk tales and ancient customs, weaving a mix of reality and illusion that resonates with readers' personal experiences. For example, almost every Chinese child has likely seen paper effigies at funerals and heard from their grandparents that these figures must not have eyes drawn on them. Why? Many are also told that if incense sticks for deities burn out prematurely, you need to burn new ones. Why? Or that if you find yourself wandering in circles down an alley without finding a way out, cursing loudly and showing no fear will break the spell. Why? These shared cultural memories form the foundation for new adventures in these novels, which are based on indigenous Chinese perspectives on life and death. They depict rituals such as forming hand seals to connect with ancestral masters and drive away evil, calculating auspicious times and locations for mining or construction, casting moon blocks to seek the will of ancestors, inviting spirits or deities to possess a body to solve problems, and even the darker practice of raising ghost children for personal gain, which inevitably leads to tragic consequences. Through these narratives, readers recall their childhood confusions, feeling the company of the dead in their daily life.

In addition to Taoism, animal totem worship is another ingrained belief in China. He Ma's *Tibetan Code* masterfully weaves together Tibetan Buddhism, the ferocious Tibetan Mastiff, mysterious local legends, and the breathtaking beauty of the Tibetan plateau. What could be more fearsome than a Tibetan Mastiff? Does a secret passage to the sacred land of Shangri-La lie hidden beneath the Potala Palace? Through the pages of *Tibetan Code*, readers embark on a journey through the shrouded mysteries of Tibetan history, the vast snowy landscapes, and the mythical realms of the region.

Beyond drawing from classical Chinese traditions, a new trend is emerging where East meets West in the storytelling styles. *The Eerie Immortal* merges Lovecraftian horror with ancient Chinese customs, drawing on thriller, time travel, suspense, and mystery to present a world of cultivation. The protagonist, Li Huo Wang, is unhinged from the very start, frequently slipping into hallucinations where he believes he's living in a modern mental institution, complete with bankrupt parents desperate to cure him and a first love waiting for his recovery. Li's consciousness jumps between ancient and modern realities, as if he has two bodies but can only perceive one at a time. In modern world, electroshock therapy is used to treat illness, while in the cultivation world, his body is tortured by unknown forces. Escaping from a fish's belly in the cultivation world corresponds to fighting with guards in the modern hospital. The novel constantly showcases the protagonist's self-doubt and suspicion through this dual narrative. The Chinese classical philosophical concept of "Zhuang Zi's butterfly dream" and the modern psychological concept of "multiple personalities" together plunge the protagonist into extreme confusion and emotional breakdown.

To Be Explored . . .

Chinese horror-themed web novels, along with popular cultural products like games and comics, have become powerful platforms for public expression and collective resonance. These works often actively discuss complex value systems and worldviews. Traditionally, tomb raiding was viewed as a severe transgression—plundering the dead's property and causing irreparable harm to historical relics. It also reflected deeply ingrained feudal superstitions that have long oppressed individuals, especially women. In contrast, modern stories tend to reframe tomb exploration as a collaborative effort with official archaeological institutions, ensuring that discoveries are properly preserved for historical and cultural purposes. Alternatively, explorers in these narratives may gather the information they need for their next adventure and then quietly depart, leaving the graves undisturbed and allowing the dead to rest in peace, their presence remaining unknown to the living world.

Meanwhile, these narratives explicitly criticize harmful remnants of feudal ideologies. The protagonists often explain the origins of traditional customs, uncovering how they've been misinterpreted over time. For instance, while it's commonly believed that pregnant women or those menstruating are prohibited from attending religious rituals or visiting ancestral graves, the original guidelines were more nuanced. In ancient times, it was thought that women's bodies, especially during pregnancy or menstruation, were closer to the yin energy, making them more sensitive to spirits. As a result, the caution was for their protection, suggesting that they could still participate in rituals with the proper care from family members and ritual practitioners. Additionally, the recommendation for pregnant or menstruating women to avoid visiting graves was primarily practical, as these visits often involved long, difficult journeys up hills, which could be physically taxing. Modern stories are now re-examining these social norms and encouraging a reconsideration of outdated practices.

Moreover, the genre is also increasingly embracing themes of diverse romantic relationships. I intentionally avoid using the term "LGBTQ+" here because it is a modern concept that doesn't neatly align with ancient Chinese philosophies. Take Taoist ideas, for example: I previously mentioned that women are often seen as closer to yin, but not equated with yin itself. This is because yin and yang are not rigidly divided by gender. Elements in nature tend to lean towards yin or yang, and when we talk about the balance between them, it refers to adjustments between individuals who possess more yin or more yang energy. It's not about fixed, absolute qualities—but a comparative and fluid concept. Modern stories are tracing back to such historical roots of Chinese social norms, advocating for diverse types of relationships. This includes not only love beyond traditional male and female roles but also questions of who bears the responsibility for childbirth and contraception. The ancient Taoist principle of "道法自然" (Dao patterns itself on what is natural) provides writers with great freedom and flexibility to explore and support new possibilities in relationships and social roles.

While some of these creations may follow formulaic patterns, I am optimistic that the rich tapestry of Chinese horror will continue to yield valuable insights and treasures for the future, offering readers a unique brand of thrills that differ from the anxieties of modern society. As one netizen humorously remarked, "If you send me a bomb, I'd just report it to the police; but if I found an embroidered shoe at my doorstep one morning, I might be so terrified that I'd rather die than wait for its owner."

Works Introduced

Cui, Zou Zhao 崔走召. *Guǐ jiào hún zhī yīnyáng xiānshēng* 鬼叫魂之阴阳先生 [The Years I Worked as a Yin-Yang Master]. Shanghai: Wenhui Publishing House, 2011.

He, Ma 何马. *Zàngdì mìmǎ zhēncángbǎn* 藏地密码 [The Tibetan Code (10 Volumes)]. Chongqing: Chongqing Publishing House, 2012.

Hu Wei de Bi 狐尾的笔. *Huǒwàng* 火旺 [The Eerie Immortal]. Guangzhou: Huacheng Publishing House, 2024.

La Mianhuatang de Tuzi 拉棉花糖的兔子 and Xiao Heibao 小黑豹. *Fēizhíyè bàn xiān* 非職業半仙 [Part-Time Half-Immortal]. New Taipei City: Pingxin Publishing, 2019.

Ma, Boyong 马伯庸. *Gǔdǒng jú zhōng jú dà quánjí* 古董局中局 [Mystery of Antiques (4 Volumes)]. Beijing: Beijing United Publishing Co., 2015.

Nanpai, Sanshu 南派三叔. *Dàomù bǐjì* 盗墓笔记 [The Lost Tomb (10 Volumes)]. Shanghai: Shanghai Culture Publishing House, 2011.

Tianxia, Bachang 天下霸唱. *Guǐ chuī dēng* 鬼吹灯 [Ghost Blows Out the Light (8 Volumes)]. Changsha: Hunan Literature and Art Publishing House, 2019.

Xia, Yi 夏忆. *Zuìhòu yīgè dàoshi* 1 最后一个道士1 [The Last Taoist Vol.1]. Nanchang: Baihuazhou Literature and Art Publishing House, 2012.

Tell Me What You See
Terena Elizabeth Bell
Whiskey Tit, 2022

Conversations about literary genres often unravel into fussy taxonomies. ("Will you read my historical-literary romance with elements of steampunk slipstream? Please?") On the other hand, a couple of thousand years ago, the author of *Ecclesiastes* observed, "Of making many books there is no end." It's hard to improve on that observation.

But there is one distinction that, if not of practical utility for professors or marketing departments, strikes me each time I pick up a book. It's the following: some writers, aware of the expectations associated with their genre (or their supposed *brand*), try to ingratiate themselves with their readers. Other writers, in contrast, challenge their readers, and do not shy away from confrontation.

Terena Elizabeth Bell belongs to the latter category. Her collection of ten stories, *Tell Me What You See*, announces as much in its title. Although this imperative phrase applies explicitly to one of the stories, it could be extended to the book as a whole, serving as both an invitation and a warning to the reader. This fiction is not for passive consumption.

There are, of course, risks to this kind of writing. If the first category I mentioned exposes itself to problems of conformity or complacency, this second mode can sometimes slip into an aloof, wannabe avant-garde pose. What does the challenge bring to the table? I ask myself. What are the rewards? To put it bluntly, as a reader: what's in it for me?

Fortunately, *Tell Me What You See* offers plenty. For all its formal fireworks, typographical effects and play of text and image, variety of genre (biblical narrative, contemporary American politics and sci-fi set in the 22nd century, to name a few examples)—above all, a taste for estrangement that is nothing if not insistent—is also interested in exploring human emotions, and its ambiguities are in the service of larger ideas, not cute puzzles.

The first story, "Welcome, Friend," effectively conjures up horror in an abandoned apartment; "Privacy Station," set on a futuristic botanical research station orbiting the earth, is a tale imbued with tenderness; "Regression," an erasure story about Alzheimer's disease, is a marvel of condensed prose. Usually I find erasures, at best, an interesting exercise, and all too often, merely an exercise—but here Bell marries form and subject and creates something truly artful and harrowing.

I struggled with the typographical experiments of "The Fifth Fear" but it is an ambitious story whose challenges are not gratuitous. A later story, "I go to prepare a place for you" is a moving piece of flash fiction that, like "Regression," depicts human vulnerability and packs a visceral punch.

The longest piece, "#CoronaLife," takes up at least a third of the volume. I admit that I didn't relish the prospect of yet another Covid story. Enough time has passed that it's now possible to speak of a "Covid genre" that emerged out of the 2020 pandemic and its aftermath, dramatizing the disruption and fear of that era. What seemed urgent back then is now cursed with a certain familiarity; there is a flattening sameness to many stories and essays on this topic.

To my relief, "#CoronaLife" is an exception. Structured as a collection of text messages, emails and tweets, along with still images, it captures the radical disconnect of the time. One could even read it against the grain as not having to be about Covid-19 at all—it's about human behavior when the façade of norms crumbles.

The concluding story, "Tell Me What You See," also addresses recent history, in this case the January 6 insurrection in Washington, D.C. And again, this highly reported event is imaginatively reconstructed and renewed, this time in the form of a little girl's eye test. As I type these words, the story feels not only like a retelling, but also like an uncomfortably prescient anticipation of what is happening now, in the same setting.

Formally inventive and politically engaged, *Tell Me What You* See is impossible to pigeonhole. It is the work of an adventurous writer, and will reward the reader who accepts its invitation.

The Guiltless Bystander
David Wheldon
Confingo Publishing, 2022

The *Guiltless Bystander* is a collection of stories by David Wheldon, a novelist, short story writer, poet, and far from least, medical doctor. It was published posthumously, though I understand its content is that of Wheldon's choosing.

In his insightful foreword, the writer Aiden O'Reilly, latterly a friend, explains how after early acclaim Wheldon's writing career fell into abeyance: how subsequently, alongside his medical duties, he continued to write but without attracting the interest of publishers. In the years before his death in 2021, both O'Reilly and the fiction writer David Rose were instrumental in bringing Wheldon's writing back to public attention, and to finding publishers for a succession of stories, culminating in the publication of *The Guiltless Bystander* in July 2022.

I confess to feeling daunted at the prospect of reviewing this collection. Wheldon's stories so beguile me that I struggle to consider them analytically. O'Reilly has used the term 'ireal' to describe the genre into which they might be placed, and certainly this resonates. It's also tempting to think of Wheldon's style as otherworldly, although that would be a simplification. Like the paintings of Eric Ravilious, the settings and behaviours on display are both very much of this world and very much not. It's as if the responses of Wheldon's characters are governed by different laws, though the reader never learns what these are. The people, and beings, who populate his stories are immediate but elusive, cerebral but quixotic, and often hold well-formed assumptions they presume universal.

Despite this, or as a result, the stories contain a pervasive element of things unknown, perhaps unknowable. This does not preclude conjecture on the part of the characters, rather it fosters it. You wouldn't have to read far to encounter unorthodox belief systems, often in the form of philosophical discourse or speculation.

On the whole Wheldon's characters seem happy with this. Inhabiting circumstances defined by a sense of unknowing, they retain agency. They do not need certainty in order to act. You might almost say uncertainty is a form of freedom.

Before long, and unlike his characters, it becomes clear that Wheldon is completely in control. Like Penelope Fitzgerald, he displays a preternatural command of detail. Also like Fitzgerald, detail is lightly but expertly deployed, made digestible, providing a counterpoint of authenticity to even the most improbable happenings.

There is, very apparently, something anachronistic about his prose. The sense of courtesy towards the reader, the precision of his word choice, and the unhurried way he allows each story to unfold all speak of an earlier approach. And yet the stories impart a sense of timelessness, of not ultimately conforming to the mores of a particular era. And just occasionally a quirk of language betrays a more modern sensibility.

The subject matter in this collection is wide ranging, the work of a discursive mind. A female chess master, incidentally an automaton, appears to achieve sentience. Medusa, the snake-haired seductress, is reimagined with tinted locks and the utmost sympathy. A medical student, 'Tall Martha', co-ordinates an original ruse to end a tedious lecture dead on time. A 'candidate' is chosen to be carried by sedan to a hilltop cell, where a brick extracted from the wall allows a conversation of the greatest intimacy with a female 'candidate' he will never meet. And, in rare instances, people in normal settings behave, almost, normally.

It might be noted that these examples all contain female protagonists, and the women in Wheldon's stories are unfailingly distinctive. Despite the limiting circumstances in which they may find themselves, they display poise and independence of character. They are well able to surprise and to initiate, and in doing so they effortlessly entice the reader's interest. Their speech patterns, and perspectives, are far from naturalistic, yet intrigue. I haven't come across anything like them elsewhere. But then you might say that of the male characters too.

There's a wonderfully accessible virtuosity in Wheldon's style, and it's hard not to share the amusement he so obviously finds in the act of writing. As with the fiction of G.K. Chesterton, though less explicitly, he relishes paradox, which appears in all manner of guises. For example, there is a formality in the way characters address one another, but what they say can be disarmingly personal. They share a trope of self-explanation, but are held at something of a distance from the reader, who is teasingly drip-fed insight into their singular manner of being in the world. In consequence one discerns, almost by osmosis, considerable depth of interiority. Wheldon's characters are not simply ideas attached to bodies.

Like other medics turned to fiction—one thinks of Maugham and Conan Doyle—there can be something of the case study in the way Wheldon's stories are set out. They tend to be front-loaded with information, and you might even wonder where this information is taking you, except that by the time you've reached that point you're spun in his web.

One senses too in Wheldon a secular mindset, nevertheless at ease with the ineffable. Where gods exist explicitly, as in the heartrending 'Medusa's Metaphors', they are corrupt: innocence can only flourish in their absence. However, in 'The Prayer Factory', prayers are hand-crafted by believers and non-believers alike, their efficacy or lack of it a different matter from their value.

In all, I can promise that this collection contains stories of rare scope. You will encounter sentences that no-one is likely to have written before or since. It's fair to say the quality varies somewhat, although even the slighter pieces combine erudition with a charming playfulness. Furthermore, for my money, 'The Automaton', first published as a chapbook by Nightjar Press, ranks with any of the great stories of the last century. Paradoxically—that term again—the non-human elicits the most human of responses.

So, despite their many quirks, Wheldon's characters invite our empathy. Idiosyncrasy is always in the foreground, and in Wheldon's hands idiosyncrasy is a trove of riches. Doubtless it's this that make his characters so improbably convincing. They are explicitly concerned with the act of living, and inhabit the human, or non-human condition according to their interpretation. This is their essence. They are interpreters of life as, ultimately, we all must be.

Sleep Decades
Israel Bonilla
Malarkey Books, 2024

Representing a life involves many forms of treason. One might read this first sentence of Israel Bonilla's debut collection of short stories as a skeleton key to the entire volume, or perhaps as a warning to the would-be interpreter against putting too much faith in the words of even the most ostensibly reliable narrator, or, for that matter, reviewer. Indeed, the nineteen stories in this remarkable book, with their various modes and manners and structuring devices, may be understood as so many forms of treason committed by their narrators against themselves and the others whose lives are recounted here, attempts to represent these lives in ways that prove their narrators' 'fine-spun theories'. Language betrays us, of course, whether we know it or not, and even if we do not intend to commit treason, the act of representation itself cannot be otherwise.

Yet language is also the substance of our self-making, the climature of those fine-spun theories, the warp and woof of the story itself—the medium in which, as the narrator of 'Confessions of an American Marihuana User' says, 'at some moment in life we enunciate a couple of sentences that epitomize us'. Bonilla has placed an epigraph from Matthew Arnold's 'Empedocles on Etna' at the beginning of his book: *And we feel, day and night, / The burden of ourselves.* In the poem, Arnold's Empedocles claims that, under the pressure of this burden, the wise man looks inside himself to find a cure, and that all fears and darkness may be dispelled by submitting to the ultimate reality of nature: *In vain our pent wills fret, / And would the world subdue. / Limits we do not set / Condition all we do. / Born into life we are, and life must be our mould.* The burden of ourselves, for Arnold's Empedocles, is distilled in the perverse human will that would impose its inordinate desires upon the world, yet ultimately lacks the power to do so.

This frustration of the pent will is in evidence throughout the volume, and represents a mode of being that characterizes the lives represented here, thrust into conflict with those *limits we do not set*: the heroic activist and ex-professor of 'Antisophers', whose uncompromising drive to change the world has led her to a stifling anti-intellectualism that conceals and compensates for her discontent with the elusiveness of such change; the narrator of 'Boca de Iguanas' who ends up discovering 'a newfound distance between the sky' and himself, 'stagger[ing] around in the darkness of [his] consciousness'; the knock-kneed boy of 'Margins,' who flees the ugliness of his body by imagining himself as pure mind—not unlike Empedocles: *Nothing but a devouring flame of thought,—/ But a naked, eternally restless mind!*—yet is left 'gasping for breath' by an encounter with a waitress. The motley cast of *Sleep Decades* push up against the limits that forge and fashion their multiform identities.

The first story in the volume, 'A Biography in Ten Objects', echews chronological narrative in favour of 'the manner of Vermeer', that is, 'a painstaking attachment to the everyday bric-a-brac', and, as the title suggests, chooses ten exemplary objects from its subject's life—glasses, lamps, a cell phone, a pen, a shopping cart, a mortar and pestle, arum lilies, homeopathic pills, a buddha statue, a bible—, portraying her life in relation to these objects. It is almost as if the *burden of ourselves* has become the burden of the objects in which our lives are externalized, a fetishism of the object which absorbs the experiences of those who have lived together with this bric-a-brac. I am reminded here of Marx's description of religion, where 'the products of the human brain appear as autonomous figures endowed with a life of their own, which enter into relations, both with each other and with the human race', and which he compares with commodities as the products of human hands. A similar note is struck in 'Levity', whose narrator describes the contents of his bedroom—a photograph of his parents, his grandfather's lamp table, the carpet—as 'the most meticulous map of a personality', a cartography of the soul, if you will. Thus a life is plotted, in the various senses of that treacherous verb.

By contrast, in 'Alive and Well', an invalid grandmother is transfigured into an object by the various quarreling factions of her family. Instead of familiar objects representing the life, will and desires of an individual, in this story an individual is transformed into an object upon which the wills and desires of others are projected. After a series of strokes, the grandmother is increasingly disabled: 'Her identity wasn't cohesive; her sense of time was ravished. The word *burden* loomed through everyone's mind. And how could it not? My grandmother was at the threshold of impersonality.' Yet as the strokes remove the *burden of ourselves* from her, she becomes not exactly a burden on others, as the cliché has it, but 'a thread to which everybody hung on', an altitudinous impersonality not unlike the 'charred, blackened, melancholy waste' where Empedocles finds himself alone in Arnold's poem, an 'inert' body against which the various characters measure their own burdens.

The title of the seventh story in the volume, 'All the Works That My Hands Had Wrought', is taken from Ecclesiastes 2:11: 'Then I looked on all the works that my hand had wrought, and on the labour that I had laboured to do; and, behold, all was vanity and vexation of spirit, and there was no profit under the sun'. In this story, which begins with an echo of Dostoyevsky's *Notes from Underground*, a mediocre man and student attempts to mold himself into a brilliant intellectual and showman like his mentor Colin, eventually organizing a disastrous meeting with an ex-acquaintance in order to prove what kind of person he had become. Ultimately, a reading of his own textbook on grammar, the crowning achievement of his career, which had caused a break with Colin, seemingly due to the latter's envy of the narrator's success, leads him to realize the vanity of his excessive ambition and the pathetic reality of his life. This calls to mind a quote from Rabbi Joseph B. Soloveitchik's essay *Halakhic Man*: 'Repentance, according to the halakhic view, is an act of creation—self-creation.' Self-making is, of course, also an act of self-unmaking, in which the will is subject to hard limits: *Born into life we are, and life must be our mould.* Or, perhaps more ominously, in Hamlet's words, *There's a divinity that shapes our ends, / Rough-hew them how we will.* Elsewhere, Rav Soloveitchik describes this self-fashioning in terms of 'the crystallization of the fleeting individual experience into fixed principles and universal norms' by means of halakha as an 'objectifying instrument' of consciousness. Of course, our narrator is far from the Rav's idea of halakhic man, yet, whether the limit be divinity, rabbinic law, or life itself, the freedom of the self-making adventure inevitably founders on the *Realitätsprinzip*.

'As the Waters Fail from the Sea' also takes its title from a biblical verse: 'As the waters fail from the sea, and the flood decayeth and drieth up: So man lieth down, and riseth not: till the heavens be no more, they shall not awake, nor be raised out of their sleep' (Job 14:11-12). In this story, narrated by the heir of an elderly bookseller, masses of dusty books pile up around the eccentric old man, who gradually pushes away those close to him as well as most of his potential customers. As in 'A Biography in Ten Objects', the bookseller is here refracted in the objects that surround him—particular volumes which he keeps in a neoclassical glass-door bookcase and which he does not wish to sell:

> I have long thought of it as his canon. It permeates his whole life: his manners, his diction, his motions, his temperament. You can see Carlyle and Hazlitt in his incoherent passion, Johnson and Tolstoy in his zealous earnestness, Emerson and Melville in his prolix mysticism, James and Hume in his pluralistic view of the universe, de Bury in his handling of books.

It is not just the content of these writers that defines the man; it is rather the dusty ponderousness, the physical nature of the books that 'builds up to a barrier, nothing else'. While the old man 'somehow ascends' and 'seems awake' only in discussing books, these same books, just as they have crowded out the people in his life, soon impede entrance to the bookshop. Yet he is resigned—'Leave them alone'—just as Job in the quoted passage resigns himself to the finality of death, and 'the door will cease to open; the tomb is finished'.

The 'many forms of treason' are echoed in the formal variety of these stories: the unorthodox presentation of 'A Biography in Ten Objects'; the epistolary form of 'Draft'; the anaphoric accumulation of 'Roulette'; the De Quinceyan paradigms of 'Confessions of an American Marihuana User'; the visionary monologue of 'Basement Blues'; and the various first-person narrators telling third-person stories or their own. This formal variety reaches its culmination in the final text of the volume, τὸ ὄν, a tour de force in which narrative technique and experimentation are pushed nearly to breaking in an attempt to explore the limits of representation, perhaps in an attempt to move beyond the necessity of treason.

Bonilla writes an exquisite and sonorous prose, Victorian in its resonance and haunting in its effect upon the reader. One strength of these stories rests upon the dialectic between the often low station of the characters and their circumstances and the careful, exacting style that eschews any lingering attachment to mere realism by foregrounding its artifice and historical antecedents. This is not a book of comforts; it is written, as the jacket copy tells us, 'in the adversative mood', and yet these stories are not devoid of hope, although perhaps they, once again like Empedocles in Arnold's poem, would beseech us to curb any unjustified extravagance:

> I say: Fear not! Life still
> Leaves human effort scope.
> But, since life teems with ill,
> Nurse no extravagant hope;
> Because thou must not dream, thou need'st not
> then despair!

REVIEW | Avital Gad-Cykman

The House in Smyrna's Keys

The House in Smyrna
Tatiana Salem Levy, translated by Alison Entrekin
Scribe UK, 2015

The House in Smyrna, written by the Brazilian writer born in Portugal, Tatiana Salem Levy, keeps being relevant to readers due to its unblinking, rather fierce look into what moves us beyond the paralysis of fear. The novel deals with the pain linked to individual and collective memory, introducing the liberating power of the review of the past and writing. The struggle to confront history, the search for solace and the hope for liberation are built into the foundations of this book.

The narrator, a young woman, is paralyzed, alone in her bed with a typewriter and a key to a house in Turkey, Smyrna, her grandfather gave her, appointing her as the person responsible for the inheritance. Four intertwined narratives emerge from her writing, during her search for a physical, mental and emotional recovery. Her paralysis, we learn, is related to her mother's illness and death, her own passionate and devastating relationship with an ex-boyfriend, the weight of her family's exile since their forced departure from the family home in Turkey, and the diasporic Jewish history in general. Another exile, beside the one from Turkey to Brazil, haunts her. During the dictatorship in Brazil, her parents fled to Portugal, where the narrator was born.

The strong emphasis on exile and history brings to mind Walter Benjamin's brilliant text "On the concept of history" (1942). Levy's narrator performs a historical archaeology, and her inquiry into the past echoes Benjamin's view that one needs to break history apart in order to reveal, understand, accept and be liberated from trapping roots and the causes of suffering.

The narrator tells her story in fragments that do not necessarily fit together with the chronological development of past situations or emotions. While certain fragments complement one another, others do not, and these frequent contradictions convey the chaos of a life and a mind. This dynamic reflects the way the narrator's memory is created and recreated between the community's recollection and forgetfulness, and her individual memories and interpretations. The birth story told from two angles is an example of contradictions regarding time, exile and birth.

First, the narrator reports that she was born outside Brazil, in exile, in winter, on a cold and gray day. Her mother, she says, went through hours of contraction, without anesthetics, because the baby hadn't turned around and the anesthetist arrived late. When the baby was born, the finally anesthetized mother couldn't hold her in her arms. Later, the mother woke up to find a vertical scar that would forever link the gap between her breasts and her pubis.

Following this story, the narrator tells the deceased mother's imaginary response. Her mother asks her to move the prism of pain, and adds that exile is not necessarily equal to suffering. According to her mother, says the narrator, the day of birth was not cold or gray, and the mother doesn't have any scar, since it was a natural birth.

Thus, the mythical point of view of the scar of exile and tortured birth giving is interacting with the mother's imaginary, realistic and pragmatic point of view. The reader is unable to determine whether one narrative has any advantage over the other.

The narrator relives memories of her mother's love and sage advice, the familiar and intimate—while she also reconstructs the troubled fate of the the past generations of her family and the Jewish people. Ever since her childhood, she has been aware of the discrepancy created by the passage of time. However, suffering, for her, is inter-generational. She feels as if she has spent her entire life in the house in Turkey, the place her family was forced to leave. Adopting this collective memory bestows her with a sense of belonging, of a home, as well as a sense of being exiled forcefully.

The whole range of sensations passes through her body and accumulates into a significant, paralyzing effect she cannot resist. The narrator feels trapped and wishes she could disconnect from the past. Her body is a map on which the past is still happening, accumulating, fragment by fragment, doubt by doubt, pain by pain, preventing her from living the present and delaying her future.

The narrator's struggle brings to mind Paul Klee's painting "Angelus Novus", and Walter Benjamin's vision of this painting articulates such experience. According to Benjamin, the angel seems to want to get away from something at which he is staring. This "something" is comprised of a chain of past events, a catastrophe

piling up ruin upon ruin. The angel, Benjamin says, is tempted to wake the dead and collect the fragments of history; hoping it will liberate him to fly. But a blowing storm from heaven clings to his wings so tightly, he cannot open them. The pile of ruins grows sky-high.

The shards of the narrator's world, her mother's illness and death, the narrator's inability to acknowledge this early death, an abusive ex-boyfriend, a broken heart and the history of exile after exile accumulate as well. It is interesting to observe that her grief carries a heavier emotional load than the pain caused by other reasons. The other storylines recede when the narrator remembers her mother. When she concentrates on this loss, she relinquishes the weight of collective history in favor of the painful the individual past.

Like Klee's angel, the narrator cannot fly. In order to lift the mass obstructing her way out, she needs to create a tolerable version of the past, a story that will allow her to renew her hope and return to life. Her recollections in writing, however, indicate that the narrator's struggle to come to terms with the past does not only drain her but also signals hope for a future that goes beyond a heap of ruins. She keeps trying to keep her wings open, even broken, and will fight to fly.

Before the first sign of healing, however, appears a sign of danger. The memory of her suffering during the time she saw her mother dying is not only a memory of pain. She recalls the great happiness of boundless affection and endless intimacy, when the slightest touch or look was a declaration of love. She says that they were so close that, at times, at the hospital, she believed she assimilated her mother's emotions and experiences. She also comments on how they were physically similar. Her great identification with her mother amounts to an assimilation. Therefore, it is conceivable that, after spending months hugging, caring, touching and interacting in great love with her mother, suffering due to the lethal illness, she craves to maintain the bond, appropriating her mother's sick body as if it belonged to her, as if the mother were her. The danger here is a brewing death wish, a longing to be one with the mother, still.

When she plunges into pain, though, the narrator hears her mother's imaginary voice begging her to embrace life and seek happiness. She resists this appeal, speaking of pain as a part of life, a characteristic of her person and a necessity. Apparently, beyond the spontaneous pain, there is a choice in pain. At first, this choice seems to contradict her desire to break the shell of suffering and recover from the paralysis, as the engine of her writing is exactly the emotion that leaves her paralyzed. However, her writing is, potentially, a tool of recovery. She may write to articulate and understand life better, channel her pain, and this way with the burden.

Toward the end of her inner journey, and without giving up the pain, the narrator chooses to keep writing and let it hurt, until the wound becomes a scar, a part of her self that does not cause her paralysis. Hence, her writing opens a door, like a key, clearly related to the key to the house in Turkey. Here, individual and collective memories and pain mix up. The house key becomes a symbol of opening, and gives her a motive to start moving forward.

Without focusing on the actual transition from paralysis to movement, the narrator starts her travel to Turkey. Arriving in the family town, she restrains her hesitation and apprehension and contacts the family elders, who stayed behind despite the danger. They are resentful but speak to her. To her utter shock, they say that the house has already been demolished, and that the family has been aware of this fact. Consequently, she realizes that her grandfather gave her the key in order to send her on a journey to the past, find out the truth, process it and learn a lesson about life. Her perspective widens, now that she is standing where the house used to. She starts questioning the meanings she had assigned to a specific, material, and possibly welcoming house. What exists is the lineage, the story, the tradition. The house takes on a more symbolic sense of a home, and this kind of home cannot be destroyed. The dream of entering this house in order to take root becomes an assimilation of her individual and collective history. Her home exists within a place that is not Brazil, Turkey or Portugal, but outside them and within each one of them.

Interestingly, even after breaking free, the narrator feels that there is pain is in everything, spread to every corner of the planet and every corner of herself. The journey, she declares, has been beautiful, interesting and even funny but it hurts. This inheritance, and everything she carries without choice hurts. Yet, she is able to take control over her life and resists obsession. Now that she writes about all the experiences that led her to her current situation, her writing enables her to open doors, go in and out, in or out, without getting stuck.

The forward movement does not stop. Now that the narrator is moving freely, she travels from Turkey to Portugal, where she experiences a fleeting love story that sustains and satisfies her. Her broken heart is mended to a certain extent, as the body that imprisoned her becomes a tool of release. Moving her body and integrating it into her emotional and mental experiences, helps the narrator accept that life continues despite losses.

The process of recovery continues through all the elements that integrated the haunting past and used to spawn anger, shame, and denial. Her past becomes a fragment of her just as much as she is a fragment of history. She finds, in agreement with Walter Benjamin that the past carries with it a secret index, by which it refers to its own resurrection. The conception of happiness resonates with that of resurrection.

REVIEW | VIK SHIRLEY

Just Like
Lee Sumyeong, translated by Colin Leemarshall
Moon Country Korean Poetry Series, Black
Ocean, 2024

The surreal meets language poetry, before undergoing complementary 'shock of translation' treatment in Lee Sumyeong's *Just Like*, the ninth book in Black Ocean's Moon Country Korean Poetry Series.

The title *Just Like* is meta: the poems are 'just like' the poems they equally *could* have been. In his extensive 'Translator's Introduction', Colin Leemarshall presents these poems through the lens of this possibility, and his translation is key to the poetics of the book. He takes Walter Benjamin's idea that a translator's job is to 'bring to light' the 'pure language' of a text through their translation to the next level, through his bespoke concept of allopoetics:

> [. . .] within and outside of the poems there are [. . .] other poems, variants of the given, secret iterations occulted in the undertows of disintegrative logic, isomorphic grammar, surreptitious homophony, and various other phenomena.

Each poem is just one of many, Leemarshall is saying, the one ghost captured on film out of multiple phantoms auditioning for the role. He leans into Lee Sumyeong's unorthodox writing with ease, as only someone in their element can (not surprising given his background as an experimental poet running innovative small press *Erotoplasty*). Lee purposely pivots from meaning and message in her poetry, consigning her poetry to the 'difficult' label and unappealing to South Korean mainstream poetry audiences. This defiant lack of 'poetic ballast' is precisely what attracted Leemarshall. With her non-literary language pool and her disinterest in lyric overfamiliarity Lee hopes to expand the 'scope of poetry' she tells her translator in the interview at the back of the book, originally published in Australian magazine *Rabbit*. Evolving Steinian tableau in the poetry and Benjaminian theory in the translation, *Just Like* is progressive on behalf of poet and translator, and, under the editorship of Korean-based poet and translator, Jake Levine, the Moon Country Series is also. All-in-all, a dream team to say the least! The books are aesthetically drool-worthy too, designer Abby Haddican's cover images are very much works of art in themselves.

The reader is plunged into Lee's 'non-literary language pool' from the outset. The 'uncanny grammar' and 'permutational richness' of the first poem, 'things like cement vegetable paper,' seduced Leemarshall, triggering a need rather than a want to translate, he explains in his introduction. For those more familiar with the Western canon think Gertrude Stein meets Russell Edson:

> A man runs a field and the field of the man running the field caves in. A man lacking a caved-in field to the man runs. Things like cement vegetable paper sweltering he haphazardly plucks a cabbage.

The detail of who the man is is irrelevant and beside the point, as is often the way with Edson. Like Stein, Lee is interested in the 'abandonment' or 'erasure' of the self. Upending a reader's pre-existing ideas around meaning encourages new ways of perceiving. These ways are rendered by the odd sentences, which unsettle and make no ordinary sense. With no emotion-soaked lyrical line in sight, expectations of poetry are purposefully defied. Those looking for neatness and answers came to the wrong place and have wandered off the safety of the main road. Good news is it's a lot more interesting!

Don Mee Choi, the Korean American poet and translator, is cited in the introduction talking about being wrong on purpose:

> I think I was wrong, to begin with, because I was Korean, but when I first came to the States, people constantly tried to correct my English spelling and pronunciation. My British English was wrong because it was uttered from a mouth attached to an unexpected face, a wrong face [. . .] translation is in a perpetual state of being wrong because it isn't the original.

Could the perpetual state of being wrong in translation be applied in *reverse* to Lee's poems? They do so many things that poems aren't meant to do, which is what makes the work so joyous. Her poems are steps to right the wrong(s) of decolonisation.

The poem 'today ah that reminds me' contains an everyday phrase in its title. 'Today' is arguably the out-of-place word: the idea of 'today' as the reminder, rather than something more tangible and specific within that day. Although invoking the everyday, this is far from an everyday poem, even as poetry is taken down a peg or two, to be level with the trivial. This creates a kind of comic irony, it opens:

> Today ah that reminds me, I have a promise to keep. Put on my gloves and feel my forehead.

The second sentence implies that putting on gloves and feeling one's forehead is a logical response to being reminded about a promise. Or even that doing this action is the promise.

The next sentence: the promise 'is ashamed' in its personification adds another layer of wrongness, like the uncomfortable field.

> Like this I want to stay with the plants that pump out plants. Want to scrub the plants until dying the hands blue. Any stuck-out tongue is blue when the promise is activated.

The verb 'activated', used in this next extract, is usually used in connection with something like a bomb, machinery, technology, something being put into action. It is this kind of strange choice of words in this assemblage, progressing the Steinian minimal phrase to an expanded tableau, that makes the writing new.

By using administrative language from the non-literary pool, rather than the 'poetic', a more unfamiliar feeling is created, one which we are not used to in poetry. So Lee is 'activating' her aim of widening the scope of poetry. Well-read readers of poetry don't want or need the familiar spelled out to them for the umpteenth time, they want and need to feel something different and to be stimulated cerebrally.

In addition to the mixing of the various language pools that we swim through every day, there is a sense that the poetry is of, about, and for an out-of-placeness in 'normal' society, that stresses that we do not/that they do not fit.

To touch on the surreality of Lee's poetry, in the extract above, which is a particularly striking image. It is interesting to note that this vibrant imagery is disrupted by language. The picture being painted is colourful, bold and energetic, yes, but what is happening is not quite clear, it is 'just like' the thread that links it together has been removed. This could be comparable to cubism in its abstract, fragmented representation of reality.

Perhaps this disruption of image is something that distinguishes Lee from other Korean female surrealists, in the Moon Country series and beyond. The poet Yi Won (b. 1968), for instance, who I will call a second-generation surrealist, started writing her poetry a generation after the original Korean feminist poets such as Kim Hyesoon (b. 1955) who wrote at a more politically turbulent and oppressive time. Yi Won is also image-led and like Lee avoids writing specifically 'about' things, unlike, for the most part, the more politically charged titan of Korean surrealism Kim Hyesoon, but whose work still makes perfect sense linguistically and within the surreal logic. Moon Bo Young (b. 1992), another Moon Country Poet, I will call third generation, writes gloriously surreal work, clear surreal images, but makes perfect sense linguistically. The image is too dispersed and fragmented to grasp with Lee because of the ruptured language and disruption of syntax.

L ee teasingly explores emotion in 'someone briefly' from a distance. Eschewing self-indulgent emotion, traces of 'raw emotion' are instead present. This is a different recipe for sadness and yearning than we are used to:

> Woke slowly. Woke crying. Tears fell without reason from within sleep.

The text is written simply, like secretarial notes. The shoulders are scattered. How can shoulders be scattered? It is a deviant collocation, like the uncomfortable field, like the ashamed promise. Lee is turning away from meaning and towards sensation. Rewiring the reader's brain with this administrative matter-of-fact breakdown of emotions and the nonsensical images as confusing as emotions themselves.

> Throwing the beach ball the girls are reiterated.

The word choice 'reiterated' is like 'activated', administrative and, like scattered shoulders, out-of-joint. It moves the reader away from sense and in the process further away from cliché, showing us new ways to emphasise and say what we want via peculiarity.

Lee aims to move away from meaning, but there is meaning if we wish to tap into it. We each bring our own meaning—Barthes' death of the author coming into play. Or new meanings are created. For example, reiterate can be used to emphasise. In that sense, they are made more like girls by throwing the ball, displaying their girlness. Girls as a costume:

> Well-known costumes were invariably established I keep wanting to be your costume.

We all wear costumes. We want to see what it is like to be someone else, and to wear that costume. So not nonsensical as seems and can scan if we wish it to. Continuing to unpack:

I want to be your empty beach ball.

Beach balls are full of air. So an empty beachball would be deflated. Useless, unusable. Nothing more than a costume. Hence to briefly be someone. But also, equally, to a certain extent, it was empty in the first place, a hollow space inside.

'I fit wherever', the final sentence, seems pertinent to the whole collection, seems to say there is nothing inside, I am malleable. And if already empty even when full, nothing visible at least—it is then a slippage between states, two states in one, and about perception and what you bring to reality. The real and unreal make our perception and make up our everyday experience. What we understand as reality is both true and untrue at once. In line with allopoetics, we have allomeanings, then. Ultimately, empty or full beach ball it's still the same, doesn't matter or make any difference.

'I want to be *your* nothing' nonchalantly supports this and discards the idea of both feeling and meaning in life. Taking the ball of nothing as a plaything rather than being worried or afraid of the nothingness.

In further support of this idea Sumyeong is very happy for there to be multiple readings of her work and in fact, hopes the poems avoid 'a single interpretive lens.' On her objects she says:

I don't think it's at all strange to read the objects in my poems under anti-capitalist, quantum mechanical, or ecopoetic lenses since my poetry, doesn't overtly provide any lenses. Readers of my poetry can interpret, it how they wish. If I have a hope, it's that the objects contained in my poetry are sufficiently diverse as to preclude a single interpretive lens.'

'most of him' displays the extreme of Lee's disinterested relation to emotion. For Lee, lyric poetry's appeals to the emotion are 'frequently a spurious means of trying to expand the self'.

The title, 'most of him', could be taken a clichéd romantic love poem, something related to *Dallas* or *Dynasty*, perhaps a power ballad penned by Tim Rice for Barbara Dickson and Elaine Page. At its most cheesy potential, a woman trying to own a man, dramatic, possessive love. Lee takes this assumption somewhere else entirely, thus expanding the scope of poetry and annihilating cliché.

The poem opens, 'Most of him is without shadow', which could mean true, without darkness: light. But there is great darkness here. The poem itself is a shadow, suggesting menace, yes, but also a shadow of another poem, the poems' other selves, allopoems, or maybe the more traditional or clichéd poem.

'Good to drain a line of him on the road'. Why 'good'? Like Edson, Lee is gleefully vague where more meaning is usually given. Lee is playing games with peoples' expectations of poetry and meaning. The line 'It would be good to set him down' reenforces the detached violence and the anti-emotion.

'Most of him crowds into other people' sounds sinister, ominous. 'Most of him unthinkingly cuts his throat' even more so. This shocking, violent image shows a violence without thought. In many ways the most dangerous violence. There is boredom, an anti-feeling and dispassion, here. Subverting expectations of both women and poetry.

Lee succeeds in her mission to 'expand the scope of poetry' by drawing from a 'non-literary' language pool and makes much other poetry appear so obvious. Colin Leemarshall's translation pushes far beyond the normal collaboration of translation and an enhanced version of Lee Sumyeong is what we are left with. Lee Sumyeong's choices mirror our confusing lives and society and do not provide us with neat answers. The undoing of cliché is more important than meaning, but what is truth and meaning anyway, the poems ask. Lee, like many of us, is bored with the old and makes the new for readers who are looking for exactly that. Bringing language poetry and neo-modernism, with its fragmentation of image, stability, time, meaning in to already subversive and exciting Korean surreal poetry scene, is what makes Lee stand out among the crowd, leaving readers all very thankful for Colin Leemarshall coming across her book that day, and making poems that are *just like*, nothing.

LOCKOUT

We finished editing *Exacting Clam 16* around ten that night, and all the editors and the selections in the issue decided to go out for a celebratory drink. A few selections had cars—"Contract With the Dead: Adventures in Chinese Horror" and "Fresh Asphalt & a Robust Spliff"—and so did Molt Ariti, the journal's new Manager of Signs. We agreed to drive out to Perec's, where they've got free popcorn and constrained beer. I usually don't lock up the book, but I had the issue keys that night because Cordelia, the Night Editor, was sick with the whats. I handed the keys off to my colleague Sigh because he was more familiar with the shut-down process. I guess Sigh wasn't feeling well *either*, though—the whats are super-contagious—so he gave the keys to the story "Preposterous Spleen." Unsure of what to do with them, Spleen gave them to "The 1971 Skydog Calculus Poem." Skydog hung the keys on the hook on the inside cover—thinking, I guess, that Nobody Trellis, our new Negative Capabilitist, would grab them on the way out. But Skydog didn't tell Nobody that—we all just tumbled out of the issue and into the freezing cold. It was only right as the cover was closing that Skydog shouted to Nobody, "You got the keys, right?" Then the cover closed and locked behind us.

"Wait—what?" said Nobody.

"Issue keys!" hollered Skydog.

"Oh shit," said "Catherine Persian Rug." They ran to the cover and tried pulling on it, but it was locked.

"Doesn't Bowcher have them?" said "Many People Were Scandalized, Some Still Are."

"I gave 'em to Sigh," I said.

"I had them, but I put them on the hook," said Skydog. "Isn't that where they go?"

"What's the deal?" sang "On Not Reading Thomas Hardy" from beside Asphalt's Kia. "We goin'?"

"We're locked out!" bellowed Rug.

Asphalt's face went sour. "We're what?"

"Oh so now no Perec's?" whined Thomas Hardy.

"Never mind Perec's—where do we sleep tonight?" said "Ode to Pie."

"*Please* let the back cover be unlocked," Nobody said under their breath.

Scandalized ran around to the back of the issue, but I knew without checking that it'd be locked—we'd been good about security since some content thefts a few issues back. Spleen and Nobody tried to pry open the front cover while I called Sigh at home to see if he had a spare key. "Far as I know there's only one key for that issue," Sigh told me. Then he launched into a coughing fit. When it passed he said, "Spleen doesn't have it?"

"Spleen gave it to Skydog, Skydog put it on the hook."

"Shee-it," said Sigh. "You know we go to press in the morning, right?" Cough.

"I realize," I said.

"I think your best bet is to call An—," cough, "—Open Book."

"What's that?"

"Booksmith," said Sigh. "We've used them before."

I looked up the number for An Open Book and dialed. "Open Book after hours line," said a gruff voice.

I told him the situation. "And this is for *Exacting Clam*?" Gruff said.

"Issue Sixteen," I said.

"Those covers are tricky," Gruff gruffed. "Issue three I broke the lock altogether." When I didn't say anything, he said, "How's tomorrow at three?"

Panic washed over me. "Don't you work twenty-four seven?"

"I do, guy, but I got five jobs ahead of you."

"We go to press first thing in the morning," I said.

"I sincerely doubt it," Gruff said.

I thanked him and told him I'd see him tomorrow. When I turned around, I saw the poem Skydog balancing on the story Spleen's shoulders near the book's spine. "What are you doing?" I shouted.

"Skydog's gonna—" grunted Spleen, their face purple, "—try and climb it."

I shook my head and pulled up my collar—it was getting cold. Then Molt came over and told me that a few selections, Pie and "I Thought We Were Friends," had given up on getting back into the issue and booked hotel rooms at the local Super 8. "I'm thinking I might do the same," he said.

Just then we heard a holler from the other side of the book. Molt and I trotted around the issue to find Nobody, Thomas Hardy and Rug huddled at the far right side. "We got an idea," said Nobody.

I looked at the corner of the cover where they were huddled. "The ISBN?" I said.

"If we can bend it," said Hardy.

"Bend the bars?" I said. "You can't."

"Some of them are pretty thin," Rug said.

"Like these two," Nobody said, pointing. "If we can bend them I can wriggle in."

"You can't print the issue with a broken code," I said.

"You can't print it without any content either," Hardy shot back.

"It's so cold," said Molt. "I can't feel my toes."

By then everyone who'd been around front, Spleen and Contract and Asphalt and Skydog, had joined us at the back of the book. I heard Rug explaining their idea to Asphalt, and Asphalt say, "The ISBN? That's crazy."

"We can at least try, can't we?" said Thomas Hardy.

"Let me get in there," Skydog said.

Thomas Hardy took hold of one bar and Skydog the other. When they pulled in opposite directions on the bars, though, neither bar budged. "Goddamn!" burred Skydog. "Spleeny, help."

Spleen stepped forward and grabbed the right bar while Rug took hold of the left. "Let's do this," said Hardy. "One. Two. Three. Go!" All four pulled, and this time the bars bent slightly. "They're moving!" I said dumbly.

"Not much they aren't," grunted Skydog.

"Put your back into it, Hardy," Rug said.

As the space between the ISBN bars widened further, Nobody dropped to the ground. "I can almost squeeze through!" they shouted.

"One more time," muttered Rug.

Skydog planted his feet on the edge of the code, leaned his head back, and let out a guttural "Gah!" as he pulled on the right bar.

"That's it— that's good!" Nobody said. Then they shimmied forward until their head and shoulders fit through the bent ISBN.

"Careful Nobe!" said Thomas Hardy.

Soon Nobody had wriggled through up to their waist, and then they disappeared into the code altogether. We all shouted our encouragement— "You got this, Nobody!", "Just go nice and slow!"—and then we got quiet and just stared at the warped ISBN. After a minute Skydog looked to Rug and said, "Now what?"

Molt leaned his forehead against the back cover. "You OK, Nobe?"

We all listened for a response.

"Nobody?" Molt hollered.

Suddenly we heard the sound of unlocking, and everyone stepped away from the back cover just in time for it to swing open. Nobody stood grinning at the end of the issue. We all yelped and hooted as we ran into the book and across the bright, warm pages.

Roy Lisker

Instructions for a Silent Listening

This is the score of a musical composition. The performer freely interprets these instructions to the audience, who themselves create the composition in their imaginations. The length of time for each stage is to be determined by the intuitions of the performer.

I. Conducted by the performer, the audience will imagine a simple melodic phrase, of a leisurely pace in the medium range, about 6 beats long. The choice of instrument is up to the listener. Repeat mentally 6 times

II. Drop the phrase a full octave and continue to listen to it

III. Over it, introduce the sound of boiling hot water filling up a bathtub

IV. Over these introduce a sustained violin tone in the upper register

V. Now bring in the sound of a handsaw cutting wood. The performer will conduct this until the mood is well established, gradually raising the volume from piano to forte

VI. Keep the sound of the handsaw, cut all the other sounds

VII. Over the saw introduce a voice coming over the public address system saying

AT-TEN-TION! YOU ARE NOT A-LONE!
AT-TEN-TION! YOU ARE NOT A-LONE!
AT-TEN-TION! YOU ARE NOT A-LONE!

(To assist his audience, the performer may imitate the physical act of using a handsaw)

VIII. Bring in some electronic "Space Age" music

IX. CUT! Silence

X. The rich sounds of birds warbling on a spring morning

XI. Contrast, in a ridiculous fashion, with the sounds of an arcade of pin-ball machines

XII. Fade out

XIII. Bring up the sounds one hears in a busy laundromat

XIV. A pair of elementary school violin students have entered the laundromat and are playing "Three Blind Mice" in a round

XV. Raise to volume of the sounds, make the screeches of the violins harsher

XVI. CUT! Silence

XVII. In the total stillness, the throbbing of a solo cello playing an anguished melody in its high register

XVIII. Over the cello bring in, once again, the sound of boiling water filling up a bathtub

XIX. Someone in the bathtub is chanting:

I AM THAT I AM!, I AM THAT I AM!, I AM THAT I AM!...

XX. Two loudspeakers broadcasting the chants:

VOICE I: *APPLE STRUDEL, APPLE STRUDEL, APPLE STRUDEL! ....*
VOICE II: *MY! MY! MY! MY! MY! MY! ....*

XXI. Raise the intensity of the combined sounds to forte!

XXII. To triple forte!

XXIII. Fade out voices in general confusion

XXIV. Sounds of noisy street traffic at a crowded intersection

XXV. Soft steam hissing from a tea kettle. Fade out. Silence

Contributors

Stephen Baily has published short fiction and plays in some sixty journals, including, most recently, *Umbrella Factory, Medicine and Meaning, BlazeVOX,* and *Millennial Pulp.* He's also the author of three novels, including *Markus Klyner, MD, FBI* (Fellow Traveler Press). He lives in France.

P.J. Blumenthal, an American writer in Munich, Germany, writes in both German and English. He is the author of *Winston Hewlett's Impotence* (Sagging Meniscus, 2024), a non-fiction book on feral man, *Kaspar Hausers Geschwister* (Kaspar Hauser's Siblings), and a German-language blog, "Der Sprachbloggeur."

Christopher Boucher is the author of the novels *How to Keep Your Volkswagen Alive* (Melville House, 201), *Golden Delicious* (MH, 2016), and *Big Giant Floating Head* (MH, 2019). He teaches writing and literature at Boston College and is Managing Editor of *Post Road Magazine.*

Christopher Clauss (he/him) is an introvert, Ravenclaw, father, poet, and middle school science teacher in rural New Hampshire. His mother believes his poetry is "just wonderful." His daughters declare that he is the "best daddy they have," and his pre-teen science students rave that he's *"Fine, I guess. Whatever."*

Marvin Cohen is the author of many novels, plays, and collections of essays, stories, and poems. He lives on the Lower East Side of Manhattan.

Kyle Coma-Thompson is the author of three collections of short stories: *The Lucky Body, Night in the Sun,* and most recently, written in collaboration with Tristan Foster, *926 Years.* He lives in Louisville, Kentucky, where he practices as a clinical mental health counselor.

Bradley David's poetry, fiction, essays, and genre-blending works appear or are forthcoming in *HAD, Denver Quarterly, Terrain.org, The Los Angeles Review* and elsewhere. He is the blended-genre senior editor at *jmww journal.* Bradley likes rocks and birds. He and his husband live in California.

W.J. Davies' essays and reviews can be found in *Literary Review, Review 31, Slightly Foxed* and elsewhere. His story 'Pest Problem' is included in Brilliant Flash Fiction's 2024 anthology, and he has been shortlisted for a Cranked Anvil fiction prize. He lives in South East England.

Matt Dennison is the author of *Kind Surgery* (Urtica Press) and *Waiting for Better* (Main Street Rag Press). His poetry has appeared in *Verse Daily, Rattle, Bayou Magazine, Redivider* and *Cider Press Review,* among others. His fiction has appeared in *ShortStory Substack, THEMA, GUD, The Blue Crow, Prole, The Wondrous Real* and *Story Unlikely.* He has also made poetry videos with Marc Neys, Jutta Pryor & Marie Craven.

Richard Dinges, Jr. lives and works by a pond among trees and grassland, along with his wife, two dogs, three cats, and seven chickens. *Old Red Kimono, Poem, Oracle, The River,* and *Alembic* most recently accepted his poems for their publications.

Scott Edwards resides in Philadelphia. He draws some of his writing inspiration from long rambling walks around the city. The characters he frequently encounters on those walks often make an appearance in his fiction. He aspires to walk a bit less and write a bit more.

Giorgio Ferretti is an Italian author and editor based in Leipzig, where he works for the literary magazine *Edit.* His short prose, poetry, and essays have appeared in various German-speaking literary magazines, and his first play *America* premiered at Schauspiel Leipzig in 2023.

Jack Foley's numerous books of poetry, fiction and criticism include *Visions and Affiliations,* a "chronoencyclopedia" of California poetry from 1940 to 2005, *Grief Songs* (SM, 2017) and *When Sleep Comes* (SM, 2020). He lives in Oakland and hosts a weekly radio show, *Cover to Cover,* on Berkeley's Pacifica station, KPFA.

Mike Fox's stories have been nominated for Best of Net and the Pushcart Prize, listed in Best British and Irish Flash Fiction (BIFFY50), and included in *Best British Stories 2018* (Salt). He is the author of *The Violet Eye* (Nightjar Press) and *Things Grown Distant,* featuring photographic illustrations by Nicholas Royle (Confingo Publishing).

Avital Gad-Cykman is the author of *Light Reflection Over Blues* (Ravenna Press) and *Life In, Life Out* (Matter Press). Her stories appear in *Spectrum, The Dr. Eckleburg Review, Iron Horse, Prairie Schooner, Ambit, McSweeney's Quarterly* and *Michigan Quarterly,* twice in *Best Short Fictions,* and elsewhere. She holds a PhD in English Literature, focused on minorities, gender and trauma, lives in Brazil and travels extensively.

Jake Goldsmith is a writer with cystic fibrosis and the founder of The Barbellion Prize, a book prize for ill and disabled authors. He is the author of *Neither Weak Nor Obtuse* (SM, 2022) and *In Hospital Environments: Essays on Illness and Philosophy* (SM, 2024).

Charles Holdefer is an American writer currently based in Brussels. His latest book is *Ivan the Terrible Goes on a Family Picnic* (SM, 2024).

Amber Isaac is a queer trans writer from the Midwest who now lives in Austin, TX. She is the Reviews Editor at *Infrarrealista Review.* Her work appears in *Prairie Schooner* and *Coachella Review.* Her first book, *Peppermint,* is forthcoming from Plancha Press.

Hank Kirton fled Arkansas and moved to Massachusetts at the age of two. His stories have appeared in several anthologies and magazines. He has written four collections. They are still available.

Jake La Botz's songs and acting have been featured in film and television, including *True Detective, Shameless, Ghost World, Rambo* (yes, *Rambo!*) and more. His debut collection of short fiction is forthcoming from the University of Wisconsin's Cornerstone Press.

Carl Landauer taught history at Yale, Stanford, and McGill. He has written broadly on intellectual and cultural history and the history of law. He has published articles and book reviews with *Salmagundi, Renaissance Quarterly, Yale Journal of Law & the Humanities, German Studies Review, Confrontations, Beat Scene, American*

Scholar, the San Francisco Chronicle, Newsday, and *Poetry Flash.*

Roy Lisker (1938–2019) was a writer, artist, mathematician, journalist and political activist. He was the author of a vast amount of literature in every imaginable form, which he largely self-distributed to friends and subscribers to his newsletter, *Ferment.* His conventionally published work includes *In Memoriam Einstein* (SM, 2016) and *Lincoln Center in July* (SM, 2016).

Jionghao Liu (刘炯浩 liú jiǒng hào) is a doctoral student specializing in Translation Studies at Binghamton University. Proficient in Chinese, Japanese, and English, her current research centers on Japanese literary adaptations of Chinese vernacular fiction, especially Shuihuzhuan 水浒传 [Water Margin].

Nate Logan is the author of *Apricot* (above/ground press, 2022) and *Small Town* (The Magnificent Field, 2021). He's a Visiting Assistant Professor of English at Marian University.

Kurt Luchs is the author of *Tributaries* (SM, 2025), *Death Row Row Row Your Boat* (SM, 2024), *Falling in the Direction of Up* (SM, 2021), *One of These Things Is Not Like the Other* (Finishing Line Press, 2019), and *It's Funny Until Someone Loses an Eye (Then It's Really Funny)* (SM, 2017). He lives in Michigan.

Mike Marks studied with poet laureate Gwendolyn Brooks in Chicago and was later awarded the first Creative Writing bachelor's degree ever tendered at Kansas State University. Now with over a hundred published poems and stories, he lives in Akron, Ohio.

Melissa McCarthy transmits from a tracking station in Edinburgh, Scotland. She's written *Photo, Phyto, Proto, Nitro* (SM, 2023) and *Sharks, Death, Surfers: An Illustrated Companion* (Sternberg, 2019).

Andrew McKeown teaches English at the University of Poitiers, France. His short stories have appeared in *Exacting Clam* and *Caliban.*

Kat Meads' most recent book is *While Visiting Babette* (SM, 2025). She lives in California.

Kirsten Mosher is an artist and writer living in Massachusetts. She is the author of *Zero (minutes to) Home* (Selektion, 2021), and *Plea$e Steal Me for 100 Plus Dollarzz* (Lily Poetry Review Books, 2023). Her stories can be read in *Minor Literature[s]* and *Exacting Clam*, among others.

Allan Peterson's most recent book is: *This Luminous, New and Selected Poems.* He lives and writes in Ashland, Oregon. www.allanpeterson.net

Jennifer M Phillips is a bi-national immigrant, painter, Bonsai-grower. Her chapbooks are *Sitting Safe In the Theatre of Electricity* (i-blurb.com, 2020) and *A Song of Ascents* (Orchard Street Press, 2022. With work in over 95 journals, she is currently a Pushcart Poetry Prize nominee.

Eric T. Racher lives and works in Riga, Latvia. He is the author of a chapbook of poetry, *Five Functions Defined on Experience: For Jay Wright* (2021).

John Repp is a poet, fiction writer, folk photographer, and digital collagist living in Erie, Pennsylvania. Seven Kitchens Press has just published his twelfth chapbook of poetry, *Star Shine in the Pines.*

David Rose born 1949, resident in Britain, is now retired after a working life in the Post Office. His short stories are published widely in the UK and US, including in *The Penguin Book of the Contemporary Short Story* (ed. Philip Hensher, 2018) and partly collected in *Posthumous Stories* (Salt, 2013). He is the author of two novels: *Vault* (Salt, 2011) and *Meridian* (Unthank Books, 2015).

M Sarki travels with his camera, disposes literary reviews, and occasionally creates a poetic artifact. His latest book, a memoir, *The Mad Habit,* is centered on his long relationship with friend, mentor, editor, and teacher Gordon Lish. Sarki also maintains and regularly contributes to his eclectic literary website aptly named the Rogue Literary Society.

Andrea Scrima, an American artist and writer based in Berlin.is the author of the novels *A Lesser Day* (Spuyten Duyvil, 2010; as *Wie viele Tage,* Literaturverlag Droschl, 2018) and *Kreisläufe* (*Like Lips, Like Skins*) (2021). Scrima has written essays for the *Times Literary Supplement, taz, Frankfurter Allgemeine Zeitung, Schreibheft, Music & Literature, The American Scholar, Hyperallergic, LitHub, Cargo, The Millions, manuskripte,* and *The Brooklyn Rail,* among others; is editor-in-chief of the New York-based literary journal *StatORec;* and publishes a regular column at *Three Quarks Daily.* In 2020, she edited the anthology *Writing the Virus,* a *New York Times* Sunday Book Review "New & Noteworthy" title of 2021.

Vik Shirley is a poet, writer, critic, and educator from Bristol now living in Edinburgh. Her books include *Corpses* (Sublunary Editions), *Notes from the Underworld* (SE), *Disrupted Blue and other poems on Polaroid* (Hesterglock), *One by One* (No Press), *Poets* (The Red Ceilings), *Strangers Wave* (zimZalla), *The Continued Closure of the Blue Door* (HVTN) and *Cassette Poems,* (above/ground press). Her most recent publication is *Some Deer* (Broken Sleep Books) and her next full-length collection, *Nervous Tic,* is forthcoming. She co-edits Firmament online and Surreal-Absurd at Mercurius. Vik has a PhD in Dark Humour and the Surreal from the University of Birmingham.

Mike Silverton is the author of *Anvil on a Shoestring* (SM, 2022), *Trios* (SM, 2023), and *Yoga for Pickpockets* (SM, 2024).

Lucian Staiano-Daniels is a historian of violent conflict who was educated at St. John's College, NYU, and UCLA.

Alex Tretbar is a Writers for Readers Fellow with the Kansas City Public Library, where he teaches free writing classes to the community. His poems and essays appear or are forthcoming in *The Cincinnati Review, Kenyon Review, Narrative, Poetry Northwest, Sixth Finch, The Threepenny Review,* and elsewhere.

David Winner is the author of *Master Lovers* (nonfiction, Outpost 19, 2023) and the novels *Enemy Combatant* (Tablo, 2021), *Tyler's Last* (O19, 2015), and *The Cannibal of Guadalajara* (Gival Press, 2010). His work has appeared in *The Village Voice, Fiction, The Iowa Review, The Millions* and *The Kenyon Review.* He is a senior editor at StatORec magazine and a regular contributor to *The Brooklyn Rail.*

www.ingramcontent.com/pod-product-compliance
Lightning Source LLC
Chambersburg PA
CBHW081326020726
47506CB00006B/1195